Models of Futures Markets

This volume presents an entirely new analysis of the economics of futures markets that will be of interest to both specialists in the area and the generalist economist seeking a new perspective. Through a combination of theoretical investigation and empirical application, three important themes are explored:

- the gains from futures trading and the efforts of emerging markets to reap these benefits
- rationality and rival hypotheses of trader behaviour, such as noise trading
- the effect of regulatory tools on price formation.

All the contributors to the volume are recognised leading authorities in the field. Together, they bring a wide expertise to bear in an analysis covering topics as significant and diverse as:

- new futures markets in China and Kazakhstan
- simultaneous modelling of the US dollar/Deutschmark market
- non-linearities and chaotic behaviour.

Barry A. Goss is Reader in Economics at Monash University, Australia, and the editor of this volume. He is widely published in the field of futures markets, co-edited the *Economic Record* Special Issue on Futures Markets 1992, and wrote the feasibility study for the establishment of the Hong Kong Futures Exchange.

Routledge Studies in the Modern World Economy

1 **Interest Rates and Budget Deficits**
A study of the advanced economies
Kanhaya L. Gupta and Bakhtiar Moazzami

2 **World Trade after the Uruguay Round**
Prospects and policy options for the twenty-first century
Edited by Harald Sander and Andás Inotai

3 **The Flow Analysis of Labour Markets**
Edited by Ronald Schettkat

4 **Inflation and Unemployment**
Contributions to a new macroeconomic approach
Edited by Alvaro Cencini and Mauro Baranzini

5 **Macroeconomic Dimensions of Public Finance**
Essays in honour of Vito Tanzi
Edited by Mario I. Blejer and Teresa M. Ter-Minassian

6 **Fiscal Policy and Economic Reforms**
Essays in honour of Vito Tanzi
Edited by Mario I. Blejer and Teresa M. Ter-Minassian

7 **Competition Policy in the Global Economy**
Modalities for co-operation
Edited by Leonard Waverman, William S. Comanor and Akira Goto

8 **Working in the Macro Economy**
A study of the US labor market
Martin F. J. Prachowny

9 **How Does Privatization Work?**
Edited by Anthony Bennett

10 **The Economics and Politics of International Trade**
Freedom and Trade: Volume II
Edited by Gary Cook

11 **The Legal and Moral Aspects of International Trade**
Freedom and Trade: Volume III
Edited by Asif Qureshi, Hillel Steiner and Geraint Parry

12 **Capital Markets and Corporate Governance in Japan, Germany and the United States**
Organizational response to market inefficiencies
Helmut M. Dietl

13 **Competition and Trade Policies**
Coherence or conflict
Edited by Einar Hope

14 **Rice**
The primary commodity
A. J. H. Latham

15 **Trade, Theory and Econometrics**
Essays in honour of John S. Chipman
Edited by James C. Moore, Raymond Riezman and James R. Melvin

16 **Who Benefits from Privatisation?**
Edited by Moazzem Hossain and Justin Malbon

17 **Towards a Fair Global Labour Market**
Avoiding the new slave trade
Ozay Mehmet, Errol Mendes and Robert Sinding

18 **Models of Futures Markets**
Edited by Barry A. Goss

19 **Venture Capital Investment**
An agency analysis of UK practice
Gavin C. Reid

20 **Macroeconomic Forecasting**
A sociological appraisal
Robert Evans

21 **Multimedia and Regional Economic Restructuring**
Edited by Hans-Joachim Braczyk, Gerhard Fuchs and Hans-Georg Wolf

22 The New Industrial Geography
Regions, regulation and institutions
Edited by Trevor J. Barnes and Meric S. Gertler

23 The Employment Impact of Innovation
Evidence and policy
Edited by Marco Vivarelli and Mario Pianta

24 International Health Care Reform
A legal, economic and political analysis
Colleen Flood

25 Competition Policy Analysis
Edited by Einar Hope

26 Culture and Enterprise
The development, representation and morality of business
Don Lavoie and Emily Chomlee-Wright

Models of Futures Markets

Edited by

Barry A. Goss

London and New York

332.645
M689

First published 2000
by Routledge
11 New Fetter Lane, London EC4P 4EE

Simultaneously published in the USA and Canada
by Routledge
29 West 35th Street, New York, NY 10001

Reprinted 2000

Routledge is an imprint of the Taylor & Francis Group

© 2000 Barry A. Goss

The right of Barry A. Goss to be identified as the Author of this
Work has been asserted by him in accordance with the Copyright,
Designs and Patents Act 1988

Typeset in Times and Gill Sans by
Prepress Projects, Perth, Scotland
Printed and bound in Great Britain by
T.J.I. Digital, Padstow, Cornwall

British Library Cataloguing in Publication Data
A catalogue record for this book is available
from the British Library

Library of Congress Cataloging in Publication Data
Goss, B.A.
    Models of futures markets / Barry A. Goss
    p.   cm. –
    Includes bibliographical references and index.
    1. Futures market–Mathematical models.   I. Title.
    HG6024.A3G658   2000
    332.64'5–dc21   99-36657
    CIP

ISBN 0415-18254-9

Contents

List of figures   x
List of tables   xi
List of contributors   xii
Brief description of this book   xvi

**1 Introduction: welfare, rationality and integrity
    in futures markets**   **1**
BARRY A. GOSS

The gains from futures trading 1
Rationality and rival hypotheses 4
*The integrity of futures markets: price limits and the
    distribution of price changes 10*

2 The gains from futures trading   **15**
DEREK FRANCIS

Introduction 15
The basic model 16
*The Pareto production gains from
    forward contracting 18*
The evolution of futures trading 20
Some initial implications 23
Gains from futures trading 24
Comparing futures trading with forward contracting 26
Dynamic welfare considerations 27
*The need for futures markets explained through quicker
    adaptation to exogenous disturbance 29*

Adaptation to the shock with only a spot market 33
The effects of futures on spot price variability 34
Overall summary 35

**3   The development of commodity futures exchanges
     in Kazakhstan and China: evidence on their role in
     market development**   **42**
ANNE E. PECK

Introduction 42
The development of commodity futures exchanges 43
The history of a wheat futures market in Kazakhstan 46
*The successful development of futures trading
     at CZCE 50*
Conclusions 56

**4   A simultaneous model of the US dollar/Deutschmark
     spot and futures markets**   **61**
BARRY A. GOSS AND S. GULAY AVSAR

Introduction 61
Specification of the model 62
*Data, unit roots and co-integration
     tests, and estimation 67*
Results: intrasample period 73
Post-sample results 77
Conclusions 79

5   Noise trader sentiment in futures markets   **86**
DWIGHT R. SANDERS, SCOTT H. IRWIN AND RAYMOND M. LEUTHOLD

Introduction 86
*A theoretical noise trader risk model for
     futures markets 87*
Empirical methodology 91
Noise trader sentiment and data 95
Noise traders' impact on futures prices 102
Summary and conclusions 112

6   Microanalytics of price volatility in futures markets   117
A.G. MALLIARIS AND JEROME L. STEIN

Introduction 117
Background literature 118
An economic theory that implies the
Lorenz system 120
Analysis of the Lorenz system 123
Empirical tests 125
Conclusion 131

7   The integrity of futures markets: the impact of price
limits on futures prices   135
ANTHONY D. HALL, PAUL KOFMAN AND ANTHONY SIOUCLIS

Introduction 135
Absorbing limits: a target zone model 139
Price limits in agricultural futures contracts 144
Concluding remarks 162

Index   168

Figures

1.1   Allocation of two goods, X and Y, depending on spot
       price ratio   2
1.2   Production of goods X and Y by producers A and B   3
2.1   Maximum quantities of X and Y that can be produced
       by A and B under the basic model   17
2.2   An Edgeworth box construction showing the Pareto
       gains from forward contracting   19
2.3   Average transaction costs as a function of volume for
       forward contracting and futures trading   27
2.4   Welfare levels for agents trading in alternative
       institutional settings   28
2.5   Effect on production of an exogenous disturbance   30
2.6   The cobweb phenomenon   34
4.1   Spot price: intrasample simulation   75
4.2   Futures price: intrasample simulation   76
4.3   Futures price: post-sample simulation   78
4.4   Spot price forecasts: post-sample   78
5.1   Extrapolative expectations, impulse response function and
       Market Vane data   102
6.1   Time series of volatility, errors and speculation for corn   126
6.2   Time series of volatility, errors and speculation for soybeans   126
7.1   June 1988 agricultural futures prices and number of
       transactions   149
7.2   Soybean futures – price limits in action   150
7.3   Volatility and jumps in futures prices   151
7.4   Liquidity measures   152
7.5   Soybean futures basis behaviour and volatility ratio   153
7.6   Folded distributions for soybean futures price
       deviations from the target price   154
7.7   S-shapes in agricultural futures returns in the fitted target
       zone models, based on the parameter estimates in Table 7.4   160
7.8   Confidence limits for corn   161

Tables

4.1	Unit root tests: augmented Dickey–Fuller	69
4.2	Unit root tests: Phillips–Perron	70
4.3	Johansen co-integration procedure: maximum eigenvalue test	71
4.4	Parameter estimates	74
4.5	Intrasample simulation of exchange rates	74
4.6	Post-sample simulation of exchange rates	77
4.7	Post-sample forecasts of spot exchange rate	79
5.1	Markets and contract months	97
5.2	Summary statistics, Market Vane Bullish Sentiment Index	98
5.3	Granger causality test, returns lead sentiment, individual markets	100
5.4	Pooled causality test, returns lead sentiment	101
5.5	Cross-sectional test.	103
5.6	Cross-sectional tests, Fama–MacBeth regressions	104
5.7	Cumby–Modest test, individual markets	106
5.8	Pooled Cumby–Modest test, Market Vane data, weekly	108
5.9	Granger Causality test, sentiment leads returns, weekly Market Vane data	110
5.10	Pooled causality test, sentiment leads returns, weekly Market Vane data	111
6.1	Interaction of variables	124
6.2	Values of coefficients from system estimation: model 2	128
6.3	Wald coefficient tests: model 2	129
7.1	Descriptive statistics	145
7.2	Sample split statistics	147
7.3	Target zone log likelihoods	157
7.4	Target zone estimates	158

Contributors

S. Gulay Avsar is a Lecturer in mathematical economics and econometrics at the School of Communications and Informatics, Victoria University of Technology, Footscray, Victoria, Australia, and a Research Fellow at Monash University, Australia. She is a graduate of the Middle East Technical University, Turkey, and holds a postgraduate qualification from Monash University. She also is co-author of several papers on futures markets that have been published in academic journals.

Derek Francis is Manager, Regulatory Economics, at Cable and Wireless Optus, Australia, and holds a Masters degree in Economics from Monash University, Australia. He also has a law degree from Monash University and previously he was employed by the Australian Competition and Consumer Commission.

Barry A. Goss is a Reader in Economics at Monash University, Clayton, Victoria, Australia, and the editor of this volume. He has a PhD from the London School of Economics and has published papers in academic journals and books on futures markets, including *The Theory of Futures Trading* (1972); (ed. with B. S. Yamey) *The Economics of Futures Trading* (1976); (ed.) *Futures Markets: Their Establishment and Performance* (1986); and (ed.) *Rational Expectations and Efficiency in Futures Markets* (1992). He also edited (with J. L. Stein) *Economic Record Special Issue on Futures Markets* (1992) and wrote the feasibility study for the establishment of the Hong Kong Futures Exchange.

Anthony D. Hall (PhD, London School of Economics, 1976) has taught econometrics at the Australian National University and the University of California, San Diego, USA, and finance at Bond University and the

University of Technology, Sydney, Australia. His work has been published in leading international journals, including *The Review of Economics and Statistics*, *The International Economic Review* and *The Journal of Business and Economic Statistics*. His research interests cover all areas of financial econometrics.

Scott H. Irwin is a Professor in the Department of Agricultural and Consumer Economics at the University of Illinois at Urbana-Champaign (UIUC). He was formerly a Professor at The Ohio State University and holds a PhD from Purdue University. Professor Irwin has conducted studies on commodity funds, market efficiency, trader behaviour and returns, futures price behaviour, hedging strategies, and assessing the value of information on futures markets. He currently heads a project evaluating the information provided by advisory services (AgMAS) and is co-operating on a project building a simulator for producer risk assessment (AgRisk).

Paul Kofman (PhD, Erasmus University Rotterdam, 1991) has taught finance and econometrics at Erasmus University, The Netherlands, Monash University, the University of New South Wales, and University of Technology, Sydney, Australia. His work has been published in *The Journal of International Economics, The Journal of Banking and Finance* and *The Journal of Futures Markets*. His research interests cover risk analysis of financial asset prices and the regulation of derivatives markets.

Raymond M. Leuthold is the Thomas A. Hieronymus Professor of Futures Markets in the Department of Agricultural and Consumer Economics at the University of Illinois at Urbana-Champaign (UIUC). He also serves as Director of the Office for Futures and Options Research. Dr Leuthold has taught graduate and undergraduate courses and conducted research on futures markets at UIUC since 1967. He has published widely in many academic journals and is a co-author of the textbook *The Theory and Practice of Futures Markets*. He has been a visiting scholar at Stanford University, USA, IGIA in France, and the Chicago Mercantile Exchange, USA.

A. G. Malliaris is the Walter F. Mullady Sr Professor of Business Administration in the Department of Economics at Loyola University, Chicago, USA. He is a graduate of the Athens School of Economics and

Business, and has a PhD in Economics from the University of Oklahoma, USA. He undertook postdoctoral studies in mathematics and economics at The University of Chicago. He has authored and co-authored articles in professional journals such as *The Society of Industrial and Applied Mathematics Review, Mathematics of Operations Research, Review of Economic Studies, Journal of Financial and Quantitative Analysis* and *Journal of Futures Markets.* He has also co-authored two books with William A. Brock: *Stochastic Methods in Economics and Finance* and *Differential Equations, Stability and Chaos in Dynamic Economics.* He specialises in financial economics.

Anne E. Peck is the Holbrook Working Professor of Commodity Price Studies at the Food Research Institute and a Senior Fellow at the Institute for International Studies at Stanford University, USA. Her research focuses principally on the evaluation of market performance. In recent studies, she has examined the delivery terms of the Chicago Board of Trade grain and oilseeds contracts, the development of the leading futures exchange in China, and efforts to develop a grain exchange in Kazakhstan. In 1999, she was a Fulbright Scholar at the Kazakhstan Institute for Management, Economics and Strategic Planning in Almaty, Kazakhstan, teaching courses on commodity markets.

Dwight R. Sanders is the Manager of Commodity Analysis for Darden Restaurants Inc. He received his PhD from the University of Illinois at Urbana-Champaign, where he worked at the Office for Futures and Options Research. Futures market research focused on behavioural finance issues as well as forecasting, basis behaviour and market efficiency. Futures industry experience includes brokerage and trading, and most recently he has worked in the areas of commodity analysis and price risk management for The Pillsbury Company and Darden Restaurants Inc.

Anthony Siouclis (B.Com. Honours, Monash University, Australia, 1996) teaches financial econometrics at Monash University. He is currently conducting PhD research on the impact of regulation in derivatives markets.

Jerome L. Stein is Visiting Professor (research) in the Division of Applied Mathematics. Emeritus Professor of Economics and Eastman Professor of Political Economy at Brown University, USA. He has been Associate Editor of the *American Economic Review* and the *Journal of Finance*. His previous books include *Economic Growth in a Free Market* (1964), *Money and Capacity Growth* (1971), *The Economics of Futures Markets* (1986), *International Financial Markets* (1991) and *Fundamental Determinants of Exchange Rates* (1995). He received the degree Docteur Honoris Causa (1997) from L'Université de la Méditerranée, Aix-Marseille II, for his research.

Brief description of this book

With six chapters written expressly for the purpose, the objective of this volume is to provide new analysis and evidence on the issues of welfare, rationality and integrity in futures markets. The major topics discussed range from the gains from futures trading and their pursuit in emerging markets, through the hypotheses of noise trading and chaos, to exchange rate forecasting and the impact of regulatory tools on price formation.

Chapter 1

Introduction

Welfare, rationality and integrity in futures markets

Barry A. Goss[1]

This volume provides new analysis and evidence on three major themes in the economics of futures markets. The issues selected for discussion are, first, the gains from futures trading and their pursuit in emerging markets; second, rationality and rival hypotheses of agent behaviour; and, third, the integrity of price formation in the presence of regulatory tools. The first and second issues are linked by the hypothesis of utility maximisation, whereas the third issue is related to the other two by the question of whether the price signals to which agents respond are distorted by regulatory intervention. These issues were selected for discussion not only because they are important unsettled questions in the economics of futures markets, but also because it is hoped that the reader will find the individual chapters provide appropriate responses to the specific challenges they address.

The gains from futures trading

Suppose, in a world with two goods X and Y, in which current consumption decisions are based on currently formed expectations of prices next period, that agent A expects the spot price ratio (P_X/P_Y) to be 2, and agent B expects this price ratio to be 0.5. Suppose further that the current allocation of these goods between A and B, at E in Figure 1.1, is based on these expectations (where P_X is the price of X and P_Y is the price of Y). If a market anticipation of this price ratio in the form of a forward (or futures) price is determined at say 1.25 and if these agents contract at this price, Pareto gains will be made; the allocation will then be at P in Figure 1.1.

Suppose that A and B are also producers of goods X and Y, and that current production decisions are based on currently formed expectations of prices next period. Assume that with identical product transformation curves T, these agents equate their respective marginal rates of substitution (MRS) to their marginal rates of transformation (MRT) under autarky. Then A will produce at Q_A and B will produce at Q_B in Figure 1.2. If the market forward price ratio is established at 1.25 and if both agents adjust to this price ratio, then aggregate production of both X and Y will be increased. Both A and B will relocate their production at R in Figure 1.2. Francis, in Chapter 2, uses these simple but powerful tools to demonstrate the gains from futures trading in what is possibly one of the first general equilibrium analyses of the welfare effects of this institutional arrangement.

Emerging futures markets

Until the early 1970s, the question of the establishment of new futures markets was analysed typically with reference to a list of feasibility conditions which were thought necessary for such markets. This list included the conditions, *inter alia*, that the commodity in question must be both storable and deliverable (see, for example, Houthakker, 1959,

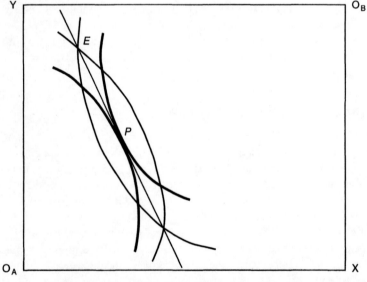

Figure 1.1 If the initial allocation of X and Y is at E, where $E(P_X/P_Y)_A = 2$ and $E(P_X/P_Y)_B = 0.5$, a futures market is formed in which $(P_X/P_Y)_M = 1.25$. If both agents trade at this price ratio, the allocation is at P, where the slope of the straight line through P is −1.25.

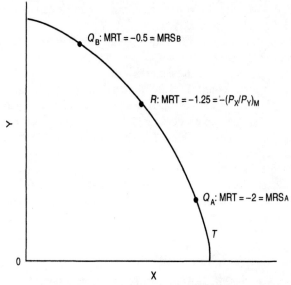

Figure 1.2 Initially, A locates at Q_A, where the MRT = MRS$_A$ = -2, and B locates at Q_B, where MRT = MRS$_B$ = -0.5. With futures trading, if both agents locate at R, where MRT = -1.25, the production of both X and Y will increase.

pp. 147–50, 158).[2] Such an analysis, however, does not constitute an economic theory and was unable to predict the introduction in 1964 of futures trading in finished live beef cattle, which are virtually non-storable, and in 1982 in share market indices, which are non-storable and non-deliverable.

By the early 1970s, this commodity characteristics approach had lost favour, and economic theories emerged that focused on key economic variables rather than on attributes of the commodity. Telser and Higinbotham (1977) argued that the net benefits from futures trading are a direct function of price variability, liquidity, turnover and commitments of traders. Empirically, these authors found *inter alia* that liquidity varies directly with turnover, whereas commission charges and margins vary negatively with turnover. Veljanovski (1986, pp. 25–6) argued that futures markets develop when they are a more efficient vehicle, in terms of transaction costs, than spot or forward markets for transferring certain property rights attached to price. Williams (1986, p. 74), in contrast, argued that futures markets emerge from a need by firms to borrow or lend commodities. For example, a short hedge (purchase of spot, sale of futures) is equivalent to borrowing a commodity and is part of an implicit loan market for the commodity.

Futures trading in emerging market economies is unlikely to have the precedents of a developed cash market and of established forward trading practices, common to futures markets in many developed Western economies, to draw upon.[3] Nevertheless, the benefits from futures trading, outlined by Francis in Chapter 2, as well as externalities,[4] are available to agents in these economies. Peck, in Chapter 3, discusses developments in two new exchanges in China and Kazakhstan with vastly different prospects: one in Zhengzhou, China, with a major mungbeans contract, has attained substantial volumes and continues to grow; the other, in Almaty, Kazakhstan, with an important wheat contract, is in decline. Peck suggests some reasons for this difference in fortunes between the two exchanges.

Rationality and rival hypotheses

Critics such as Isard (1987) and Meese (1990) have claimed that traditional economic models of exchange rate determination have performed poorly in recent decades, in that they are unable to explain a significant proportion of exchange rate variation and are unable to outperform a naive random walk model in post-sample forecasting. Perceived deficiencies in traditional models to which critics have drawn attention include undue reliance on single equation methods and inadequate modelling of expectations. A low point was reached, perhaps, a few years later when Krugman (1993, p. 7) claimed that '...for the most part international monetary economists have given up, at least for now, on the idea of trying to develop models of the exchange rate that are both theoretically interesting and empirically defensible.'

Prior research, of course, had already cast very serious doubts on the informational efficiency of the foreign exchange market. Although Bilson (1981), Frenkel (1981) and Baillie et al. (1983) did not reject the unbiasedness hypothesis for major currencies with single equation estimation, Bilson (1981) and Bailey et al. (1984) did reject that hypothesis with SURE estimation for a group of major currencies. Hansen and Hodrick (1980) rejected the semistrong efficient markets hypothesis (EMH) for the Deutschmark, Swiss franc and Canadian dollar, against the US dollar, when the set of publicly available information was defined as lagged forecast errors for own and other major currencies. Although Hansen and Hodrick (1980) did not reject the EMH for the British pound/US dollar exchange rate, Bailey et al. (1984) cast doubt on the rationality of expectations in that market when they found autocorrelated residuals in their single equation estimates.

Unbiasedness embodies the joint hypotheses of rational expectations and risk neutrality, and the predominance of rejections, especially with wider information sets, has been interpreted by some researchers as evidence of market inefficiency (for example, Bilson, 1981; Taylor, 1992) and by others as evidence of a time-varying risk premium (for example, Hodrick and Srivastava, 1984, 1987). (On these various interpretations, the reader is referred to the surveys in Hodrick, 1987; Baillie and McMahon, 1989; Taylor, 1995.)

Although academic research can do little to rectify any lack of speculative efficiency in the foreign exchange market, it can at least address the first set of issues. This is the objective of Goss and Avsar in Chapter 4, who develop a simultaneous model of the US dollar/ Deutschmark market. This model contains behavioural relationships for short hedgers and long hedgers, for short speculators and long speculators, and for agents with unhedged spot market commitments (an alternative way of closing this model is by the introduction of a spot rate equation, as in Goss *et al.*, 1998). Expectations of spot and futures exchange rates are obtained as fitted values on a set of public information defined as all predetermined (current exogenous and lagged endogenous) variables in the model. This method of empirical representation of a rational expectation of an economic variable is based on McCallum (1979), and any test of the rational expectations hypothesis based upon this methodology is a joint test of the expectations hypothesis and the appropriateness of the model (Maddock and Carter, 1982). The post-sample forecasts of the spot rate produced by this model are compared with the forecast provided by a naive random walk model and with that implicit in a lagged futures rate. The first comparison has the clear policy implication that those who would improve economic forecasts of spot exchange rates should take into account information from both spot and futures markets in the context of simultaneous determination because the model presented here by far outperforms a random walk. The second comparison permits a test of the semistrong EMH (Leuthold and Hartmann, 1979). If the model outperforms the lagged futures rate as a predictor of the spot rate, this is evidence against the EMH because the model evidently contains information that is not reflected in the futures rate. This outcome, however, is a necessary but not sufficient condition for rejection of the EMH. The sufficient condition requires a demonstration that the model in question can be used to produce risk-adjusted profits (Rausser and Carter, 1983; Leuthold and Garcia, 1992).

However, if the lagged futures price outperforms the model in predicting the spot rate post-sample, this is not necessarily a demonstration of market efficiency, but may be simply a reflection of an inappropriate model.

Noise traders

In the early 1980s, the hypothesis emerged that security prices fluctuated to an extent that was too large to be justified by news on market fundamentals alone. Furthermore, evidence accumulated to support the view that non-information events caused the demand for shares and, hence, their prices to change: for example, it was found that the share market was less volatile on Wednesdays when the exchange was closed, that maximum volatility did not coincide with most important news days, and that shares which were added to the Standard and Poors 500 Index exhibited price increases (Shleifer and Summers, 1990, pp. 19, 22–3).

The noise trader theories of asset pricing, which attempt to explain these outcomes, typically postulate that security prices are determined in a world that comprises rational investors and noise traders (or 'ordinary investors'). Rational investors fully and efficiently utilise new information and have rational expectations of security prices. Noise traders, on the other hand, respond to non-information, such as the advice of brokers, or they follow fads; alternatively, they may exhibit extrapolative expectations by chasing trends, using technical analysis or 'stop loss' orders. Noise traders are assumed, therefore, to misperceive the distribution of security prices. The impact of noise traders on prices will only be significant, of course, if their responses to non-information are correlated.

Although rational investors can make significant returns by arbitrage on the difference between the correct and the misperceived distribution of security prices, such arbitrage is assumed usually to be risky. The result is that the impact of noise traders on prices is not fully eliminated by rational arbitrage. Indeed, argue Shleifer and Summers (1990, p. 24), noise traders may be more aggressive and more confident and, hence, take more risk than rational investors. Noise traders also, therefore, may earn significant returns (see also Benos, 1998).

This outcome has two implications in noise trader theory. The first is that if security prices respond to new information *and* to changes in noise trader sentiment, it follows that prices fluctuate more than is warranted by news on fundamentals (see also Arrow, 1982). Second, if the impact of noise traders on prices is not fully eliminated by rational arbitrage, it may not be optimal for rational investors simply to forecast fundamentals;

it may be optimal for such investors also to predict the change in noise trader sentiment.

Noise traders who exhibit extrapolative expectations, for example by buying securities after they have risen and by selling securities after they have fallen, are 'positive feedback traders'. This behaviour, especially if reinforced by the actions of rational investors, is consistent with positive short-run autocorrelation of returns (see Shleifer and Summers, 1990, p. 29).

To what extent is noise trading characteristic of futures markets? This is the question addressed by Sanders, Irwin and Leuthold in Chapter 5. These authors first develop a theoretical model of futures price determination in the presence of noise traders, which is based on a model of De Long *et al.* (1990). The model presented in Chapter 5 comprises two assets: a safe asset with a fixed price, and a risky asset with a variable price. This model also comprises two types of economic agent: rational investors and noise traders, the latter of whom misperceive the price of the risky asset. Both rational investors and noise traders are assumed to maximise utility.

At maturity, the price of a futures contract in this model equals the fundamental value of the asset, this result being brought about by rational arbitrage. Before maturity, however, the equilibrium futures price may differ from fundamental value. If noise traders are on average bearish, there will be a downward bias in futures prices, and the model predicts that futures prices will rise as maturity approaches (reminiscent of the test of the normal backwardation hypothesis used by Telser, 1958). In contrast, if noise traders are on average bullish, futures prices will exceed fundamental value, and these prices will fall as maturity approaches. The model, therefore, provides predictions about returns, based on the average sentiment of noise traders.

Sanders, Irwin and Leuthold use the Vane market index as a measure of noise trader sentiment. This index, which is based on newsletters, brokers' recommendations, etc., provides a measure of the degree of bullishness. These authors are able to demonstrate that sentiment follows returns for each of twenty-eight futures markets, and so they are confident that this index is representative of noise traders. Sanders, Irwin and Leuthold then address the issue of whether noise traders have an impact on prices by testing for the presence of bias in futures prices, using cross-section analysis, and by investigating whether returns follow sentiment, using time series techniques. The reader may then reflect upon what proportion of agents in futures markets is made up of noise traders, and if, as assumed, noise traders are able to optimise their own utility, whether they may ultimately learn to optimise the use of information. The reader may wish to reflect, also, upon the more important question of the reasons for any differences between the outcomes reported in Chapter 5 and those obtained for equities markets.

Hypotheses about dynamic systems

Attempts have been made to explain and predict the time paths of financial variables using hypotheses based on two types of models. First, hypotheses have been derived from models of stochastic variables, i.e. of variables that change in an uncertain way so that their future time paths can be described only in a probabilistic manner. Second, hypotheses have been derived from deterministic models, i.e. from models, broadly speaking, without exogenous variables and, recently, a particular type of these models, namely chaotic models, has been used. Although a precise definition of chaotic models is lacking (Medio, 1992, p. 4), some deterministic models are capable of generating complex time paths of *apparently* random behaviour. Although the existence of such models was known in the nineteenth century, recent developments in this area are assumed to date from the work of Lorenz (1963) and emerged in the study of atmospheric turbulence.

Although locally unpredictable, chaotic systems may be globally stable. In such a case, an *attractor* or limit time path exists. This may be a single equilibrium point, or it may be a *strange attractor* or set of points, toward which time paths starting in its neighbourhood are attracted (see Baumol and Benhabib, 1989, pp. 91–2; Medio, 1992, p. 81).

If a variable x follows a generalised Wiener process, then the change in x, for a small time interval Δt, is

$$\Delta x = a\Delta t + b\varepsilon\sqrt{\Delta t} \tag{1.1}$$

where a and b are constant; a is the drift rate per unit of time, $\varepsilon \sim N(0, 1)$ and $b\varepsilon\sqrt{\Delta t}$ represents volatility. Then $x \sim N(a\Delta t, b^2\Delta t)$, and the variance increases with the time interval. As $\Delta t \rightarrow 0$, equation 1.1 becomes:

$$dx = adt + bdz \tag{1.2}$$

where $dz = \varepsilon\sqrt{dt}$. Although a linear first-order differential equation, such as equation 1.2, cannot generate a chaotic time path, a *non-linear* first-order differential equation can represent chaotic behaviour. Similarly, although first- and second-order linear difference equations can, under certain conditions, generate oscillations, a first-order *non-linear* difference equation can generate a chaotic time path (Baumol and Benhabib, 1989, p. 81). The justification for the use of non-linear equations in research on financial markets is found in the lack of proportionality between cause and effect; for example, a given change in interest rates can have effects of different magnitudes in different economies (for an example, see Chorafas, 1994, Chapter 1). Evidence of non-linear relationships has been found in price data for futures contracts and for other financial markets, and some of this evidence is consistent with deterministic chaos (see the survey in Clyde and Osler, 1997, pp. 491–2).

In Chapter 6, Malliaris and Stein develop a system of first-order non-linear differential equations to study the relationships between the following three variables:

1 excess price volatility (i.e. the noisiness of the system) x;
2 the extent of informed speculation z;
3 the variance of the Bayesian errors y [a Bayesian error, which has the same meaning here as in Stein (1986), is due to misuse of information, and signifies that agents are still learning the true model driving the economy].

Malliaris and Stein hypothesise *inter alia* that the greater the excess volatility the greater is the variance of the Bayesian errors, and that an increase in the measure of informed speculation (for example, because of the entrance of more large speculators) will lead to a decline in variance of Bayesian errors. Depending on the values of the parameters, this system can result in chaotic behaviour with a strange attractor, or in asymptotic stability.

Baumol and Benhabib (1989, pp. 101–2) discuss methods of testing for chaos in economic time series. Among the methods discussed are the reconstruction approach, which seeks to reproduce an economic time series by a non-linear deterministic model, and the 'dimension' approach, which seeks to distinguish chaotic from stochastic dynamics. The method of testing for the presence of chaos, used by Malliaris and Stein in Chapter 6, does not coincide precisely with either of these methods, but is closer to the first approach. Malliaris and Stein obtain least-squares estimates of the parameters of their model, in difference equation form with data from US corn and soybeans markets, and they test the hypotheses *inter alia* that the system is non-linear (against the alternative that it is linear) and that volatility is related to the Bayesian error (against the alternative that it is not so related).

The integrity of futures markets: price limits and the distribution of price changes

The leptokurtic nature of the frequency distribution of daily price changes in securities markets, including futures markets, is well known (see, for example, Mandelbrot, 1963). The main rival hypotheses put forward to account for this phenomenon are that the observations are drawn from a stable Paretian distribution or, alternatively, that they are drawn from a mixture of normal distributions (normal distributions with changing means and variances).

Although Mandelbrot (1963) argued that empirical frequency distributions for cotton favoured the stable Paretian rather than the normal distribution, more recent evidence tends to favour the mixture of normals against the stable Paretian. For example, Hall *et al.* (1989) used the stability under additions test of the characteristic exponent to discriminate between the stable Paretian and mixture of normals hypotheses with commodity futures price data. The data were randomised because successive daily price changes evidently were not independent, and tests favoured the mixture of normals hypothesis. Similarly, Hsieh (1988) used empirical frequencies within subsamples to reject the hypothesis that observations on daily price changes in spot exchange rates, for five major currencies, are drawn from a fixed leptokurtic distribution. He argued that changes in monthly mean and monthly variance accounted for rejection of the hypothesis that the observations were independent and identically distributed (i.i.d.) for the Canadian dollar, Deutschmark and Swiss franc, although i.i.d. had been rejected also for the British pound and Japanese yen. Nevertheless, his evidence suggested that variances were time varying for all five currencies.

Further evidence that tends to favour the mixture of normals hypothesis has been found with intraday (transactions) data. For example, Harris (1987) proceeded upon the following assumptions: (1) that price change and volume, after each information event, are jointly i.i.d.; (2) that the number of such events varies each day; and (3) that the number of information events, although unobservable, bears a constant ratio to the number of transactions. He found, *inter alia*, with data for equities that, although daily price changes are indeed leptokurtic, as transaction intervals increase the distribution of price changes approaches normality.

The evidence in favour of mixtures of normals, however, is not conclusive, and the debate is not finished; other distributions are not ruled out (see also Hall *et al.*, 1989, p. 112). What is also unknown is the effect of regulatory tools, such as price limits, on the probability of price changes, and ultimately on the efficiency of markets. This is the issue investigated by Hall, Kofman and Siouclis in Chapter 7. Here, again, the emphasis is on intraday data because price limits are valid for one day only, being set as a percentage of the closing price of the previous day.

Acknowledgements

Thanks are due to Robert Brooks and Jeffrey Williams, who provided comments on some of the chapters in this volume; they are not, however, responsible for any remaining errors or omissions. I am indebted to Gary Swinton and Sue Drummond of the Geography Department at Monash University, who prepared the diagrams and graphs; they used modern technology and personal skill to create a tailored product. I am indebted, also, to Elizabeth Kwok for her help in preparation of the manuscript; it seems that she can always fit another task into an already crowded day, without any sacrifice in her meticulous standards. Finally, I would like to acknowledge the contribution of the editorial team at Routledge, in particular of Alan Jarvis, who encouraged the preparation of this volume, of his successors Craig Fowlie and James Whiting, and especially of Liz Brown, whose skills of diplomacy and planning converted obstacles into smooth sailing. In addition, this volume has benefited, at the copy-editing stage, from the input of David MacDonald and the group at Prepress Projects, to whom thanks are due.

Endnotes

1 I am indebted to Jerome Stein for comments on an earlier version of this chapter; he is not responsible for any remaining errors or omissions.
2 This point of view was not universally accepted, and Bakken (1966, p. 20) made the then radical statement that he could foresee trading in a 'universal contract based on index numbers'. At the same time, Gray (1966, pp. 117–22) distinguished between feasibility and success of a futures contract, and referred to contractual characteristics that may hinder success.
3 Futures trading in emerging markets also may not have an appropriate legal system for contract enforcement (see Williams, 1995, p. 1).
4 For example, futures prices may provide a guide to forward contracting or production decisions by agents not trading on the futures exchange.

References

Arrow, K.J. (1982) 'Risk perception in psychology and economics', *Economic Inquiry* 20: 1–9.

Bailley, R.W., Baillie, R.T. and McMahon, P.C. (1984) 'Interpreting econometric evidence on efficiency in the foreign exchange market', *Oxford Economic Papers* 36: 67–85.

Baillie, R.T. and McMahon, P.C. (1989) *The Foreign Exchange Market: Theory and Econometric Evidence*, Cambridge: Cambridge University Press.

Baillie, R.T., Lippens, R.E. and McMahon, P.C. (1983) 'Testing rational expectations and efficiency in the foreign exchange market', *Econometrica* 51: 553–63.

Bakken, H. H. (1966) 'Futures trading (origin, development and economic status', in *Futures Trading Seminar*, vol. III, Madison: MIMIR Publishers, pp. 1–24.

Baumol, W. and Benhabib, J. (1989) 'Chaos: significance, mechanism, and economic applications', *Journal of Economic Perspectives* 3: 77–105.

Benos, A.V. (1998) 'Aggressiveness and survival of overconfident traders', *Journal of Financial Markets* 1: 353–83.

Bilson, J.F.O. (1981) 'The "speculative efficiency" hypothesis', *Journal of Business* 54: 435–51.

Chorafas, D.N. (1994) *Chaos Theory in Financial Markets*, Chicago, IL: Probus Publishing.

Clyde, W.C. and Osler, C.L. (1997) 'Charting: chaos theory in disguise?', *Journal of Futures Markets* 17: 489–517.

De Long, J.B., Shleifer, A., Summers, L.H. and Waldemann, R.J. (1990) 'Noise trader risk in financial markets', *Journal of Political Economy* 98: 703–38.

Frenkel, J.A. (1981) 'The collapse of purchasing power parities during the 1970s', *European Economic Review* 16: 145–65.

Goss, B.A., Avsar, S.G. and Fry, J.M. (1998) 'Expectations and forecasting in the US dollar/British pound market', Mimeograph, Clayton, Victoria, Australia: Department of Economics, Monash University.

Gray, R.W. (1966) 'Why does futures trading succeed or fail: an analysis of selected commodities', *Futures Trading Seminar*, vol. III, Madison: MIMIR Publishers, pp. 115–28.

Hall, J.A., Brorsen, B.W. and Irwin, S.H. (1989) 'The distribution of futures prices: a test of the stable Paretian and mixture of normals hypotheses', *Journal of Financial and Quantitative Analysis* 24: 105–116.

Hansen, L.P. and Hodrick, R.J. (1980) 'Forward exchange rates as optimal predictors of future spot rates: an economic analysis', *Journal of Political Economy* 88: 829–53.

Harris, L. (1987) 'Transaction data tests of the mixture of distributions hypothesis', *Journal of Financial and Quantitative Analysis* 22(2): 127–41.

Hodrick, R.J. (1987) *The Empirical Evidence on the Efficiency of Forward and Futures Foreign Exchange Markets*, Chur: Harwood.

Hodrick, R.J. and Srivastava, S. (1984) 'An investigation of risk and return in forward foreign exchange', *Journal of International Money and Finance* 3: 1–29.

Hodrick, R.J. and Srivastava, S. (1987) 'Foreign currency futures', *Journal of International Economics* 22: 1–24.

Houthakker, H.S. (1959) 'The scope and limits of futures trading', in Abramovitz, M. *et al.* (eds) *The Allocation of Economic Resources*, Stanford, CA: Stanford University Press, pp. 134–59.

Hsieh, D.A. (1988) 'The statistical properties of daily foreign exchange rates: 1974–83', *Journal of International Economics* 24: 129–45.

Isard, P. (1987) 'Lessons from empirical models of exchange rates', *International Monetary Fund Staff Papers* 34: 1–28.

Krugman, P. (1993) 'Recent thinking about exchange rate determination and policy', in Blundell-Wignall, A. (ed.) *The Exchange Rate, International Trade and the Balance of Payments*, Proceedings of a Conference, Sydney, Reserve Bank of Australia, pp. 6–22.

Leuthold, R.M. and Garcia, P. (1992) 'Assessing market performance: an examination of livestock futures markets', in Goss B.A. (ed.) *Rational Expectations and Efficiency in Futures Markets*, London: Routledge, pp. 52–77.

Leuthold, R.M. and Hartmann, P.A. (1979) 'A semi-strong form evaluation of the efficiency of the hog futures market', *American Journal of Agricultural Economics* 61: 482–9.

Lorenz, E.N. (1963) 'Deterministic non-periodic flow', *Journal of Atmospheric Science* 20: 130–41.

McCallum, B.T. (1979) 'Topics concerning the formulation, estimation and use of macroeconomic models with rational expectations', in *Proceedings of the Business and Economic Statistics Section*, Washington, DC: American Statistical Association, pp. 65–72.

Maddock, R. and Carter, M. (1982) 'A child's guide to rational expectations', *Journal of Economic Literature* 20: 39–51.

Mandelbrot, B. (1963) 'The variation of certain speculative prices', *Journal of Business* 36: 394–419.

Medio, A. (1992) *Chaotic Dynamics Theory and Applications*, Cambridge: Cambridge University Press.

Meese, R. (1990) 'Currency fluctuations in the post-Bretton Woods era', *Journal of Economic Perspectives* 4: 117–34.

Rausser, G.C. and Carter, Colin (1983) 'Futures market efficiency in the soybean complex', *Review of Economics and Statistics* 65: 469–78.

Shleifer, A. and Summers, L.H. (1990) 'The noise trader approach to finance', *Journal of Economic Perspectives* 4 (2): 19–33.

Stein, J.L. (1986) *The Economics of Futures Markets*, Oxford: Basil Blackwell.

Taylor, M.P. (1995) 'The economics of exchange rates', *Journal of Economic Literature* 33: 13–47.

Taylor, S.J. (1992) 'Rewards available to currency futures speculators: compensation for risk or evidence of inefficient pricing', in Stein, J.L. and

Goss B.A. (eds) *Economic Record: Special Issue on Futures Markets*, pp. 105–16.

Telser, L.G. (1958) 'Futures trading and the storage of cotton and wheat', *Journal of Political Economy* 66(3): 233–55.

Telser, L.G. and Higinbotham, H.N. (1977) 'Organized futures markets: costs and benefits', *Journal of Political Economy* 85: 969–1000.

Veljanovski, C.J. (1986) 'An institutional analysis of futures contracting', in Goss, B.A. (ed.) *Futures Markets: Their Establishment and Performance*, London: Croom Helm, pp. 13–41.

Williams, J. (1986) *The Economic Function of Futures Markets*, Cambridge: Cambridge University Press.

Williams, J. (1995) 'The new commodity contracts in China', paper presented to Western Economic Association International Conference, San Diego, July.

Chapter 2

The gains from futures trading

Derek Francis

Introduction

A function of markets is to gather, process and disseminate diffuse elements of heterogeneous private information. This enables traders to co-ordinate their plans at mutual least cost.[1] In this chapter, it is shown that futures markets naturally emerge to facilitate this role. Specifically, they evolve as the institution that minimises the transaction costs of exchange of different private information sets concerning the future. This allows people to alter present planning in light of a more comprehensive information set about the future. This leads to market participants making better current period decisions and achieving Pareto gains from futures trading.[2]

Trading in futures involves a standardised contract to receive or supply a good at some specified future date at a mutually agreed price. In practice, the obligation is generally extinguished by carrying out the reverse transaction in the standard contract at some later stage, before delivery or receipt of the good becomes necessary.[3] Thus, one person's gain from futures trading must equal the other's loss, or futures trading taken in isolation is a zero sum game. Where are the gains from this trade?

It is the aim of this chapter to develop a theoretical general equilibrium framework to demonstrate how the gains from futures trading arise.

This chapter attempts to clarify some major deficiencies in the literature concerning futures markets. Specifically, the following questions are addressed:

1 Where and how do the gains from futures trading arise?
2 What is the effect of futures markets on prices?
3 Why do futures markets emerge for some goods and not others?
4 What are the welfare implications of futures trading?

In the first section, the basic general equilibrium model is presented. Given the heterogeneity of private information, traders form different expectations concerning the future relative prices of goods. Exchange of this information through forward contracting allows people to make Pareto gains through increased current production of the two goods. Futures trading then naturally evolves as the institution that minimises the transaction costs of forward contracting. The theoretical implications of this result are discussed in relation to current economic theory on futures trading.

In the second section (pp. 24–36), the gains from futures trading are explored. In particular, the analysis investigates the nature of heterogeneous information and its relationship to the gains from futures trading. The relationship between exogenous disturbances and intertemporal resource allocation decisions in alternative institutional settings is also examined. The insights gained from the analysis provide a basis for the direct quantification of the welfare effects of futures trading in different circumstances.

The model developed is related to existing theories in the literature on futures trading, such as those relating to unbiasedness, spot price variability, rational expectations and expectation formation.

THE BASIC MODEL

The basic model has two representative agents A and B; two goods X and Y; and two periods 1 and 2. The agents have identical production transformation curves between the two goods. The maximum quantities of X and Y each agent is able to produce are shown in Figure 2.1. The curve is assumed to be concave to the origin.[4]

Production decisions are made in period 1. The output becomes available for consumption in period 2. Agents attempt to maximise expected consumption utility in period 2. A has a consumption bias towards X, and B has a symmetrical consumption bias towards Y. This provides the basis for the gains from trade.

Assume that all agents are initially in autarky, unable to exchange information. Each agent equates their marginal rate of transformation (MRT) X for Y with their personal marginal rate of substitution (MRS) X for Y. MRS is equated with MRT to maximise period 2 utility in autarky.

By way of illustration, assume that A produces 10X and 5Y in period 1, where $MRTA_{XY} = 2$, and assume that this is being consumed in period 2, $MRSA_{XY} = 2$, and the utility achieved is UA (Figure 2.1). Assume B produces 10Y and 5X, $MRTB_{XY} = 0.5 = MRSB_{XY}$ in period 2, and B achieves utility UB (Figure 2.1).

Suppose now that the two agents are brought together, while maintaining the assumption of no communication before the production decision is made. A will produce (10,5) and B will produce (5,10). This decision is based solely on private information. Therefore, aggregate production for (A + B) is (10,5) + (5,10) = (15,15).

Allowing the agents to trade in period 2 will generate consumption reallocation gains. As MRSA > MRSB, A can exchange Y for X with B, and the utility levels of UAC and UBC can be achieved (see Figure 2.1). In period 2, this trade price $P_X/P_Y = 1$ corresponds to the perfectly competitive equilibrium price, given period 1 production and large numbers of agents.

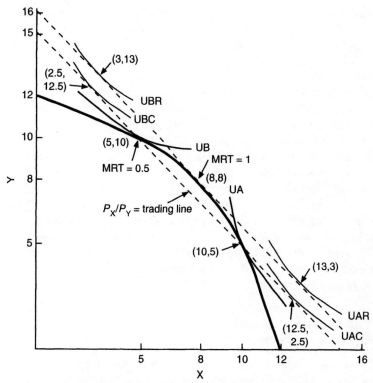

Figure 2.1 Agent A, initially in autarky, locates production in period 1 at (10,5), where MRS = MRT = 2. Agent B locates (5,10), where MRS = MRT = 0.5. In period 2, agent A can trade down the $P_X/P_Y = 1$ line, from (10,5) to (12.5,2.5), achieving utility UAC; agent B does the opposite, achieving UBC. Through futures trading, they can both relocate production to (8,8) and achieve UAR and UBR respectively

This is not a Muth (1961) rational expectations equilibrium (REE). Such an equilibrium would require the expectations of agents, and thus their production decisions, to be consistent with the solution to the true model.[5] That is to say, if agents could have correctly foreseen in period 1 that the period 2 P_X/P_Y would equal 1, they could have relocated production at (8,8) and thus increased their utility levels. This REE could then have been achieved (Figure 2.1).[6]

With *forward contracting*, the REE is *achievable*. Specifically, through forward contracting in period 1, Pareto gains can be made via the exchange of private information, leading to better production.

In autarky, agent A, when restricted to private information, extrapolated that the expected period 2 $P_X/P_Y = 2$, with expected utility UA. B's expected period 2 $P_X/P_Y = 0.5$, with expected utility UB. Consequently, there are gains to be had from forward contracting in period 1 at any price between these private expectations.

If agent A agrees to supply B with 2.5Y in exchange for 2.5X, the utility levels Uac and Ubc are attained with certainty, given production of (10,5) and (5,10) (Figure 2.1). These utility levels represent the consumption exchange gains as outlined previously. The forward contracting price of $P_X/P_Y = 1$ is established.

Given this forward price, there are further gains to be derived from altering production. A and B can make Pareto gains by relocating their period 1 production decision to where their MRTs equal this common forward price ratio – at (8,8) on the transformation curve MRT = 1. Agent A, by relocating at (8,8) and forward selling 5Y for 5X, can shift his period 2 consumption point to (13,3), achieving the higher utility level UAR with certainty. B, by relocating at (8,8) and selling 5X forward for 5Y, can achieve UBR. If large numbers of As and Bs engaged in costless forward contracting at the start of period 1, this competitive REE could potentially be achieved.[7,8]

The Pareto production gains from forward contracting

I wish now to focus on the gains that result from better production. Unless traders have homogeneous expectations of the forward price, there will always be gains from forward contracting. Agent A originally expected period 2 P_X/P_Y would equal 2. Therefore, he originally located his production decision where MRT = 2, whereas B located where MRT = 0.5. The total amount produced equalled (10,5) + (5,10) = (15,15) (Figure 2.2a).

Through the medium of forward contracting, the agents establish an expected forward price that lies between their respective independent expectations. As both individuals relocate production at the common expected future price, a *net production gain* occurs. Agent A gives up 2X and produces an extra 3Y, whereas B gives up 2Y and produces an extra 3X. Production increases to (8,8) + (8,8) = (16,16).

This Pareto gain results from producers equalising their MRTs through the exchange of different information about the future. Production decisions became mutually consistent, and also consistent with (in this model) the global information set concerning the future. Thus, *whenever producers have different expectations concerning the future relative price of a good, there are always Pareto gains to be made from forward contracting.* These gains are exhausted when producers' MRTs are equalised and present production decisions are altered to equal this common MRT. A net increase in production necessarily occurs.

In summary, the three assumptions necessary to drive the model are as follows.

1 The product transformation curve is concave down, i.e. this means the supply curve for the good is upward sloping.

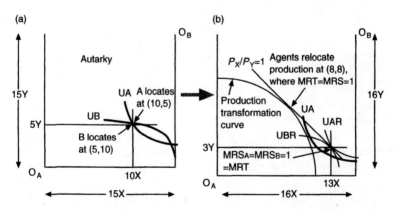

Figure 2.2 An Edgeworth box construction showing the Pareto gains from forward contracting. (a) Agent A initially locates at (10,5), where MRS = 2. Agent B initially locates at (5,10), where MRS = 0.5. (b) After engaging in futures trading, both agents equalise their future price expectation and relocate their production decision to this common MRT = 1 at (8,8) on the production possibility frontier. The dimensions of the Edgeworth box expand because of the net increase in production from forward contracting to equalise producers' MRTs. The REE is achieved with forward contracting.

2 Different expectations of the relative future price of the good.
3 Production of the good is not instantaneous, so that when the decision to produce occurs a spot market commitment is made.

In Figure 2.2a and b, achievement of the REE is illustrated. In autarky, agents A and B plan production at (10,5) and (5,10) respectively. Through forward contracting, they establish the futures price $p_X/p_Y = 1$,[9] which lies between their own price expectations. Given the forward price, both agents relocate the production decision at (8,8), where MRT = MRS = 1, and make certain increases in expected utility to at least UAR and UBR respectively. Net production increases, and thus the dimensions of the Edgeworth box increase to (16,16), as shown in Figure 2.2b. The new equilibrium is Pareto optimal.

The evolution of futures trading

The discussion now turns to why futures trading naturally evolves as the institutional trading arrangement that economises on the transaction costs of forward contracting.[10] This result implies futures trading makes it possible to provide the market with more information about the prevailing future price than forward contracting. Thus, futures trading naturally evolves as the superior instrument for exchanging different information sets concerning the future. The technical analysis here largely follows the work of Houthakker (1959) and Veljanovski (1986).

Consider Figure 2.1 and the optimisation problem presented previously. Initially, A locates at (10,5), with an expected utility of UA. The expected future price of A is based on that agent's private information sets. B thought the opposite and thus located at (5,10), giving B an expected utility of UB. Suppose agent A and B pair off and agree to deliver 5Y and 5X, respectively, to the other person in period 2. Both agents relocate production at (8,8). They thereby shift their initial endowment points from (10,5) and (5,10) to (13,3) and (3,13), respectively, and raise their expected utilities with certainty to at least UAR and UBR (Figure 2.1). Even if the forward contract does not predict the future price very well, the collective utility level of these forward contractors will necessarily be higher because of the Pareto improving production.[11]

As other agents observe the higher utility of A and B, they will wish to engage in forward contracting themselves. However, there are substantial transaction costs in forward contracting. First, search costs associated with the double coincidence of wants – each A must find a B who is prepared to buy what he wants to sell, and sell what he wants to buy. Second, they incur scrutinising and enforcement costs. Each A and B must specify the grade and quality of the good to be traded, scrutinise the integrity and reliability of the person with whom they are trading, and further may incur costs over time ensuring forward contracts are not breached. Finally, there is the cost of delivery.

Given such transaction costs, it seems natural that a broking agent will emerge to facilitate forward trade.[12] He will search for As and Bs who wish to forward contract. The agents will list with the broker, who can initially pair them off. This reduces individual search costs. There are increasing returns to this activity: as more traders list, the probability of finding mutually beneficial trades increases. This in turn increases the tendency for As and Bs to want to list with the broker. We may also expect some economies of scale in contractual specification, scrutiny and enforcement. Thus, the broker may specialise in scrutinising the individual traders and guaranteeing the specified contracts. He will in turn be paid by the traders to perform this role.

In attempting to economise on enforcement, delivery and capital costs, it seems better for individual traders to pay and receive margins depending upon their positions and the movement of the forward price, rather than agreeing to deliver prespecified amounts when forward contracts fall due.

For example, suppose in period 1 agent A contracts with B to supply 5Y in return for 5X, establishing a futures price $p_X/p_Y = 1$. Suppose the spot price in period 2 is $P_X/P_Y = 1.67$. At the start of period 2, when the futures contract matures, each party could carry out their obligation by delivery. Alternatively, the equivalent transaction could be performed by B simply paying A 2X because 5Y exchanges for 3X in the market. The relevant accounting transactions are: in period 1, agent A sells 5Y futures to B for 5X futures; in period 2, agent A buys back the 5Y futures for 3X futures. Agent A gains 2X from futures trading whereas B loses 2X.[13]

The introduction of the clearing house

Alternatively, consider the same transaction with a third party acting as the clearing house between A and B. Agent A sells 5X futures to the clearing house and receives 5Y futures in return, whereas B engages in the opposite transaction with the clearing house. The broker requires a small margin from both parties to cover their positions for adverse movements in the futures price (for example, the broker may demand

2Y from A and 2X from B). If the futures price does not move, the parties engage in the reverse transaction with the clearing house at the start of period 2. The clearing house returns the margin deposits and the obligations are extinguished.

Suppose the future price moves to $P_X/P_Y = 1.67$ before period 2. The broker could transfer 2X from B's account to A's account and require B to make an additional deposit margin to keep his futures trading position open.[14] Through doing this, the broker performs numerous valuable services: he better guarantees the integrity of the exchange process, economises on capital tied up in futures trading by requiring only deposit margins, and he eliminates the delivery costs of forward contracting.

Contract standardisation

Standardised futures contracts will develop to economise on the transaction costs of exchange. Increasing returns accrue from use of a standard contract as a medium of exchange: as use of the standard contract expands, confidence in the medium is enhanced, which in turn promotes further expansion in use. Thus, inferior types of forward contracts in goods X and Y will be progressively driven out of the market by trade in the standard contract.

This is a similar conclusion to the theoretical work of Brunner and Meltzer (1971) on the benefits of an economy moving from barter to money. These benefits relate to minimising the transaction costs of exchange caused by the uneven distribution of information through society.

The authors' thesis is the following: in a barter economy, in attempting to go from an initial endowment to a final endowment, people will trade in intermediate goods (mediums of exchange). As traders learn about the properties of different potential mediums of exchange, they will choose those intermediate goods about which it is easiest to acquire information in order to minimise the cost of the transaction. Once a particular good is in frequent use, the cost of acquiring information about it further declines, which increases the probability of its general acceptance as a medium of exchange. This induces clustering of transaction chains to a common pattern and, finally, to a dominant medium of exchange. This is as a result of the increasing returns nature of the model.[15]

The introduction of speculators

As delivery is no longer required under a standard contract, people can participate in speculative activity even if they do not produce or have stocks of X and Y. Profits can be made by speculators if their predictions concerning the future price are better than the prediction of the futures market. This could arise, for example, if they had selective access to unique information. In their attempt to exploit such profit opportunities, speculators help facilitate a more complete transmission of information concerning the future price. Further, they will increase market liquidity and probably reduce futures price volatility.[16]

Short summary

With the adoption of a standardised contract, the evolution of an impersonal market is complete. A central broker can substantially facilitate exchange by developing a standardised contract and requiring deposit margins from the traders who buy and sell in the contract.

Futures traders deal only with the broker and do not worry about contractual specification, search, scrutinising or enforcement. Traders also use less liquid capital than with forward trading. They will pay the broker for facilitating these exchanges. Futures markets evolve to perform the function of forward contracting at a lower cost. The analysis suggests that the brokerage is a potential natural monopoly because of the increasing returns nature of the activity.[17]

Some initial implications

The present analysis differs from the traditional literature, which emphasises risk shifting and risk premiums. This literature suggests that the primary reason for futures trading is *insurance*: producers pay speculators a *premium* for bearing the risk of an adverse movement in spot prices. This is embodied in the *normal backwardation hypothesis* whereby producers, who are short hedgers, trade with long speculators, and the futures price trends upwards as maturity approaches.[18] This theory predicts that producers, by transferring a risk premium to speculators, can obtain certainty *at the cost* of a lower average return.

In contrast, this chapter suggests that producers, through futures trading, can obtain *both* a higher average and more certain return through improved production decisions. Furthermore, the analysis suggests futures traders *do not* take systematic positions according to their identity, i.e. producers or speculators; rather, they take futures positions according to their unique private information to maximise expected future utility. And, by doing so, traders reveal the aggregate period 2 supply and demand functions before period 1 production decisions are made, thus leading to higher total production.

In addition, the analysis suggests that the futures price will *not* trend upwards through time; rather, it will be an unbiased predictor[19] of the future price because any evidence of a risk premium would be bid away to extract further Pareto production gains.[20] That is to say, the returns from futures trading will be highest in total when the futures price is an unbiased predictor. Speculators can only make a profit if they assist this price discovery process by providing the futures market with more accurate information concerning the correct future price.

Further, anyone who obtains new information concerning the future price could undertake futures trading and profit from this information. Thus, the price movements of futures should reflect this new information and be consistent with the REE.[21]

Thus, the analysis suggests that the 'normal backwardation hypothesis' literature may be misleading by characterising futures trading as a quasi-insurance market, rather than emphasising trading's role in improved decision-making about the future through the exchange of heterogeneous private information.

GAINS FROM FUTURES TRADING

In this part of the chapter, it is demonstrated that the gains from futures trading vary directly with the degree of heterogeneity of present information about the future. The effects of the establishment of a futures market on trading volume, and the ability of futures markets to more speedily impart new information to spot markets, will be discussed.

There follows an analysis of the welfare implications of the following institutional settings in which the exchange of information may occur: a spot market only, a spot market with forward contracting and a spot market with futures trading. The model will be subjected to an exogenous disturbance. Possible adjustment paths in various alternative institutional settings are posited, and also alternative assumptions about expectation formation. This analysis will indicate when futures trading is likely to be most beneficial.

> Proposition 1: the more heterogeneous information is concerning the future the greater will be the gains from futures trading.

This proposition can be verified quite simply. The more divergent the information on which producers base their production decisions the greater will be the difference in their individual MRTs. The greater the difference between current valuations of future output the greater will be the gains from futures trading. That is to say, effective futures markets increase production by equalising the MRTs of producers,[22] and this increase (or the gains from trade) will be greater the bigger the initial difference in producers' individual MRTs.

Proposition 2: futures markets increase trading volume compared with forward contracting. This is a result of traders exchanging their private information at a lower transaction cost than with forward contracting. Increased trading volume implies that a greater amount of private information about the future is conveyed to the market.

In the basic model, traders adjusted their expectations of the future price to the futures market price because this price represented a global pooling of information.

Suppose individual expectations of the future spot price do not adjust to the futures market prediction. Specifically, agent A expects P_X/P_Y to remain at 2, whereas B expects P_X/P_Y to remain at 0.5. If both agents attempt to maximise the value of production on the basis of these expectations, they will continue to trade in futures. Agent A continues to sell Y futures and to buy X futures at $P_X/P_Y = 1$. In principle, there is no limit to this process and the volume of futures trade may exceed the existing stock of output several times over.

Within this framework, we would expect a greater flow of private information about the future to increase the trading volume in futures. For example, consider agent A, who obtains additional information that leads him to be more certain of the future price $P_X/P_Y = 2$. This information motivates agent A to buy more X futures and to sell more Y futures. The excess supply of Y futures and excess demand for X futures will raise the p_X/p_Y price ratio for futures.

New information about the true model is beneficial. Extra trading in futures reflects additional private information sets. If these information sets are a more comprehensive reflection of the true model, futures trading will enhance market performance by imparting improved information about the future to the market.

This theoretical analysis is consistent with a major empirical result of Rutledge (1986), who attempted to identify the direction of causation between futures trading volume and spot price variability. Rutledge found that thirty-one out of the thirty-three cases studied were consistent with the hypothesis that futures trading volume responds to spot price variability, *rather than* causing it.[23] Increased spot price variability is evidence of additional information being conveyed to the market. The analysis carried out in this chapter predicts that an exogenous disturbance (i.e. increased spot price variability) enhances the potential gains from futures trading and thus increases the trading volume in the futures market, which is consistent with Rutledge (1986).

Comparing futures trading with forward contracting

Forward contracting will not perform as well as futures trading in imparting new information to the market because of the higher transaction costs of performing exchange: the problems caused by double coincidence of wants, enforcement[24] of contracts and delivery could be expected to rise as trading volume increases (or at least remain significantly higher than the per unit transaction costs of futures trading). Valuable information will be excluded from the market process (as a result of these transaction costs) and, thus, forward contracting will not fully exploit the opportunities to gain from the exchange of private information about the future.

Figure 2.3 shows the average transaction costs as a function of volume for forward contracting and futures trading. Initially, the costs of setting up a futures market may be substantial. Once this (largely) fixed cost is overcome, transaction costs of trade are small. The components of marginal cost (of trade) are brokerage fees and loss of interest on funds held as margins against the risk of default, although this last component can be minimised through the use of Treasury Bills.

Contrast this with forward contracting. There is little fixed cost but a higher marginal cost (of trade), reflecting the following costs: double coincidence searches, delivery and enforcement. There is an optimal trading volume at which it will be more economical to switch from a forward contracting market to a futures exchange when all trade should be carried out via futures. In practice, this may not happen because a forward contracting market could crowd out the establishment of a futures market.[25]

Short summary

Trading volume is related directly to the gains from imparting new information to the market. The greater the exogenous disturbances to a market the stronger is the case for the development of a futures market to facilitate future production and allocation decisions for that good.

The larger the forward trading volume the greater will be the relative loss from forward contracting compared with the alternative institutional arrangement of futures trading. Large trading volumes in futures constitute

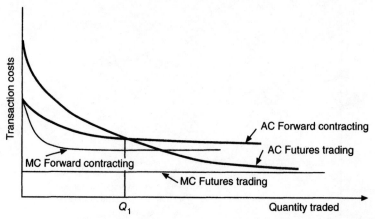

Figure 2.3 At quantity Q_1, it is optimal to switch over from a forward contracting market to a futures exchange. AC, average cost; MC, marginal cost.

corroborative evidence that efficiency gains are occurring from the exchange of additional information about the future production and consumption decisions for a good.

Figure 2.4 illustrates welfare levels for agents trading in alternative institutional settings. Assuming the (marginal) transaction costs of futures trading have been netted out[26] in the diagram, the period 2 REE results from futures trading at point *P*. The welfare level given by utility of UAR is achieved.

The equilibrium utility level is UAF with forward contracting. The difference between A's and B's expected price with this inferior equilibrium is representative of the higher per unit transaction costs of forward contracting compared with futures trading. This expectational difference remains in period 1 because attempts to profitably arbitrage this difference are not possible. Thus potential arbitrageurs will incur transactions costs from facilitating exchanges that are higher (per unit traded) than the difference between the ask-bid spread in Figure 2.4.

Dynamic welfare considerations

Suppose we have the standard optimisation problem as presented above, but with repetition, and also assume allowing agents to adjust their expectations to past happenings. It would seem reasonable for agents to adjust their individual expectations towards the REE.

The speed with which agents can adapt their expectations will

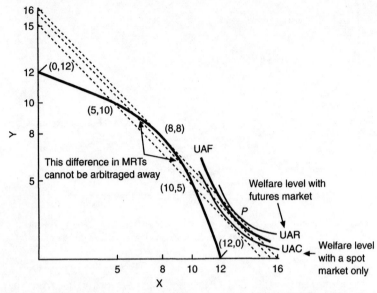

Figure 2.4 The welfare level with forward contracting is UAF. The difference between A and B in the expected P_X/P_Y equals the difference in transaction costs per unit of forward contracting versus futures trading. This cannot be arbitraged away profitably. The welfare level with futures trading is UAR; point P is achieved in the diagram.

determine the loss from having only a spot market. For example, consider the standard adaptive expectations equation:

$$\text{Expected } P_{t+1} = \text{Expected } P_t + \lambda(P_t - \text{Expected } P_t) \qquad (2.1)$$

where $0 < \lambda < 1$ and t is time.

If λ equals 1, this corresponds to weak form rational expectations: agents take full account of information as contained in past prices. With only a spot market, and one repeat of this model, all agents would have an expected future price $P_X/P_Y = 1$. The REE is achieved rapidly. With continuous repetition of the model and no exogenous shock, the REE equilibrium is maintained and the need for a futures market disappears.

Alternatively, consider $\lambda = 0.5$. With one repeat (and only a spot market), A-type agents expect $P_X/P_Y = 1.5$, whereas B-type agents expect $P_X/P_Y = 0.75$. With successive repetition, the equilibrium will converge to the REE. As λ becomes smaller, the convergence to the REE is slower and the welfare loss is larger with only a spot market, and the greater would be the gains from having a futures market over time.

Thus, the less traders exploit new public information, as embodied in the change in present price, the more likely would be the emergence of a futures market, which would motivate the traders to behave as if they fully used a global information set. In other words, the less traders make use of new information the greater the need for an institutional regime that will motivate traders to use information more completely. Futures trading provides this regime: traders have strong incentives to learn the true model quickly and thereby readily gain tangible and certain increases in expected future utility.[27]

The dynamic analysis with forward contracting is similar to that for a spot market alone, although we would expect the model to converge to the REE more rapidly because of increased information flows.

The need for futures markets explained through quicker adaptation to exogenous disturbance

Suppose we have 100 agents, 50 As and 50 Bs, and the REE as presented previously, where $P_X/P_Y = 1$. This equilibrium will be exposed to an exogenous disturbance and possible dynamic reactions to the shock will be suggested.

The specific shock to which the model will be exposed is that half of the Bs change their consumption preferences to that of agents A. That is to say, 75 traders now have the consumption preferences of agents A, whereas 25 have their original B preferences.

Let us suppose that given this change in consumption preferences for some of the traders the new REE is at $P_X/P_Y = 1.5$. The value of production is maximised on the transformation curve at location (9,6.8). The 75 traders with A preferences consume (11,3.8), achieving utility UAS, whereas the 25 traders with B preferences consume (3,15.8), achieving UBS at the REE, as shown in Figure 2.5.

Now, we analyse the adjustment path from the old REE to the new REE with and without a futures market.

With a futures market

Case 1: agents are purely passive, attempting to maximise on the basis of private information; the REE is achieved rapidly

As soon as the B agents become As, they will wish to obtain UAR for certain in period 2. Thus, they will change their demand and supply for futures. At $p_X/p_Y = 1$, these agents will now wish to buy 5X futures and

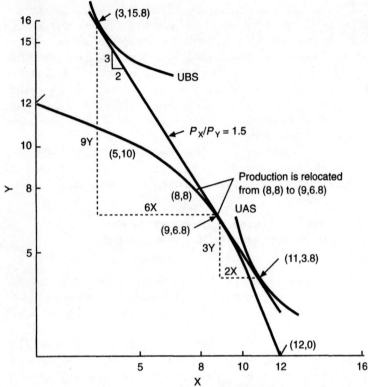

Figure 2.5 With the shock, there are now 75 As and 25 Bs. They each relocate production from (8,8) to (9,6.8). Agents A sell 3Y futures for 3X futures, agents B sell 6X futures for 9Y futures. Consumption shifts to (11,3.8) for the As, achieving utility UAS, whereas the Bs shift to (3,15.8), achieving UBS. $P_X/P_Y = 1.5$; production = 900X + 600Y, which gives consumption = $(75 \times 11 + 25 \times 3)X + (75 \times 3.8 + 25 \times 15.8)Y$.

sell 5Y futures. This results in an excess demand for X futures and an excess supply of Y futures at $p_X/p_Y = 1$. Thus, the futures price p_X/p_Y increases.

The A agents are assumed to adjust to the futures price and maximise accordingly. The rationale is that they have limited private information so they logically (or passively) will adapt their future price expectation to the futures market price to maximise utility. This is because they know the futures price represents a global pooling of information that will be more comprehensive and complete than their unique private information.[28] Thus, the futures price would be a better predictor than their limited private information set. As the futures price increases, they will move around the transformation curve from A to B as shown in Figure 2.5, reducing their demand for X futures and supply of Y futures. They will simultaneously increase X production and decrease Y production.

The remaining B agents will be happy that the futures price ratio is increasing. They will also passively adjust their production to this futures price while increasing their demand for Y futures and their supply of X futures. This adjustment process to the REE will continue until the demand and supply of futures are brought into equilibrium – at the futures price $p_X/p_Y = 1.5$. The 25 B agents each sell 6X futures, buy 9Y futures and produce (9X, 6.8Y). B's final endowment is (3,15.8) and utility level is UBS. The 75 A agents each sell 3Y futures for 2X futures and also produce at (9,6.8), while consuming at (11,3.8).

On the assumption of passive adaptation, the REE is located quickly. If production goes ahead once the futures price has settled in period 1 at $P_X/P_Y = 1.5$, the REE will be realised. There is no welfare loss. Society has intertemporally responded to this exogenous shock with perfect efficiency by using futures trading to quickly register and adapt to the new information. Note the result holds if each of the traders using futures imparts their particular and limited private information through futures trading, which allows them to, in aggregate, discover the true model driving the market market.[29]

Therefore, the case for a futures market is more compelling if, through time, there is a significant amount of new information that vests among different groups of traders. In such situations, traders will feel more compelled to have *passive*[30] expectations concerning the future price, while using the futures market to maximise utility. By doing this, traders will also simultaneously register their particular private information to the futures market, which allows the true model to, in aggregate, become discoverable through futures trading and the global pooling of distinct private information. In such situations, traders will be more likely to 'passively' adjust their private expectations of the future price to the futures market price because they know that it embodies this global pooling of discrete private information.

Case 2: agents do not respond passively to the shock

Suppose the model has performed for numerous periods at the old REE, where $P_X/P_Y = 1$. Traders may adjust their private information sets to this and thus their futures price expectation becomes $p_X/p_Y = 1$.

When the 'change in consumption preference' shock occurs, the market may exhibit much inertia in response. The agents whose preferences have changed may not feel compelled to register the information through futures trading because they expect $P_X/P_Y = 1$ in the future (i.e. if both spot and futures markets have been trading at $P_X/P_Y = 1$ for numerous periods, it could be expected that the incentives to engage in futures trading would significantly diminish through time as it presents little gain on pure spot trading).

Alternatively, if some agents do register the information, as soon as there is any increase in the futures price, other agents may offset this by buying more Y futures and selling more X futures. Why may this be the case? Agents may develop rigidity in their thinking concerning the expected future price, and think the correct future price is what has prevailed in the past, i.e. $P_X/P_Y = 1$. They may thus buy and sell futures according to this expectation. For these reasons, it is unlikely that the change in the true model will be rapidly imparted into the futures market. The longer the REE has been at $P_X/P_Y = 1$ the greater the likelihood of inertia in response to an exogenous disturbance.

This suggests that a futures market may provide less benefit if there is infrequent new information about the future entering individual trader's information sets. That is to say, the REE changes little through time. This will be the case for two reasons: (1) as the REE changes less through time, the lower will be the aggregate productive and allocational gains to be picked up from adopting futures trading with its quicker adaptation process in discovering these new REEs; (2) the less rapid will be the particular adaptation process of the futures market in discovering new REEs.

Futures trading will provide greater opportunities for gains in markets in which futures prices fluctuate because of frequent, diverse and large exogenous disturbances caused by new information coming to the market. In such cases, traders will be more likely to utilise the futures market while registering their private information and automatically adjusting their future price expectation to the futures market price. This is because in such an environment traders would be more aware of the limitations and deficiencies of their own private information sets, thus the more likely and rapidly the futures market can locate the REE. High futures trading volumes and futures price volatility are probably evidence that the futures market is doing its job in registering this new information.

This discussion is consistent with the Brunner and Meltzer thesis (1971). They suggest that the productivity of a 'transaction dominating medium of exchange' (for example, a futures contract) is related to the unevenness and heterogeneity in the spread of information, i.e. 'the degree of uncertainty about market conditions...accelerated technological changes or innovations...and larger fluctuations in economic activity' (Brunner and Meltzer, 1971, p. 800). Thus, if, as was argued earlier in the chapter, futures trading is the transaction dominating medium of exchange of information about the future for a particular good, we would expect futures trading to be greatest when the above conditions are prevalent.[31]

Adaptation to the shock with only a spot market

With only a spot market, the adaptation to the shock, i.e. the change in the preferences of the 25 Bs, will depend on how the information of the consumption preference change is imparted to the market. The principal source of welfare loss arises from those agents whose preferences have changed not being provided with a forum to register this new information about the future.

Assuming the shock to preferences has not been registered in period 1, the supply of 800X, based on expected future $P_X/P_Y = 1$, reacts with demand X shock to create a period 2 spot of, for example, $P_X/P_Y = 1.8$ in Figure 2.6. The welfare loss from the non-maximisation of the sum of consumer and of producer surplus can be calculated in the standard way. What occurs next depends upon how traders form their expectations.

Case 1: rational expectations

Consider that agents expectation formation process is such that:

$$\text{Expected } P_X/P_{Y \text{ period}(t+1)} = P_X/P_{Y \text{ period}(t)} \qquad (2.2)$$

We then get the familiar cobweb result. With repetition of the model, the period 3 expected price for period 4 is $P_X/P_Y = 1.8$. This increases supply of X to 960, creating a period 4 price of 1.2. Provided the demand curve is flatter than the supply curve, the system will approach the REE in decreasing oscillations, as shown in Figure 2.6.[32]

Case 2: mildly adaptive expectations

Consider:

$$\text{Expected } P_X/P_{Y \text{ period}(t+1)} = \text{Expected } P_X/P_{Y \text{ period}(t)} + 0.6(P_X/P_{Y \text{ period}(t)}$$
$$- \text{Expected } P_X/P_{Y \text{ period}(t)}) \qquad (2.3)$$

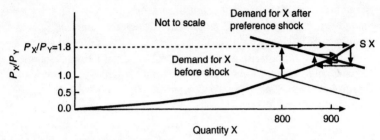

Figure 2.6 A cobweb phenomenon results from full incorporation of the change in past prices into expected future prices.

Then, in period 3, the expected P_X/P_Y for period 4 is 1.48. The disequilibrium path approaches the REE more rapidly. Interestingly, this illustrative result provides a justification for adaptive expectations: the incomplete incorporation of public information (as embodied in present price) is a deliberate adjustment made by agents. They realise the tendency for the disequilibrium price to overshoot the REE when information is being imparted into the system in large and discontinuous blocks.

As shown previously, the more weakly adaptive the expectation formation process the slower the model will approach the REE. Intertemporal resource misallocation will be substantial without a futures market.

The adaptation to the shock could also be analysed if there was a forward contracting market instead of futures trading. The economy would settle below the REE in period 2, the welfare loss being proportional to the difference in transaction costs of forward contracting compared with futures trading.

The effects of futures on spot price variability

The above analysis suggests futures markets should decrease spot price variability, and increase the spot market's ability to track better the REE, because it provides the mechanism to impart new information more rapidly to the market about the true model. Empirical evidence on this matter is generally supportive of this conclusion. The tests that have been used study the variability of spot prices for a given commodity for two time periods: one in which an active futures market for the commodity exists and one in which there is no such market.[33] The tests generally indicate a reduction in spot price variability when the futures market exists.

Overall summary

When individuals have heterogeneous information about the future for a good, there are mutual gains from trading this information through forward contracting. Futures markets emerge as the superior mechanism to facilitate this trade through minimising transaction costs of exchange.

People use the futures market to trade their private information sets concerning the future for a good. They replace their individual present decisions concerning the future, based on private information, with a decision based on the global information set as embodied in the futures price. Traders' decisions become mutually consistent and more prescient about the future. A certain Pareto gain results from higher total production.

The greater the heterogeneity in private information and the more frequent and large the exogenous disturbances to which a good is exposed, the greater the gains from futures trading. Futures trading volume will increase in response to this new information and traders will be more motivated to atomistically and automatically use, and respond to, the futures market to maximise future utility. This enables the futures market to converge to the REE more rapidly. This should decrease spot market volatility.

As futures trading volume increases, the average transaction costs of exchange using futures decrease, whereas in the forward contracting market average cost of exchange may increase (or remain approximately constant). This implies an optimal switchover from a forward contracting market to a futures market.

The more weakly adaptive are traders' expectation formation processes the greater the gains from futures trading.

If there is only spot market trade, cobweb phenomena may occur and large intertemporal resource misallocation will result. This may be especially the case if traders adjust future expected prices instantly to the current price, and in doing so overshoot the true REE. A more adaptive expectational approach may locate the REE more quickly.

The following is a list of conditions under which futures trading is more likely to be beneficial for a particular good.

1 A large amount of new information about the future enters individual traders' information sets.
2 This information is dispersed through the trading community as widely and unevenly as possible.
3 This private information is as heterogeneous (or inconsistent) as possible; for example, there should be as great a difference as possible in individual expectations concerning the future price of the good.

4 The less capable the spot market is in incorporating this information the better. For example, as illustrated, if traders' future supplies and demands for a good change rapidly and significantly through time, spot markets will experience considerable problems in quickly incorporating this information correctly into the present price.

Thus, futures trading extends the gains society obtains from mutually beneficial market trade. In particular, futures markets give traders an improved forum to exchange their private information sets about the future. This allows traders' present plans for the future to become mutually consistent and Pareto efficient, and more prescient with respect to an otherwise less knowable future.

Acknowledgements

The author thankfully acknowledges the kind help and ideas of Barry Goss, supervisor of the thesis on which this chapter is based. The author also thanks D. K. Fausten, Y.-K. Ng and J. Freebairn for suggestions, corrections and help with the presentation of the arguments. Errors are, of course, the author's own,

Endnotes

1 This idea and the basic rationale of the paper comes from Hayek (1945).
2 Pareto gains occur when no one is worse off and at least one person is better off.
3 Veljanovski (1986, p. 31) quotes a figure of generally less than 1% of futures contracts being settled by delivery.
4 This reasonable assumption can be explained by a number of alternative routes, as follows.

   (a) The different factors of production are specialised: for example, factor L may be relatively better at producing good X, whereas factor K is relatively better at producing good Y, i.e. they are imperfect substitutes in the production process. This characteristic will generally lead to diseconomies of scale (DOS) in the production process for both goods, which is a sufficient condition for a concave production function. For example, if the economy produces all X, those factors that are relatively the best at producing Y can be redeployed to produce Y, with only a small sacrifice in the production of X. However, as this process continues, more X must be sacrificed to produce extra Y because those factors that are relatively less specialised in producing Y must be redeployed to its production, thereby leading to greater forgone X.

Even if there is no specialisation of the factors of production, a concave production function will still occur if one of the following happens.

(b) Both goods are produced under conditions of decreasing returns to scale (DRS). DRS exists if a doubling of all inputs produces less than a doubling of output. This will often be the case at reasonable output levels where the factor(s) of production has diminishing marginal product.

(c) One good is produced under DRS, the other under constant returns to scale.

(d) One good is produced under strongly DRS, the other only weakly increasing returns to scale.

5 For a discussion explaining Muthian rational expectations equilibrium, see Harrison (1992 pp. 80, 84–94).

6 This model is similar to what Houthakker (1959, pp. 141–2) describes as social uncertainty – 'uncertainty due exclusively to the fact that many individuals take part in production and consumption'. He agrees that this problem can be solved by forward contracting but fails to explore the resulting implications of this, and further suggests this should not be confused with futures trading!

7 Houthakker (1959, p. 143) supports this view in a brief discussion but fails to develop the analysis.

8 This potential result is supported by the evidence from experimental futures markets that set up optimisation problems similar to those outlined above. See, in particular, Friedman *et al.* (1983), in which, in a multiperiod model without a futures market, agents take numerous repeats to learn the true model, whereas with the futures market the REE is achieved rapidly.

9 Lower case p_x/p_y is the notation used to represent the futures price.

10 This is the basis of Veljanovski (1986, p. 13).

11 With extreme prices, some forward contractors could be worse off, but the expected value from forward contracting is necessarily higher than that from not forward contracting, so (UAR > UA, UBR > UB), and also UAR = UBR is greater than the exposte average utility with no forward contracting UAC and UBC.

12 See Houthakker (1959, pp. 146–7) for a good discussion of these points.

13 Note, notwithstanding the movement in P_x/P_y, both agents can trade in the market at $P_x/P_y = 1.67$ to attain the endowment points of (13,3) and (3,13), and thus attain at least utility of UAR and UBR respectively.

14 See Veljanovski (1986, p. 24) for a good general discussion on the use of margins by the clearing house.

15 This view also corresponds to the work of Telser and Higinbotham (1977). Their focus is slightly different, being concerned primarily with the benefits of facilitating exchange among strangers rather than the exchange of heterogeneous information.

16 In this model, speculators are assumed to behave crudely. Based on their information, they buy futures if they think the futures price is too low and sell if they think it is too high. Thus, they can only make profits if they

intertemporally smooth prices. Even if they do not do this, it may be shown that other traders will gain from their destabilising behaviour following Friedman *et al.* (1983). The problems associated with not trading on fundamentals and the creation of speculative bubbles, noise trading etc. are not considered in this chapter.

17 A natural monopoly occurs when a good (performance of the brokerage function in this case) can be produced more cheaply by a single firm than by any combination of firms. See Veljanovski (1986, pp. 25–8) for a discussion of the natural evolution of futures trading from forward contracting.

18 This idea was first presented by Keynes (1930), was developed by Kaldor (1939) and Hicks (1953), and was first refuted by Telser (1958). Support can also be found from, specifically, Cootner (1960) and Houthakker (1959, pp. 153–4). For an interesting discussion, see Gray (1961).

19 An unbiased predictor is one that is neither, on average, too high or too low in predicting the future price.

20 This assumes agents, given their own expectations derived from their private information set, will prefer to follow the futures price as a more reliable guide (because it represents the global information set). This assumption is discussed later in this chapter.

21 It may be argued that speculators must earn a return on the capital tied up in their investment in futures (the Cootner crinkle) and this cannot occur if the futures price follows an REE. However, futures trading, through the use of margins, allows the investor incredible economies with respect to the size of a position and the capital tied up in the position. Typically, the broker requires a margin of between 1% and 5%. Thus, if a speculator held a $1million position, he may only require a $10,000 margin; if he is to earn a real rate of return of say 5% per annum, and he holds his position for 2 months, he requires a return of about $90. In other words, excluding brokerage fees, the spot price need only favourably change by 1:10,000 (for example, from $100 to $100.01) to give the speculator a sufficient return. Thus, this analysis suggests speculators primarily trade in futures to take advantage of their access to unique information about the future price, and this information could be very insignificant (so long as it is on average a better reflection of the REE) and still afford the speculator a good profit opportunity.

22 This is based on the assumption of a concave production function.

23 This is based on the premise that the future can not cause the past in determining causation.

24 Given an adverse price movement, risks of default and costs or ability to deliver become more significant the larger the position (trading volume) taken by a futures trader.

25 This can be contrasted with the position taken by Veljanovski (1986, p. 18), in which he suggests that the alternative institutional frameworks can happily coexist through minimisation of transaction costs – from equalising at the margin the costs of forward contracting and futures trading. This analysis suggests that the production technology used to facilitate futures trading volume is a natural monopoly, i.e. as futures trading volume increases

the average transaction costs of futures trading falls. Once the futures market is set up, this analysis suggests all forward trade should occur using futures to minimise the transaction costs of exchange. Further, a substantial forward market may impede the efficient development of a futures exchange because there remains insufficient incentive to invest in the large fixed costs to set up the exchange. This could be the case notwithstanding the futures exchange could facilitate the entire forward trading market at a lower total cost than the forward contracting market.

26 This assumes for simplicity either that transaction costs are zero with futures trading or that they have already been subtracted from the diagrams without worrying about the small difference in location points of the As and the Bs.

27 This can be related to a curious empirical result found by Williams (1987). In studying experimental double auction markets, he found that individual trader's expectation formation process was adaptive. However, he found that when agents traded among each other in aggregate the markets converged to a competitive equilibrium. Thus, the contracts written between people, in an aggregate sense, behaved as if the subjects had rational expectations, although the individual trader's forecasts did not have this same convergence property. The answer to this puzzle probably lies in 'the intensive learning process that goes on "continuously" within each trading period. Individual's forecasts were made at the beginning of each period before any such learning had taken place. Observed market prices, however, were the result of that learning process'. This point is taken from Harrison (1992, p. 93).

28 Alternatively, agent A had an original expectation $P_X/P_Y = 2$. As long as the futures price p_X/p_Y is less than this, they will maximise utility by buying X futures, selling Y futures and relocating production so that their MRT is equal to p_X/p_Y.

29 Present period consumption and stocks could be added to this model without changing the intuitive results. As the futures price p_X/p_Y increases, people will wish to buy X spot, store it and sell X futures, thus making riskless profit. This will raise the present price of X, reducing present consumption demand for X. Thus, the spot price of X is tied to the futures price by the maximum contango possible – the cost of storing X. People will wish to store less Y and thus will supply more of it now and decrease the present price of Y, which will increase the present and future demand for Y *ceteris paribus*. Thus, those who simply use the spot market free ride on this information concerning the future and further make their present plans consistent with this information concerning the future. This present period consumption and storage adaptation is a further gain from futures trading.

30 Passively is used here to mean traders that expect the future price $P_X/P_{Y\,(t+1)}$ to adjust automatically to equal the futures price p_X/p_Y. They do not try to second guess the futures price, instead believing it is the best predictor of the future price.

31 This view also corresponds to the work of Telser and Higinbotham (1977). Their focus is slightly different, being concerned primarily with the benefits of facilitating exchange among strangers rather than the exchange of heterogeneous information.

32 It may be legitimately questioned whether this formulation actually
    represents weak form rational expectations: agents, in completely adjusting
    their expectations by their expectational error, consistently over- or
    undershoot the true REE. A more adaptive approach in forming expectations
    would locate the REE more rapidly.
33 Rutledge (1986, pp. 141–2) provides a list of the tests carried out and the
    potential methodological objections to these tests.

References

Brunner, K. and Meltzer, A.H. (1971) 'The uses of money: money in the theory
    of an exchange economy', *American Economic Review* 61: 784–805.
Cootner, P.H. (1960) 'Returns to speculators: Telser vs Keynes', *Journal of
    Political Economy* 68: 396–404.
Friedman, D., Harrison, G.W. and Salmon, J.W. (1983) 'The information role of
    futures markets: some experimental evidence', in Streit, M.E (ed.) *Futures
    Markets: Modelling, Managing and Monitoring Futures Markets*, Oxford:
    Blackwell, pp. 124–64.
Gray, R.W. (1961) 'The search for a risk premium', *Journal of Political Economy*
    69(3): 250–60.
Harrison, G. (1992) 'Rational expectations and experimental methods', in Goss,
    B.A. (ed.) *Rational Expectations and Efficiency in Futures Markets*, London:
    Routledge, pp. 78–108.
Hayek, F.A (1945) 'The use of knowledge in society'. *American Economic
    Review* 35: 519–30.
Hicks, J.R. (1953) *Value and Capital*, 2nd edn, Oxford: Oxford University Press.
Houthakker, H.S. (1959) 'The scope and limits of futures trading', in Abramovitz
    M. *et al.* (eds) *The Allocation of Economic Resources*, Stanford, CA: Stanford
    University Press.
Kaldor, N. (1939) 'Speculation and economic stability', *Review of Economic
    Studies* 7: 1–27. Reprinted in Kaldor, N. (1961) *Essays on Economic Stability
    and Growth*, London: Duckworth, pp. 17–58.
Keynes, J.M. (1930) *A Treatise on Money*, vol. 2, London: Macmillan, pp. 142–
    4.
Muth, J.F. (1961) 'Rational expectations and the theory of price movements',
    Econometrica 25(3): 315–35.
Rutledge, D.J.S. (1986) 'Trading volume and price variability: new evidence on
    the price effects of speculation', in Goss, B.A. (ed.) *Futures Markets: Their
    Establishment and Performance*, reprinted from Chicago Board of Trade
    International Research Seminar Proceedings, 1978, Chapter 6.
Telser, L.G. (1958) 'Futures trading and the storage of cotton and wheat', *Journal
    of Political Economy* 66: 233–55.
Telser, L.G. and Higinbotham, H.N. (1977) 'Organized futures markets: costs
    and benefits', *Journal of Political Economy* 85: 969–1000.

Veljanovski, C.J. (1986) 'An institutional analysis of futures contracting', in Goss, B.A. (ed.) *Futures Markets: Their Establishment and Performance*, London: Croom Helm, pp. 13–41.

Williams, A.W. (1987) 'The formation of price forecasts in experimental markets', *Journal of Money, Credit and Banking* 19: 1–18.

Chapter 3

The development of commodity futures exchanges in Kazakhstan and China

Evidence on their role in market development

Anne E. Peck

Introduction

The renewed emphasis on prices and markets throughout the world, especially in the centrally planned economies of China, the former Soviet Union and Eastern and Central Europe, has been accompanied by the opening of an uncountable number of new commodity markets. Many, if not most, are local or regional markets, and some are surely no more than markets in name only. At the same time, trade is developing on some of the new markets. Moreover, some have developed new futures markets too. In China alone, some forty commodity futures exchanges were started in 1992. In Kazakhstan, more than one hundred markets opened in 1992, and at least one of these developed a futures market. At least two exchanges in Poland, the Warsaw Board of Trade and the Poznan Commodity Exchange, are planning futures markets. In Hungary, the Budapest Commodity Exchange opened in 1989 and although its principal contracts are financial ones it also trades futures in various agricultural products. There are many new commodity exchanges in Russia and several have listed futures contracts. For example, the Russian Non-Ferrous Metals Exchange and the Russian Ferrous Metals Exchange in Moscow offer trading in metals futures. However, in spite of all the apparent development activity, only a very few of the new markets have succeeded in maintaining futures trading in any amount.

This chapter reports in some detail on the experience of two new exchanges that also developed futures markets, the China Zhengzhou Commodity Exchange (CZCE) and the International Kazakhstan Agro-Industrial Exchange (IKAE).[1] CZCE, a major grain wholesale market in Zhengzhou, China, opened futures markets in 1993; IKAE, the principal exchange in Almaty, Kazakhstan, where all agricultural and industrial product exports were registered, opened futures markets in 1996. Trading on CZCE has grown nearly continuously since opening; that on IKAE has ceased. In their early development, the two exchanges shared many common needs, such as for the development of clearing rules, a margin system, a trading environment, etc.; needs that all new futures exchanges must accomplish. Another common need was for precise settlement terms for the contracts. This chapter reports on these developments at CZCE and IKAE and draws comparisons with each other and with other markets.

Opening a new market is of course only the first phase of development for a new exchange. Educating potential users, attracting and training members, and managing the ensuing trading are themselves major undertakings, and here the experiences of CZCE and IKAE were vastly different. Thus, the chapter also discusses many of the initiatives of CZCE exchange officials, initiatives and management that have been critical to their continuing success. The chapter begins with a discussion of the early history of the development of futures markets, noting both their early proliferation (much like that seen everywhere in formerly centrally planned economies) as well as the more recent and lengthy history of subsequent consolidation (a pattern which will also be evident in the years to come in these countries). The experience of the IKAE is then reported, followed by that of CZCE. The final section draws comparisons and conclusions.

The development of commodity futures exchanges

Contracts for future delivery of grains appeared in the USA in the mid-nineteenth century. By the end of the century, trading in futures had evolved to the point that it was recognisably distinct from the buying and selling of grain typical of busy agricultural markets at major transportation centres. Forward contracts for delivery of wheat were recorded in New York in the 1840s, whereas contracts for future delivery for wheat and corn were recorded in Chicago in the 1850s. As trading in them grew and their value in assisting both buyers and sellers to make marketing plans became ever more apparent, the exchanges struggled with managing the new trading. In particular, it quickly became apparent that a new system of accounting and financial control was required to ensure as nearly as possible that all participants would honour their contractual obligations. And, although a system of voluntary margining appeared early on at the Chicago Board of Trade (CBOT) market, it was not until the 1890s that the Minneapolis Grain Exchange developed the organised clearing house and formal margin system that is recognised today throughout the world as characteristic of organised futures markets.

As well, the early exchanges operated without explicit regulatory oversight. Nevertheless, they had to deal with numerous episodes of threatened manipulation, make adjustments to the delivery terms of their contracts, and generally monitor the trading of their members. In the USA, formal federal oversight of the exchanges did not begin until the 1920s, and their regulatory authority dates only until the 1930s.

Perhaps because the development of these early futures markets was evolutionary, taking place over nearly eighty or so years, we are often taken by surprise by the speed with which new exchanges emerge and new contracts develop. Although most of the growth in recent years in futures markets and contracts has been for financial products, many new agricultural and metals exchanges also have been started, and many of these offer trading in contracts for commodities traded on previously established exchanges. Both of these developments are new for commodity exchanges. Whereas multiple futures markets and contracts for individual agricultural commodities were the norm during the period of market development from the mid-nineteenth to the early twentieth century, consolidation has been the dominant trend of the modern era. For example, well into the 1930s, there were three major international wheat futures markets: one in the USA (Chicago), one in the UK (Liverpool), and one in Argentina (Buenos Aires). Moreover, within the USA, in addition to the CBOT, there were wheat futures markets in Duluth, Kansas City, Milwaukee, Minneapolis, Portland and St. Louis. Of these, only the Chicago, Kansas City and Minneapolis markets remain.[2] Similarly, markets for cotton futures were active in New York, New Orleans, Memphis, USA, and Liverpool, UK; only that in New York remains.

The trend towards consolidation among agricultural exchanges was so dominant that for many years it seemed virtually unthinkable that a new wheat or cotton futures market might open and be successful. Constantly improving transportation and communication systems served to link markets ever more closely together and the advantages of increased liquidity from trading that was consolidated in one market generally outweighed the advantages individual users might gain in pricing specificity from separate regional or national exchanges. The contrasting experience of financial exchanges and products, in which many new exchanges have opened around the world and have built significant trading bases, only reinforced the argument: whereas each country's financial assets were unique, prices varied independently and, hence, separate markets could grow and thrive, the prices of wheat in one country were so closely linked to prices in others that there really was a single world price with only transportation differences to account for and, thus, numerous independent markets could not survive.

In recent years, however, many new agricultural exchanges have begun trading futures contracts or have them in development. Perhaps the most successful new contracts to date have been the corn and soybean futures contracts at the Tokyo Grain Exchange (TGE), a market that is open at times when the Chicago market is closed. The contracts also differ from those of the CBOT in their delivery terms. The corn contract specifies delivery at Japanese ports and is, in effect, pricing US corn with cost, insurance and freight (CIF) paid to Japan. The soybean contract specifies delivery of US-produced soybeans in designated warehouses in Japan. Thus, both provide alternative representations of world corn and soybean prices than are reflected in the CBOT contracts, with the TGE corn contract the more transparently international because delivery is on a CIF basis rather than in-store in Japan. In 1997, the volume of corn futures traded on the TGE was 13.8 million contracts, more than 80% of the volume of the CBOT corn contract; the volume of TGE soybean futures was 10.0 million contracts, nearly 70% of CBOT volume.[3]

Nor is the Tokyo exchange alone in developing new agricultural futures markets. For example, the London International Financial Futures Exchange continues trading the wheat contract developed on the London Commodity Exchange. In the planning stages are new agricultural exchanges in locations as disparate as Germany, Argentina and Central America. And, as noted in the introduction, the most interesting and surely most prolific scene for new exchange development has been in the formerly centrally planned economies. There are now a dozen or more new futures exchanges in China, all dealing in physical commodities and some with significant trading volume. Among countries in the former Soviet Union and Eastern and Central Europe, new commodities exchanges have been started in, among others, Russia, Hungary, Poland and Kazakhstan.

Along with the expansion of interest in new agricultural markets and with evidence of some successes of new contracts for the major international commodities for which there are already major markets, there is now wider discussion of the potential value of several exchanges trading a single agricultural commodity, each with unique contract terms. Several factors have been adduced to explain the early successes of at least some of the new contracts. First, there are the effects of time differences, in which an exchange such as that in Tokyo can provide a market in hours when the Chicago markets are not open (although there are off-hours trading possibilities in Chicago). Second, there is no a priori reason why the price of grain in Chicago should be the most representative reflection of world prices. Indeed, during the 1990s, the CBOT struggled with the need to redefine the delivery terms of its grains contracts precisely because they had become unrepresentative.[4] And, as TGE's success has shown, if an exchange develops a contract with a more representative contract, trading may well grow beyond the needs of traders locally and capture significant international business. Third, there is increasing recognition that agricultural prices within countries can fluctuate markedly from international prices, either in circumstances created by government policy interventions (whether in prices directly, in the conditions of production or use, or in macroeconomic policies affecting, for example, exchange rates or their convertibility) or when transport costs are substantial and actual trade flows are intermittent. Fourth, there are many commodities that are of substantial regional importance for which an international market does not exist. Finally, and perhaps most important for the new exchanges in countries where markets are themselves only just emerging, the successful development of a futures market can facilitate the development of the underlying markets themselves. And, even if unsuccessful, a new exchange can facilitate the subsequent development of markets by increasing understanding of the needs of a market system. The experience of CZCE as a successful market and of IKAE as an unsuccessful one are illustrative.

The history of a wheat futures market in Kazakhstan[5]

The Republic of Kazakhstan, formerly a part of the Soviet Union, has been an independent country only since December 1991; it has had its own currency only since 1993. As was very common throughout the former Soviet Union, exchanges of one kind or another emerged virtually immediately and in substantial number once the countries were independent. In Kazakhstan, more than one hundred exchanges were established in Almaty, the former capital, alone – a truly amazing number in a country of only sixteen million people and a city of about one million. But, by mid-1993, only four of these remained, and in November 1995 the four were merged to form the IKAE (Euroconsult, 1994). Further, the principal exchanges in other cities were made subsidiaries of IKAE. Twenty or more of these branches continue operations, but the exchange in Almaty became the leader, especially in developing markets. Occasionally, a news report of trading in one commodity or another suggests that a few of the exchanges in other cities also remain, but the reports have been sporadic at best.[6]

There is no doubt IKAE was the principal commodity exchange in Kazakhstan. In its comparatively short history, it has served several different roles in the marketing of agricultural and industrial products and also has become a part of the development of the new national securities exchange. Early on, it was given responsibilities for the registration and licensing of export transactions, and, for the grains, ensuring that minimum price targets for exports were being met.[7] Export contracts for grain must still be registered at IKAE, although there no longer are minimum price requirements (Danagro Advisor, 1997). Because of the registration requirement, however, IKAE continues to provide much information on a regular basis about exports of a wide range of commodities. In addition, the exchange was active trying to develop spot market trading in each of the commodities for which it had reporting responsibilities and, by 1996, was holding trading sessions three times per week. Comparatively little trade actually developed on the exchange.

As an important step in their efforts to develop market-based trading, IKAE also designed and launched a futures market. On 14 May 1996, IKAE began trading in the first agricultural futures contracts in Kazakhstan; these were contracts for wheat, which was the leading agricultural export crop.[8] The choice of wheat may seem odd as there are successful wheat futures markets elsewhere, but this is perhaps the clearest case of a market whose prices can fluctuate independently of world prices to a significant degree. Most Kazakhstani wheat is exported to neighbouring countries in the former Soviet Union, principally Russia but also Uzbekistan and Tadjikistan. In 1996, estimates put the cost of transporting wheat from the Kazakhstan border to Moscow at $35 per ton, whereas costs of transporting wheat from the US Gulf ports to Moscow were $50 per ton (Danagro Advisor, 1996, p. 69). The calculation of a simple import/export parity band indicates prices in Kazakhstan could have varied that year by well over $75 per ton relative to prices in Moscow and $150 per ton relative to prices in the USA, where the latter is an amount of variation greater than the price of wheat in Kazakhstan. Obviously, such extreme variation is unlikely. Nevertheless, the calculation does indicate there is scope for substantial independence in wheat prices in Kazakhstan and that a futures market for wheat could serve an important role in facilitating pricing and intertemporal marketing decisions for grains within the country.

The development of futures markets at IKAE required a major investment in exchange staff time and resources. First, the exchange needed to create clearing arrangements, a margin system and general exchange regulations, all of which needed approval by the Kazakhstan Commission on Commodity Exchanges.[9] In these, it borrowed from exchange practice everywhere. The clearing house was a separate entity within IKAE. It collected a transaction fee of 250 tenge[10] for each trade, established the minimum initial margin for all participants in each market (for trades in wheat futures, it was 10,000 tenge), and was responsible for margin adjustments as contract maturity approached or price volatility increased. The clearing house also established the maximum permitted daily price changes and position limits for each market. The limit on an individual trader's position in wheat was 150 contracts.

Second, IKAE needed to create a trading environment, and it chose a mixed system of open outcry and screen trading in which traders assembled in a single room and bids and offers were recorded by exchange personnel and posted on screens over the trading floor for all participants to see. Then, as trading occurred, changes in the posted bids and offers were recorded on the screen. Trading sessions were held on the same three days per week as the cash markets, with cash markets open in the morning and futures in the afternoons. Each commodity was traded separately, one after the other, for a five- to ten-minute period within the trading session, similar to trading at the London Metals Exchange.

Third, the exchange needed to develop the specific delivery terms for the wheat futures contract, work that was especially challenging because there was virtually no history of commercial trade practice from which to draw on for the details of contract specification. Such trading as existed was more often than not barter trade, exchanging wheat for electricity or for fuel. Moreover, the exchange was not located in the main centre of wheat production, which is in the northern part of the country whereas Almaty is in the southeastern corner. Neither is Almaty a major transit centre because most of the wheat is exported to Russia, i.e. to the west and north. These circumstances contrast sharply with patterns observed in the development of exchanges generally, and futures markets specifically, in most other countries. Of course, with advances in modern communications technology, it is no longer true that the locations of futures exchanges need to be closely tied to the location of the physical market. Nevertheless, the difficulty of the task confronting officials at IKAE in designing sensible contract terms for a wheat futures market in the absence of virtually any history of market trade cannot be overstated.

For initial contract terms, officials at IKAE determined par delivery would be of #3 soft wheat, free-on-track in Akmola, the major transshipment centre in the northern wheat production area of Kazakhstan (IKAE, 1996b) (Akmola is also the new capital of the country). Actual delivery was expected to come from sellers representing individual production units, essentially the former state farms. If intending to deliver, the seller was required to file a notice of intention to deliver at the beginning of the delivery month. Wheat for deliveries was to be in rail cars at the production unit, with freight paid to Akmola. Individual buyers taking deliveries, who were also required to identify themselves at the beginning of the delivery month, were responsible for paying charges for the shipment of wheat from Akmola to their location.[11] The exchange would match buyers and sellers based on the delivery notices and would notify each.

During conversations with IKAE officials, it was clear that they would have preferred to begin trading with a contract calling for delivery of grain in storage. Officials indicated that there was a significant amount of elevator storage space in Akmola, clearly enough to accommodate the delivery requirements of a futures market as would be expected in a location of substantial grain production and shipping activity. Storage delivery was not possible for two reasons. First, warehouse receipts, whereby a receipt identifying the specific characteristics of grain put into storage is issued by the storage facility and becomes itself a legally binding promissory note to provide grain of the same quality, did not yet exist in the country. Second, elevator ownership was highly concentrated and, although in the midst of substantial reorganisation via official privatisation initiatives, it was expected to be some time before ownership was significantly less concentrated. By all accounts, elevators simply were not yet active middlemen in the buying, selling and storage of grain (for details, see Carana Corporation, 1995; Danagro Advisor, 1996). Officials at IKAE developed the needed authorisations for a warehouse receipt system to be implemented at the same time as they began work on a futures market, but, to date, legislation has not been enacted to permit such dealings.

The IKAE contract was perhaps most similar to the call-on-production contract used in the soybean meal market on the CBOT or the world sugar market on the New York Coffee, Sugar and Cocoa Exchange, rather than to the storage-based delivery contracts typical of other grain futures markets. Although the resulting terms are unusual in direct comparison with other grain futures contracts, the development of them was not. That is to say, the terms were taken directly from existing trade practice. During the first nine months of 1996, official registrations of wheat sales for export amounted to some 404 contracts (IKAE, 1996a). Of these, 382 were for soft wheat; of these 382, 341 were for #3 grade and 249 were priced 'ex works', the state farm equivalent of farm gate prices.

The wheat futures contracts imitated these arrangements closely, creating an ex works delivery with freight paid to a central location, thereby retaining the most commonly observed trade practice while creating a central pricing arrangement.

Initial levels of trading were low and remained so throughout 1996. During this period, exchange officials also became involved in the development of a new securities exchange, in part a response to initiatives of the Kazakhstani government to privatise the pension system along the lines of the Chilean system. In August 1996, IKAE joined with other organisations and registered the International Kazakhstan Stock Exchange (IKSE). In December, IKSE was merged with another securities exchange to form the Kazakhstan Securities Exchange (KASE), which has grown to become the principal securities exchange in the country. Meanwhile, the futures market appears to have been closed (although, as noted, IKAE itself remains open and continues to have export registration and other responsibilities), undoubtedly as much because of the demands of these new exchange initiatives as because of any change in the wheat market.

Since 1996, there has been little progress in the development of wheat markets at IKAE. Nationwide, overall levels of production of wheat continue to decline, as do exports. Moreover, most trade is still accomplished through barter arrangements, not exchange trading. Recent estimates indicate that in early 1998 agricultural enterprises had debts totalling as much as approximately $1.4 billion and that arrears as well as current wages continued to be paid in kind, with grain or other commodities (ACDI/VOCA, 1998). Of the total harvest of 12.3 million metric tons, some 7.8 metric tons were committed for fuel and electricity, 1 metric ton for seed and forage loans, and 2 metric tons for seed for next year's crop. A warehouse receipt system is still not in place. ACDI/VOCA has expressed interest in assisting in the development of a warehouse receipt system in Kazakhstan, and should this project be implemented IKAE might be able to rekindle interest and reopen its futures market.

The successful development of futures trading at CZCE[12]

In contrast to the experience of IKAE in Kazakhstan, the development of futures markets in China was planned in much greater detail both by the government and by CZCE. In 1992, after many years of study and in accord with their increasing emphasis on markets over central planning, China's reformers authorised futures exchanges on an experimental basis.

Almost immediately, more than forty organisations in various localities began calling themselves futures exchanges (Wall and Wei, 1994). By the end of 1993, there was actual trading at thirty-three such exchanges, with a total turnover of more than 715 billion yuan, some $90 billion (Fry, 1994). In 1994, total turnover had grown to 3,200 billion yuan, even with a fall in the number of exchanges. In mid-1995, the government officially limited trading to those exchanges with sufficient membership and sufficient volume in at least one listed contract, classifying those that passed the standards as 'experimental' markets.[13] By the end of 1995, fourteen experimental exchanges remained, with a total turnover of nearly 10,000 billion yuan (Li, 1996). The most successful of these has been the CZCE, the only exchange whose levels of trading have continued to grow.

Futures exchanges in China are electronic, each having developed its own customised central computer system. The CZCE has, nevertheless, retained a trading floor, believing that the commotion provides a useful sense of the market's tenor. Growth in trading at CZCE has been rapid, from a single trading floor in 1993 to four trading floors within the city of Zhengzhou and nineteen smaller remote sites in 1996. Construction of all new facilities was completed in early 1997 and includes a main futures trading hall with 460 sites for almost 300 members and 650 trading stations. The CZCE trading floor comprises rows of terminals where the equivalent of floor brokers take orders by telephone, access their computer screens for the desired commodity and delivery month, observe the prevailing bid and ask prices, and execute the order with several keystrokes. The computerised trading is continuous over each of two trading sessions, morning and afternoon, and some traders seem to be developing into the equivalent of scalpers.

The ease of duplicating screens for another commodity compared with populating another pit encouraged many Chinese exchanges to list numerous commodities, often without regard to the comparative advantage of their region for marketing a specific commodity or to the listings on other exchanges. In contrast, the CZCE initially listed only five commodities: wheat, corn, soybeans, sesame and mungbeans. CZCE officials held out the most hope for wheat, given Zhengzhou's location in the wheat belt of north central China, but in the event trading in mungbeans soon dominated. Since its opening, the CZCE has experimented with listing various additional commodities, including domestic treasury notes, aluminium, peanuts, red beans, rice and cotton yarn. After a regulatory review in mid-1995, CZCE officials suspended trading in most of these listings for lack of volume. More recently, they have been encouraging trading in one new commodity at a time, for example wheat, and adding an auxiliary trading period in which only that commodity is traded.

As noted, CZCE's contract for mungbeans was its initial success. Much like soybeans, mungbeans are planted in spring or early summer. They are harvested in the early autumn, but generally are marketed a month or so later. Most consumption occurs in the subsequent spring and summer. Because mungbeans deteriorate with age without careful storage, little of one crop is carried over into the next crop year. The main producing areas are in the northwest and, increasingly, in the northeast of the country, more or less within the orbit of Zhengzhou. Because the large total production is scattered across many farmers in many provinces, few dominant commercial flows have emerged. Mungbeans, as well as grains, still move in bags, although facilities for bulk handling are being built. They are transported mostly in generic open-bed trucks, although rail shipment is possible from hubs such as Zhengzhou. As both wholesale and futures markets have developed, commercial firms have begun to specialise, some in aggregating farmers' production, others in transporting commodities to larger centres, and still others in processing or larger-scale exports. At each stage of this marketing chain, ownership usually changes. Prices are quoted in metric tons, although the standard lot of 10 tons (some 370 bushels) corresponds to the approximate size of an open-bed truck. Also, CZCE officials selected this relatively small lot size in part to encourage smaller speculators, who they wanted in the market for the liquidity they could provide. Larger processors, who tend to deal in lots of 60 metric tons, which is the size of a rail car, simply deal in multiples of six futures contracts.

Grade standards for delivery on a mungbean futures contract are the recognised national standards regarding moisture, broken beans and foreign matter. Many lots of mungbeans fail to meet the national standards, foreign matter being the most common problem. Because mungbeans are stored in bags, there is not the opportunity for mixing and cleaning while in store as in US grain elevators. Cleaning is carried out when the mungbeans arrive at the warehouse, where it is usually obvious whether they are best for the general wholesale market or for the futures market. Because the CZCE has strictly monitored delivery standards, it has enhanced the usefulness of the futures contracts to the larger mungbean processors, who prefer uniformly high quality. According to participants in mungbean wholesale markets, the CZCE's emphasis on meeting the national standards for deliverable mungbeans has improved quality overall.

Following the start of wholesale trading on CZCE on 12 October 1990, trading in mungbean futures began on 28 May 1993. Not surprisingly, although trading started rather slowly, the volume of trading increased much more rapidly than did the number of contracts that traders were willing to carry even overnight. Volume continued growing though the first half of 1994, before a marked decline in the last half of 1994, coincident with a period of central government scrutiny of all the new futures markets. Not long after the China Securities Regulatory Commission officially designated the CZCE as an 'experimental' exchange in October 1994, mungbean trading recovered and grew substantially until the spring of 1995. Since then, monthly (not to mention daily) volume has shown considerable variation, but at stable levels.

Since spring 1995, complete data on open interest are also available from the exchange. They show that there has been continued and substantial growth in the open interest more or less steadily through 1995 and 1996.[14] The open interest of around 300,000 contracts in late 1996 represents approximately three times the national production of mungbeans. By way of comparison, the open interest on the CBOT's wheat, corn or soybean futures markets represents less than half US annual production. (Put differently, converting metric tons to bushels and adjusting for the contracts' sizes, the CZCE's mungbean open interest represents a quantity that is about 35% of the CBOT's wheat open interest.) Thus, it would seem that the CZCE has attracted considerable speculative interest, including short speculation, which is a necessary component of a successful futures market (Gray, 1979).

Finally, it is important to note that the growth in open interest has been both in absolute amount and relative to the volume of trading. In early 1995, the volume of trading during the average trading day was usually greater than the open interest at the end of the day; whereas by the third quarter of 1996, the open interest was typically twice the average volume. This relative increase suggests the increasing presence of longer-term positions in the open interest, as would be characteristic of firms hedging inventory or forward commitments in mungbeans. Interviews with commercial firms describing their increasing use of futures underscored the increasing presence of commercial firms in the market. At the end of 1995, the CZCE counted 256 member firms (up from 170 at the end of 1994 and from sixty-eight at the end of 1993), of which 129 (50%) were specialised futures firms, ninety-four (36%) were commercial firms (including both cereals-related and industrial firms), and the remainder included investment, finance and miscellaneous other firms.[15] Firms are not, however, specialising in mungbeans; instead, they commonly also handle soybeans, wheat, corn and sometimes even industrial commodities. In short, the CZCE has been successful in developing a diverse membership, one in which commercially based firms, and not just trading companies, are important.

That commercial firms were not all active from the first instant should not be surprising. Rothstein's (1983) evidence from the early history of the grain futures markets in Chicago suggests many grain-handling firms there took decades to devise strategies relying on those markets. By this standard, the growth of commercial firms' use of the CZCE futures contracts, most of whom had never even thought in terms of prices before, is nothing short of remarkable. It also augers well for the future, as commercial use is arguably the key determinant of the market's ultimate size (Working, 1954). In less than four years, the CZCE and its mungbean contract has developed both breadth and depth in both speculators' interest and commercial firms' participation.

CZCE's success also owes much to the initiatives of CZCE officials in developing trading and in managing all aspects of trading after the markets opened. For example, CZCE developed education and outreach programmes covering all aspects of the markets in order to assist all potential users in gaining knowledge about the new system of trading. Additionally, in just the few years that the contract has traded, CZCE officials have responded thoughtfully and aggressively to delivery problems, to several attempts at manipulation, and to violations of position limits, incidents expected on all new exchanges and not unlike those that confronted officials of the Chicago Board of Trade during the early years of trading of grain futures.[16]

For the initiation of trading in June 1993, the CZCE specified six delivery months, namely January, March, May, July, September and November.[17] Originally, four warehouses were registered. The first problems with deliveries arose in November 1993. Traders short the November 1993 contract arrived at registered warehouses, often from some distance, with truckloads of newly harvested mungbeans to make delivery on their contracts, only to have the mungbeans rejected for water content of 14–15% instead of the stipulated 13.5%. CZCE officials, although concerned about these early problems, resisted changing the deliverable grade to something less than the national standard; instead, they encouraged registered warehouses to expand their drying capacity.

CZCE officials contended with their first attempted manipulation in the July 1994 contract. One long, a broker/speculator based in Zhengzhou, held more than 1,000 contracts at the start of July, close to the entire open interest remaining. CZCE officials responded in three immediate ways. First, they met with the long, in the fashion of all futures exchanges, to alert him to their concern and their resolve. Second, they altered the price-move limits to make them tighter with each successive day, so as to cap the amount of variation margin the shorts would have to pay each day through the clearing house. Third, they encouraged the shorts to acquire mungbeans and to ship them to registered warehouses. The outcome by the end of July was chastening losses to the shorts, some, but not large, profits (and a lot of mungbeans) to the long, and no default.

With the immediate crisis of the July 1994 contract behind them, CZCE officials considered more substantive changes to the contract terms to deter manipulation. They imposed position limits that become tighter one month before the delivery period. They increased the additional original margin both longs and shorts must deposit at the start of the delivery month, which had been variously 30%, 20% and 15%, to the current 50% of the settlement price.[18] They instituted a regulation that one trader cannot take more than 20% of the deliveries in any one month. They also rethought their premise that deliveries on the contract should be difficult to accomplish. (US exchange officials commonly hold the view that deliveries are and should be rare, despite the evidence to the contrary; see, for example, Peck and Williams, 1991.) To the original four warehouses, they began adding many others outside the immediate Zhengzhou area as eligible delivery points. In all, twenty-one warehouses are now regular for delivery on CZCE contracts.[19] Officials also allowed for delivery of age-blackened beans, although at a stipulated discount, yellowish and greyish mungbeans at par, and also 'bright' mungbeans at a 5% premium. Their alterations in the contract expanded the 'deliverable supply' considerably.

CZCE officials also have been vigorous in monitoring members for sudden increases in trading volume, tracking margin funds through banking channels, and performing background checks on new members. In May 1995, officials uncovered a large speculator who was trading through multiple accounts and forced him to trade out of his positions in excess of the limits. CZCE officials also uncovered a trader with multiple accounts in the autumn of 1996, a trader who had previously been very active in the Beijing futures market. In February 1997, the CZCE revoked this trader's privileges, the first such disciplinary action taken by a Chinese exchange.

Finally, CZCE officials have taken many steps to continue to develop the cash and wholesale markets throughout the region. The wholesale market at CZCE itself continues to be a very active market in which all products and by-products of grains and oilseeds, feeds and raw materials can be traded. They have developed the Jicheng Information Network, an electronic network linking major grain wholesale markets, large provincial and private grain enterprises, and state grain reserve depots throughout the country. The network not only provides members with market-wide news information, it also permits them to exchange information and even to conclude deals. Clearly, all these initiatives support the development of markets throughout China as well as the new futures markets.

Conclusions

Like IKAE and CZCE, all modern exchanges can actively design new futures contracts. They need not rely on informal forward trading to 'ripen into organised trading in futures' and then for the organised trading to 'show considerable evolution before reaching its full stature' (Irwin, 1954, p. 5). However, their success is ever more dependent upon aligning the contract with trade practices for the physical commodity and, as the contrasting experiences of IKAE and CZCE show, on active management and development of trading in both the cash and the futures markets.

The importance of close links between physical trade practice and the success of a new futures contract has been well documented. For instance, the frozen pork belly contract succeeded in the mid-1960s only after the Chicago Mercantile Exchange aligned provisions regarding shrinkage allowances, grading and storage techniques with trade practices; revisions that took careful exchange management (Powers, 1967). When introducing a plywood futures contract, the CBOT deliberately copied the prevailing physicals trade (Sandor, 1973). The Minneapolis Grain Exchange's failure with the high-fructose corn syrup contract (Thompson *et al.*, 1996) only reiterates the lesson that if a futures contract is not well aligned with what commercial practices are or ought to be or if it does not attract commercial use as part of regular merchandising operations it will fail.

No doubt, exchange officials everywhere also recognise in CZCE's story the corollary to their dependence upon existing trade practice: futures exchanges can deliberately improve trading practices in physicals trading to the ultimate benefit of futures trading. The CZCE has supported a wholesale market in Zhengzhou itself, it has offered an electronic bulletin board for news about mungbeans as reported by market participants, developed an information system for the dissemination of prices at other wholesale centres, recruited members from the commercial trade region-wide, registered futures delivery warehouses in a variety of locations, advertised the grade standards eligible for delivery, encouraged investments in cleaning and drying facilities, specified rules for the wholesale trading of registered warehouses, and drafted laws related to forward contracting and futures trading.

By contrast, IKAE officials, responding to national priorities, became involved in the development of another market system at precisely the time that many development initiatives needed to be pursued to support its new wheat futures market. Legislation recognising warehouse receipts has languished. Education and outreach programmes for producers and warehouse managers were not implemented. Investment in grain storage and handling facilities was not facilitated. Interest appears to be reappearing in many of these issues, with a market information project under way through the European Union Technical Assistance programmes and the possibility of a project through ACDI/VOCA on developing warehouses. Perhaps the market development initiatives of IKAE will regain momentum and it too can become a leader in market development not just in Kazakhstan but throughout the countries of the former Soviet Union, like the leader CZCE has become among exchanges in China.

Endnotes

1 Also referred to as the Kazakhstan International Agro-Industrial Exchange.
2 Each exchange trades a different variety of wheat, and although their prices are related there is enough independent variation in prices that all three exchanges have survived. Working (1954) reports on the near closure of the Kansas City market when it changed its contract to permit delivery of the same variety of wheat as is traded in Chicago. Gray (1967) analyses the trading linkages among them.
3 Futures Industry Institute (1998). CBOT contracts, each 5,000 bushels, are slightly larger than TGE contracts (each 100,000 kilograms), so the percentages overstate slightly the comparative amount of trading at the TGE.
4 For a discussion of the history of the delivery terms of the Chicago Board of Trade grains and oilseeds contracts and their recent problems, see Peck and Williams (1991).
5 The author visited IKAE in September/October 1996, during the period that wheat futures were offered for trading. Subsequent visits to Kazakhstan have permitted the collection of much information about market development but have not included a visit to the exchange.
6 Separately, there has been a two-year project under way since 1996, funded by the European Union's Technical Assistance Programme, to develop wholesale markets as well as a price reporting system in several cities in Kazakhstan.
7 At one time, export quotas were used and IKAE was also charged with conducting auctions for quota sales. IKAE had offices in all the oblasts and

their representatives were closely associated with the regional Department of Agriculture (Danagro Advisor, 1996).

8 Launch of the wheat futures contract in May was preceded by initial trading in an experimental currency contract in January 1996 and accompanied by the opening of an interest rate contract.

9 The Commission on Commodity Exchanges was created on 30 May 1995 and given broad powers to license exchanges, review exchange rules and review trading. It comprises twelve members, including representatives of the exchanges, the ministries of the economy, agriculture, industry and trade, the state committee on pricing, and others. See Republic of Kazakhstan (1995) for details.

10 In 1996, when IKAE began trading, the exchange rate was approximately 70 tenge to $1.

11 If the two were located so as to be able to arrange shipment without including transit through Akmola, the exchange rules specified a cost-sharing arrangement which depended on the total transportation cost (if it was less than the cost of transit from the producer to Akmola, the seller paid the buyer the amount of the difference; if it was more, the buyer paid the seller).

12 The author visited CZCE in 1995 and 1997. Much of the material in this section is also reported in Williams *et al.* (1998).

13 The standards were membership of at least fifty and trading of at least 5,000 contracts per day in at least one listed contract.

14 The open interest of individual delivery months follows the pattern seen in most other futures markets, namely low when the delivery period is distant, a peak a few months before the delivery period, and a fall as the delivery period approaches. Most open interest is in the nearest two or three delivery months.

15 The number of member firms continued to grow in 1996, reaching 316 by the end of the year. Of these, only 273 could trade until construction of the new facility was completed in 1997. Information about member firms comes from CZCE (1994–1995).

16 For example, Taylor's (1917) history of the CBOT documents some fifteen incidents of attempted manipulations, warehouse irregularities and so on over just the decade beginning in 1865 in the wheat futures market alone.

17 Like the concept of a one-month-long delivery window, CZCE copied many contractual terms from the Chicago Board of Trade's grain contracts, which CZCE officials had studied carefully.

18 Except for the delivery period, the original margin for mungbeans was 7% until September 1994 and has been 5% thereafter.

19 In a typical month, some fifty CZCE members make or take delivery. Although some members take delivery in small quantities on behalf of their brokerage customers, some large processors use the futures delivery system as a major source of supply. Those taking delivery often trade the receipts by delivery location, in twice-weekly sessions provided by the exchange. The CZCE will soon have a new system in which a generic warehouse receipt is issued to someone standing for delivery; the recipient will then express preferences among the twenty-one registered warehouses, a preference that the CZCE will try to match as closely as possible among the specific receipts tendered by the shorts.

References

ACDI/VOCSA (Agriculture Co-operative Development International/Volunteers in Overseas Co-operative Assistance) (1998) *Kazakhstan Grain Storage and Marketing Project: A Proposal*, Washington, DC: ACDI/VOCA.

Carana Corporation (1995) *Kazak Grain and Bread Systems Analysis*. Report prepared for US Agency for International Development, 30 October 1995, Almaty: Carana Corporation.

CZCE (China Zhengzhou Commodity Exchange) (1994–1995) *Annual Report*, Zhengzhou: China Zhengzhou Commodity Exchange.

Danagro Advisor (1996) *Strengthening the Implementation of Agriculture Sector Reforms*, 2 vols. Asian Development Bank, Government of Kazakhstan Technical Assistance 2356, Final Report, Manila: Asian Development Bank.

—— (1997) *Farm Restructuring and Development Project: Phase I Report*, Asian Development Bank, Government of Kazakhstan Technical Assistance 2737, Manila: Asian Development Bank.

Euroconsult (1994) 'Agricultural Sector Mission Kazakhstan', in *Field Report, Agricultural Marketing*, Almaty: The World Bank.

Fry, J. (1994) 'The regulation of commodity exchanges: an international comparison', in *Landell Mills Commodities Studies*, R878, Trowbridge, UK: manuscript version only.

Futures Industry Institute (1998) *FII Fact Book*, November 1998 edn, Washington, DC: Futures Industry Institute.

Gray, R.W. (1967) 'Price effects of a lack of speculation', Food Research Institute Studies 7 (suppl.): 177–94.

Gray, R.W. (1979) 'The emergence of short speculation', in *Proceedings of International Futures Trading Seminar*, 21–22 May. CBOT: 6, Chicago: Chicago Board of Trade.

IKAE (International Kazakhstan Agro-Industrial Exchange) (1996a) *Statistics of the Export Contracts at the International Kazakhstan Agro-Industrial Exchange*. Office of Statistics, no. 8, Almaty: IKAE.

—— (1996b) *Temporary Rules for Futures Trade at the International Kazakhstan Agro-Industrial Exchange*. City of Almaty ruling, 26 August, Almaty: IKAE.

Irwin, H.S. (1954) *Evolution of Futures Trading*. Madison, WI: Mimir Publishers.

Li, J. (1996) 'Development, problems and strategies of China's futures markets', in *The Proceedings of the Sixth Annual Asia-Pacific Futures Research Symposium*, winter 1995, Chicago: Chicago Board of Trade, pp. 313–24.

Peck, A.E. and Williams, J.C. (1991) 'Deliveries on Chicago Board of Trade wheat, corn, and soybean futures contracts, 1964/65–1988/89', *Food Research Institute Studies* 22: 129–225.

Powers, M.J. (1967) 'Effects of contract provisions on the success of a futures contract', *Journal of Farm Economics* 49: 833–43.

Republic of Kazakhstan (1995) 'Concerning the approval of regulations concerning the Republic's commission on commodity exchanges, on licensing of commodity exchanges and the approval of the Republic's commission of commodity exchanges', in *Resolution no. 755 of the Cabinet of Ministers of the Republic of Kazakhstan*, 30 May, Almaty: Government of Kazakhstan.

Rothstein, M. (1983) 'The rejection and acceptance of a marketing innovation: hedging in the late nineteenth century', *Review of Research in Futures Markets* 2: 200–14.

Sandor, R. (1973) 'Innovation by an exchange: a case study of the development of the plywood futures contract', *Journal of Law and Economics* 16: 119–36.

Taylor, C.P. (1917) *History of the Board of Trade of the City of Chicago.* Chicago: Robert O. Law.

Thompson, S., Garcia, P. and Wildman, L.D. (1996) 'The demise of the high fructose corn syrup futures contract: a case study', *Journal of Futures Markets* 16: 697–724.

Wall, D. and Wei, J. (1994) *Futures Markets in China*, Sussex, UK: University of Sussex, The Chinese Economy Programme.

Williams, J., Peck, A., Park, A. and Rozelle, S. (1998) 'The emergence of a futures market: mungbeans on the China Zhengzhou Commodity Exchange', *Journal of Futures Markets* 18:427–48.

Working, H. (1954) 'Whose markets? Evidence on some aspects of futures trading', *Journal of Marketing* 19: 1–11.

Chapter 4

A simultaneous model of the US dollar/Deutschmark spot and futures markets

Barry A. Goss and S. Gulay Avsar

Introduction

Traditional economic models of exchange rate determination have performed poorly in recent decades in that they are unable to explain a significant proportion of exchange rate variation and are unable to outperform a naive random walk model in post-sample forecasting. Critics such as Isard (1987), Meese (1990) and others have discussed these issues and have drawn attention to perceived deficiencies in traditional models, including undue reliance on single equation methods, inadequate modelling of expectations and insufficient attention to capital flows (see Isard, 1987, pp. 3, 15, 16; Meese, 1990, p. 117). This chapter addresses these questions. A simultaneous model of the US dollar/Deutschmark exchange rate is developed using information from both spot and futures markets. The model contains separate functional relationships for short and long hedgers, for short and long speculators in futures, and for unhedged spot market commitments. This chapter has its foundations in the theoretical model of Peston and Yamey (1960) and in the empirical commodity market models of Giles *et al.* (1985) and Goss *et al.* (1992), and extends the work of Goss and Avsar (1996) on foreign exchange from minor to more active markets.

During the past two decades, empirical analysis of major foreign exchange markets has received much attention from researchers, with emphasis on the question of informational efficiency. Studies of exchange rates during this period have, mostly, used data sets from the floating rates period of the 1970s, although some have used data from the fixed rates period of the 1960s or from the floating period of the 1920s. Investigations of the efficient markets hypothesis in the US dollar/Deutschmark market have resulted in a predominance of rejections, especially with wider information sets.

Although Bilson (1981), Baillie *et al.* (1983) and Bailey *et al.* (1984) did not reject the unbiasedness hypothesis for the US dollar/Deutschmark (USD/DM) market with single equation estimation, Bilson (1981) and Bailey *et al.* (1984) did reject that hypothesis with SURE estimation for a group of major currencies. Rejection of unbiasedness has been interpreted by some authors as evidence of market inefficiency (see, for example, Bilson, 1981; Taylor, 1992), and by others as an indication of the presence of a time-varying risk premium in the presence of rational expectations (see, for example, Hodrick and Srivastava, 1984, 1987). Hansen and Hodrick (1980) rejected the semistrong efficient markets hypothesis (EMH) for the US dollar/Deutschmark market, in which the publicly available information set was defined as prior forecast errors for own and other major currencies. By comparison, Geweke and Feige (1979), again using prior forecast errors for a group of currencies (their 'realised rate of exchange gain in the forward market'), did not reject the semistrong EMH for the USD/DM market considered separately, but did reach the conclusion, with SURE estimation, that the group of markets was inefficient. (See also the excellent surveys by Hodrick, 1987, pp. 54–6, 140–50; Baillie and McMahon, 1989, pp. 162–79; Taylor, 1995, pp. 13–21.)

The remainder of this chapter is organised into the following sections: the specification of the model is discussed; discussion of the data, unit root and co-integration tests and estimation methods; presentation of intrasample and post-sample results; and, finally, the conclusions are presented.

Specification of the model

Short hedgers

Consider first the position of short hedgers. These agents, such as US exporters to Germany or German investors undertaking capital inflow to the USA, are long in spot Deutschmarks, and are hedging the risk of a fall in the spot rate: they are, therefore, sellers of Deutschmark currency futures (both spot and futures exchange rates are defined as US dollars per one Deutschmark, so that a rise in price means devaluation of the US currency). In his classic works, two of the main categories of hedging distinguished by Working (1953a, 1962) are carrying charge hedging and selective hedging. On the carrying charge hypothesis, spot market commitments are hedged in a one-to-one ratio, and the futures market commitments of short hedgers would vary directly with the current forward premium (defined as futures rate minus spot rate), and negatively with the expected forward premium. On the selective hedging hypothesis, a proportion only of spot market commitments is hedged, and the futures commitments of short hedgers would vary directly with the current futures rate and negatively with the expected futures rate. It is an acknowledged fact that the variance of the actual change in the spot rate is greater than the variance of the forward premium. The reason for this is possibly that although the forward premium is interpreted as the expected change in the spot rate the actual spot rate change reflects news, including noise elements. It is noteworthy that of all currencies studied by Bilson (1981) the USD/DM rate has by far the highest ratio of spot rate variance to variance of forward premium at 14:1 (see Bilson, 1981, p. 437). This is a ground for expecting that short hedgers in this market are likely to be fully hedged, so that the carrying charge hypothesis would be appropriate. On the other hand, it is well known that financial markets exhibit not only time-varying volatility, but also volatility clustering (Engle, 1982, 1983). If agents pursue an optimum hedge ratio (Ederington, 1979; Kahl, 1983), and this optimum varies over time, the selective hedging hypothesis would be appropriate to accommodate variations in the hedging ratio. The last hypothesis has been used here for short hedgers because of its greater flexibility.

The futures market positions of short hedgers are expected also to vary directly with measures of their spot market commitments, such as US exports to Germany; hence, the specification of this equation is:

$$SH_t = \theta_1 + \theta_2 P_t + \theta_3 P^*_{t+1} + \theta_4 X_t + e_{1t} \qquad (4.1)$$

where SH is the futures market positions of short hedgers; P is the current futures rate; P^*_{t+1} is the rational expectation of the futures rate at time $(t+1)$, formed at time t; X is US exports to Germany; t is time in months; e is the error term; θ_1 is constant; and θ_2, $\theta_4 > 0$, and $\theta_3 < 0$.

Much has been written on the theoretical and empirical aspects of the rational expectations hypothesis (REH) since the publication of Muth's classic paper (Muth, 1961). It is not intended to repeat or summarise these discussions here. On the assumptions and implications of the REH, the interested reader is referred to Sheffrin (1985) and Minford and Peel (1986); Maddock and Carter (1982) stress the joint nature of hypothesis tests of the REH and the economic model in which the REH is embedded; and there are helpful discussions on the formation of rational expectations in Blume *et al.* (1982), Frydman (1983) and Bray and Savin (1986). Experimental evidence in support of the view that financial markets converge under realistic conditions to a rational expectations equilibrium can be found in Plott and Sunder (1982) for securities markets in general, and in Friedman *et al.* (1983) and Harrison (1992) for futures markets in particular. Much evidence has accumulated in the foreign exchange area against the REH (see, for example, Stein, 1995, pp. 191–197), although the question remains open on whether there is support for the REH in a simultaneous model with explicit representation of expectations variables. The preference of the economist, however, among alternative models, must always be for that model which provides the most powerful test, i.e. power to reject a false hypothesis. It should be noted that the method used to represent expectations empirically in this chapter (see *Estimation*) is consistent with both REH in the sense of Muth (1961), in which the system converges to a rational expectations equilibrium, and a situation in which agents are still learning the true model that is driving the economy. In the latter case, a concept such as Stein's (1986, pp. 150–1) asymptotically rational expectations may be relevant, in which the subjective distributions of agents converge to the objective distribution of the system with repeated sampling of information.

Because the two major aims of this chapter are to illuminate the process of exchange rate determination and to provide a model for out-of-sample forecasts of exchange rates, the survival of the strict REH is not critical to this chapter.

Long hedgers

These agents, such as US importers from Germany or US investors undertaking capital investment in Germany, have a commitment to buy Deutschmarks spot and are hedging the risk of a rise in the spot rate. They are, therefore, buyers of Deutschmark futures.

It is often assumed that the market position of a long hedger is the mirror image of that of a short hedger, but this is not necessarily so (Yamey, 1971, p. 423). Working (1953b) developed the concept of operational hedging especially to explain the market behaviour of long hedgers. Under this concept, long hedgers, in the context of this chapter, can use the futures rate as a guide to the DM contract price of planned imports, and can use the forward premium as a guide to the timing of DM spot purchases (because long hedgers gain from an increase in the forward premium). The operational hedging concept assumes that hedgers cover fully their spot market commitments (in a one-to-one ratio), and this hypothesis is used here rather than the selective hedging hypothesis. The two reasons for this are that the absence of time-varying volatility (see below) in the long hedging function rendered the selective hedging hypothesis less relevant, and that the high ratio of variance of spot price changes to variance of forward premium, discussed above, is a ground for expecting these agents to be fully hedged. The futures market positions of long hedgers, therefore, would be expected to vary negatively with the current forward premium and directly with the expected forward premium. Long hedgers' futures positions would be expected to vary directly also with a measure of their spot market commitments, such as US gross domestic product, which is used here as a proxy for US imports from Germany and US capital outflow to Germany. Hence, the specification of this function is:

$$LH_t = \theta_5 + \theta_6(P_t - A_t) + \theta_7(P_{t+1} - A_{t+1})^* + \theta_8 GDP_t + e_{2t} \qquad (4.2)$$

where LH is the futures market positions of long hedgers; A is the current spot rate; $(P_{t+1} - A_{t+1})^*$ is the rational expectation of the forward premium at time $(t + 1)$, formed at time t; GDP is the US gross domestic product; and $\theta_6 < 0$, and θ_7, $\theta_8 > 0$.

Short speculators

Short speculators in futures, assumed risk averse, expect the futures rate to fall; they are, therefore, sellers of Deutschmark currency futures. The futures market positions of these agents are assumed to vary directly with the current futures exchange rate, and negatively with the expected futures rate. Traditionally, the market commitments of short speculators have been assumed also to vary negatively with the marginal risk premium (Brennan, 1958; Kaldor, 1960). The specification of this equation is:

$$SS_t = \theta_9 + \theta_{10}P_t + \theta_{11}P^*_{t+1} + \theta_{12}r_t + e_{3t} \qquad (4.3)$$

where SS is the futures market commitments of short speculators; r is the marginal risk premium; and $\theta_{10} > 0$, and θ_{11}, $\theta_{12} < 0$.

Long speculators

Long speculators in futures, on the other hand, expect the futures rate to rise, and they buy Deutschmark currency futures. The market commitments of these agents, also assumed risk averse, would be expected to vary negatively with the current futures exchange rate and marginal risk premium, and positively with the expected futures rate.

The specification of this function is:

$$LS_t = \theta_{13} + \theta_{14}P_t + \theta_{15}P^*_{t+1} + \theta_{16}r_t + e_{4t} \tag{4.4}$$

where LS is the futures market commitments of long speculators; and θ_{14}, $\theta_{16} < 0$, and $\theta_{15} > 0$.

Unhedged spot market commitments

Other agents have current long positions, unhedged, in spot Deutschmarks either because they are importing goods from Germany to the USA or because they are US investors undertaking capital investment in Germany. As these positions are unhedged, they are equivalent to long speculation in spot. Such positions, therefore, could be expected to vary negatively with the current spot rate, positively with the expected spot rate, and negatively with the US-German nominal interest differential.[1] This function is consistent with the original model of Peston and Yamey (1960), which included holders of unhedged inventories of commodities, and is similar to speculative demand functions in the spot market used in Brennan (1958) and Kaldor (1960). The specification of this equation is:

$$U_t = \theta_{17} + \theta_{18}A_t + \theta_{19}A^*_{t+1} + \theta_{20}ID_t + e_{5t} \tag{4.5}$$

where U_t is the unhedged spot market commitments in Deutschmarks by US agents; A^*_{t+1} is the rational expectation of the spot rate in period $(t + 1)$, formed in period t; ID is the US-German nominal interest differential; and θ_{18}, $\theta_{20} < 0$, and $\theta_{19} > 0$.

This model, with seven endogenous variables, is completed with the following two identities:

$$U_t \equiv (M_t + AKO_t) - LH_t \tag{4.6}$$

$$SH_t + SS_t \equiv LH_t + LS_t \tag{4.7}$$

where AKO is US capital outflow to Germany.

Equation 4.6 is an identity that states that unhedged long spot commitments in Deutschmarks comprises all such commitments, less those that are hedged. Under equation 4.6, with a high ratio of long hedging to total long commitments, U_t can be negative: this would imply that these agents are reducing their Deutschmark-denominated assets in the current period. Equation 4.7 is a futures market clearing identity, which states that total sales of futures must equal total purchases of futures in each period.

Conventional identification conditions are not applicable to simultaneous, linear rational expectations models with forward expectations. The reasons for this are, first, that expectations of endogenous variables are replaced by functions of observed variables (see *Estimation*). Second, the reduced form parameters are highly non-linear functions of the structural parameters, and rank conditions for global identification cannot be derived (for a discussion of these issues, see Pesaran, 1987, pp. 120, 157–60). Nevertheless, local identification is possible, and Pesaran (1987, p. 160) derives the practical order condition that the number of predetermined variables in the model should be at least equal to the total number of endogenous, predetermined and expectational variables in the equation under consideration minus one. This model satisfies that condition, on an equation-by-equation basis, and estimation with the programme used (see *Data, unit roots and co-integration tests, and estimation*) would not proceed if such a condition were not met.

Data, unit roots and co-integration tests, and estimation

Data

The data used are outlined under the headings *Endogenous variables* and *Exogenous variables*. The intrasample period is from 1983 (02) to 1989 (12) comprising 83 observations, whereas the post-sample period is from 1990 (02) to 1992 (11), comprising 34 out-of-sample observations.

Endogenous variables

Data for the spot rate (*A*) are daily observations (interbank rate) on the last trading day of each month, quoted in US dollars per Deutschmark from the Deutsche Bundesbank (1983–92, series 5). Data for the futures rate (*P*) are daily observations on the last trading day of each month, quoted in US dollars per Deutschmark, for a contract which is on average two months before delivery.[2] These quotations are from IMM (1983–9) and from *Asian Wall Street Journal* (1990–2).

Commitments of traders for the variables *S*, *LH*, *SS* and *LS* are end of month open positions in number of contracts of DM125,000 each from CFTC (1983–92). These data are collected by the CFTC for 'reporting' (large), 'commercials' (hedgers) and 'non-commercials' (speculators), and for 'non-reporting traders' for both long and short positions. Data for 'non-reporting (small) traders' are not classified as between hedging and speculation, and it has been suggested that for some commodities and for some time periods these positions should be treated as all speculative (see Peck, 1982), whereas in other studies the open positions of small traders have been divided between hedging and speculation as the positions of reporting traders (see Goss *et al.*, 1992). This last approach has been adopted here. Unhedged spot market commitments (U) have been calculated from equation 4.6 and converted to contracts of DM125,000.

Exogenous variables

Data on exports (X) are monthly observations on US exports to Germany in DM million from the Deutsche Bundesbank (1983–92, series 4). Import data (M) are monthly observations on US imports from Germany, in DM million from the same source as export data, converted to contracts of DM125,000. Data on US capital outflow (AKO) are monthly observations on unofficial direct and portfolio capital movements from the USA to Germany in DM million, from the Deutsche Bundesbank (1983–92, series 3), converted to contracts of DM125,000. Observations on German capital inflow to the USA (GKI) are monthly data on unofficial direct and portfolio investment, in DM million, from the same source as AKO data.

Interest differential data (ID) are monthly observations on US interest rates (money market: day-to-day money) less monthly observations on German interest rates (money market: day-to-day loans), from OECD *Main Economic Indicators* (1983–92, Tables R2/07 and R2/01 respectively). The marginal risk premium is measured by the difference between the monthly average US ninety-day commercial paper rate and the monthly average ninety-day Treasury Bill rate, in per cent per annum, both rates being taken from the *Federal Reserve Bulletin*.[3] GDP is the US gross domestic product, observed quarterly in US$ million, from the *Survey of Current Business*, and interpolated to monthly observations with the program TRANSF (Wymer, 1977).

Unit root tests

To investigate whether the variables in this model are stationary, tests for a single unit root were conducted, using both augmented Dickey–Fuller tests (ADF) (see Dickey and Fuller, 1979, 1981; Said and Dickey,

1984), and Phillips–Perron tests (see Phillips and Perron, 1988). ADF tests were executed using the following general model:

$$\Delta Z_t = \mu + \beta t + \gamma Z_{t-1} + \phi_j \Delta Z_{t-j} + e_t \qquad (4.8)$$

where Z is an economic variable; μ is constant; β, γ, ϕ are coefficients to be estimated; j is equal to 1, 2, …, k; e_t is assumed to be NID $(0, \sigma^2)$. Inclusion of a time trend and lagged values of ΔZ_t in the model for a specific test was determined according to whether serial correlation was present in e_t, and by general to specific modelling (see Maddala and Kim, 1998, pp. 19, 78). The hypothesis of a single unit root in Z_t is addressed by testing the hypothesis $H(\gamma = 0)$ in equation 4.8. Calculated ADF test statistics and 5% critical values from MacKinnon (1991) for each variable in the model are given in Table 4.1. These results suggest that the variables SH, P, A, X, M, ID and r are $I(1)$ at the 5% level of significance, the remaining variables $(P - A)$, LH, SS, LS, U, AKO, GKI and GDP being stationary. In the case of M and r, where the calculated test statistic is very close to the critical value, the choice of significance level is obviously vital to the outcome. Nevertheless, the 5% significance level is more relevant to the moderate sample size in this chapter than either the 10% or 1% levels.

The low power of the ADF tests is well known (Evans and Savin, 1981). For this reason, Phillips–Perron tests were also conducted, and the results of these tests are presented in Table 4.2. It is generally agreed

Table 4.1 Unit root tests: augmented Dickey–Fuller

Variable	Calculated ADF statistic	5% Critical value	Order of integration
SH	−0.9963	−2.8976	I(1)
LH	−4.1293	−3.4659	I(0)
SS	−4.7365	−3.4645	I(0)
LS	−3.0062	−2.8967	I(0)
U	−4.3422	−3.4659	I(0)
P–A	−5.2377	−2.8972	I(0)
P	−2.1341	−3.4652	I(1)
A	−2.1819	−3.4652	I(1)
X	−1.1455	−2.8976	I(1)
M	−2.8857	−2.8972	I(1)
AKO	−3.8189	−2.8981	I(0)
GKI	−4.9115	−2.8967	I(0)
ID	−2.3663	−2.8972	I(1)
r	−3.3829	−3.4645	I(1)
GDP	−4.0707	−3.4666	I(0)

Table 4.2 Unit root tests: Phillips–Perron

Variable	Calculated test statistic	5% Critical value	Order of integration
SH	−5.0240	−2.8963	I(0)
LH	−9.7394	−3.4639	I(0)
SS	−8.3054	−3.4639	I(0)
LS	−3.5392	−2.8963	I(0)
U	−9.1823	−3.4639	I(0)
P − A	−7.5169	−2.8963	I(0)
P	−1.9586	−3.4639	I(1)
A	−1.9919	−3.4639	I(1)
X	−3.4400	−2.8963	I(0)
M	−4.7838	−2.8963	I(0)
AKO	−4.5712	−2.8963	I(0)
GKI	−2.9695	−2.8963	I(0)
ID	−2.0039	−2.8963	I(1)
r	−3.6221	−3.4639	I(0)
GDP	−4.4872	−3.4652	I(0)

that the Phillips–Perron tests have greater power than the ADF tests (see Banerjee *et al.*, 1993, p. 113), and for this reason the Phillips–Perron tests are taken as definitive. The greater power of the Phillips–Perron tests is seen in Table 4.2, in which the hypothesis of a single unit root has been rejected for *SH, X, M* and *r*; whereas the ADF tests had indicated that these variables were non-stationary. In other cases, the Phillips–Perron tests confirm the results of the ADF tests. The outcome of the unit root tests, therefore, is that the variables *P, A* and *ID* are regarded as non-stationary, all other variables being taken as I(0). [In addition, the expectational variables *P*, A**, derived as fitted values, are I(1); see *Estimation.*]

Co-integration tests

Each of the equations 4.1 and 4.3–4.5 in this model contains a mixture of stationary and non-stationary variables. Nevertheless, if a linear combination of these I(1) variables, in each of the respective equations, is stationary, i.e. if the I(1) variables in each equation are co-integrated, then the residuals of those equations will be stationary.

To investigate whether the I(1) variables in these equations are co-integrated, augmented Engle–Granger tests, as analysed by MacKinnon (1991), could be used. The Engle–Granger procedure, however, has been criticised on the grounds, *inter alia*, of, first, that the distribution of test

Table 4.3 Johansen co-integration procedure: maximum eigenvalue test

Equation: I(1) variables	Test statistic	5% Critical value	No. of co-integrating vectors: m
4.1, 4.3, 4.4	25.444	15.41	$m = 0$
P_t, P^*_{t+1}	0.386	3.76	$m \leq 1$
4.5	58.757	42.44	$m = 0$
A_t, A^*_{t+1}, ID	26.208	25.32	$m \leq 1$
	6.500	12.25	$m \leq 2$

statistics is not independent of the nuisance parameters of the particular application and, second, that the procedure is capable of identifying only one co-integrating vector (which varies according to the normalisation). The Johansen procedure overcomes these difficulties and is capable of identifying all co-integrating vectors in a set of $I(1)$ variables (see Johansen, 1988; Johansen and Juselius, 1990). The Johansen procedure includes two tests: the trace test and the maximum eigenvalue test. The first of these tests the hypothesis that the number of co-integrating vectors m is at most equal to q [where $q < n$, the number of $I(1)$ variables in the relationship] against the general alternative that $m \leq n$. The maximum eigenvalue test addresses the hypothesis that $m \leq q$, against the specific alternative $m \leq q + 1$.

In this chapter, the maximum eigenvalue test of the Johansen procedure has been used. For completeness, this test was executed for all $I(1)$ variables in each of the equations 4.1 and 4.3–4.5, and the results are reported in Table 4.3. It will be seen that this test suggests that there is one co-integrating relationship between P_t and P^*_{t+1} in each of the equations 4.1, 4.3 and 4.4 because the hypothesis $m = 0$ is clearly rejected at 5%. Similarly, the test indicates that there are two co-integrating vectors between A_t, A^*_{t+1} and ID in equation 4.5 because the hypothesis $m \leq 1$ is rejected at 5%.

Estimation

To make the REH operational, it is necessary to define the set of publicly available information that agents utilise in forming their expectations. In this model, an instrument for a rational expectation of an endogenous variable at time $(t + 1)$, formed at time t, is obtained as a fitted value on all predetermined (i.e. exogenous and lagged endogenous) variables in the model at time t. This procedure follows McCallum (1979). In equation

4.3, for example, an instrument is obtained by ordinary least squares (OLS) for P^*_{t+1} as a fitted value on the information set at time t, ϕ_t, so that:

$$P^*_{t+1} = E(P_{t+1}|\phi_t) \text{ and}$$

$$P_{t+1} = E(P_{t+1}|\phi_t) + \eta_t$$

where, under rational expectations, $E(\eta_t = 0)$ and η_t is uncorrelated with the elements of ϕ_t.

The estimation of simultaneous rational expectations models with forward expectations, by full information methods, although potentially more efficient, is less robust to specification errors than limited information methods and is computationally more demanding (Pesaran, 1987, p. 162). For these reasons, this model is estimated by the limited information methods discussed by McCallum (1979), Flood and Garber (1980) and Cumby *et al.* (1983); these methods can nevertheless produce consistent estimates. With an expectational instrument obtained as outlined above, consistent estimates of the coefficients of an individual structural equation can be obtained by instrumental variable (IV) estimation, if there is no serial correlation of the error term of that equation. This procedure has been used for equations 4.2 and 4.5 of this model.

If there is evidence of serial correlation in the error term, however, a simple correction for autocorrelation with IV estimation will not produce consistent estimates (Flood and Garber, 1980). Nevertheless, consistent estimates can be achieved if fitted values are obtained, on the appropriately dated information set, for all variables in the autoregressive transformed equation, and that equation is estimated by non-linear least squares. This procedure was discussed by Cumby *et al.* (1983) and has been used for equation 4.3 in this model. After these estimation procedures, there was no evidence of further dependence in the error term (see *Results: intrasample period*). The residuals of regression equations of financial time series are frequently heteroscedastic and exhibit volatility clustering. These phenomena can be modelled according to the autoregressive conditional heteroscedasticity (ARCH) method of Engle (1982, 1983). The ARCH LM test (see *Results: intrasample period*) suggested the possible presence of ARCH effects in equations 4.1–4.4 only, and the residuals of these equations were modelled as ARCH processes and the equations re-estimated by maximum likelihood. This procedure, however, indicated that there were significant ARCH effects, and of low order, in equations 4.1 and 4.4, but not in equations 4.2 and 4.3. According to the Schwartz Bayesian information criterion (see Maddala and Kim, 1998, pp. 19, 78), the error term of equation 4.1 was modelled as an ARCH (1) process, whereas that of equation 4.4 was represented as an ARCH (2). These specifications were confirmed by general to specific modelling (see also McKenzie and Brooks, 1997, p. 80). These estimations were executed using the program E VIEWS 2.0 (Lilien *et al.*, 1995).

Results: intrasample period

Results are presented and discussed in this section under the following headings: parameter estimates, intrasample simulation and diagnostic tests.

Parameter estimates

Estimates of the structural parameters, together with asymptotic *t*-values, adjusted coefficient of determination and Durbin–Watson statistics for the individual equations are given in Table 4.4. It will be seen that the signs of all fifteen parameter estimates are as anticipated, and fourteen are significant at the 5% level (one-tail test). Several aspects of these estimates deserve comment. First, there is support for Working's (1953a) selective hedging hypothesis for short hedgers, and for his (Working, 1953b) operational hedging hypothesis for long hedgers. Second, the significance of $\hat{\theta}_3, \hat{\theta}_7, \hat{\theta}_{11}, \hat{\theta}_{15}, \hat{\theta}_{19},$ while providing support for the REH, should not be interpreted to mean that agents necessarily form fully rational expectations (hypothesis tests in *Post-sample results* will further illuminate this question).[4] Third, US exports to Germany and US gross domestic product appear as valid proxies for the spot market commitments of short and long hedgers respectively. Fourth, the estimates of θ_{12} and θ_{16} being negative and, in the case of θ_{12}, significant provide support for the traditional view of the risk premium as analysed by Brennan (1958) and Kaldor (1960). Finally, the estimate of θ_{20}, the coefficient of the interest differential, suggests that a relative rise in US nominal interest rates leads to a decline in spot purchases of DM. If the reduction in DM spot purchases is the result of a rise in the spot exchange rate (i.e. depreciation of the US dollar), this would be consistent with the monetary model of the exchange rate. However, if the decline in spot purchases of

Table 4.4 Parameter estimates: equations 4.1–4.5

Equation	Coefficient	Variable	Estimate	Asymptotic t-value
4.1	θ_1	Constant	1676.5	0.376
	θ_2	P_t	187,467.5	2.748
	θ_3	P^*_{t+1}	−164,775.1	−2.459
	θ_4	X_t	9.364	71.548
		α_0	1.14×10^8	1.348
		α_1	0.501	2.109
4.2	θ_5	Constant	−42,822.94	−5.432
	θ_6	$P_t - A_t$	−855,339.2	−2.729
	θ_7	$(P_{t+1} - A_{t+1})^*$	448,294.5	1.702
	θ_8	GDP_t	200.509	8.410
	$\bar{R}^2 = 0.4742$	DW = 2.131		
4.3	θ_9	Constant	−5090.24	−1.737
	θ_{10}	P_t	303,693.0	5.300
	θ_{11}	P^*_{t+1}	−263,092.0	−5.081
	θ_{12}	r_t	−5340.46	−1.908
		ρ_3	0.228	1.611
	$\bar{R}^2 = 0.4392$	DW = 1.837		
4.4	θ_{13}	Constant	25,114.3	6.834
	θ_{14}	P_t	−136101.1	−2.417
	θ_{15}	P^*_{t+1}	123,825.8	2.076
	θ_{16}	r_t	−3189.56	−1.493
		α_0	63,155,593	5.385
		α_1	0.609	2.547
		α_2	−0.214	−1.748
4.5	θ_{17}	Constant	−544.51	−4.743
	θ_{18}	A_t	−1186.09	−1.956
	θ_{19}	A^*_{t+1}	1489.75	2.396
	θ_{20}	ID_t	−76.918	−2.380
	$\bar{R}^2 = 0.1765$	DW = 1.720		

Table 4.5 Intrasample simulation of exchange rates

Variable	Correlation coefficient	Theil's IC	% RMSE
A	0.9970	0.0077	1.714
P	0.9961	0.0089	2.060

DM is the result of a fall in the expected spot rate (expected appreciation of the US dollar), this would be consistent with the Mundell–Fleming interpretation of the Keynesian model (see Baillie and McMahon, 1989, p. 72).

Intrasample simulation

Table 4.5 provides a summary evaluation of intrasample simulation, by the model, of spot (AS) and futures (PS) exchange rates, and these simulations are illustrated in Figures 4.1 and 4.2. According to the criteria of correlation coefficient, Theil's inequality coefficient and per cent root mean square error (RMSE) (for definitions of these last two concepts, see Pindyck and Rubinfeld, 1981, pp. 362, 364), these simulations must be regarded as quite good, with that of the spot rate being slightly superior according to all three criteria. This general picture is confirmed in Figures 4.1 and 4.2, which indicate that the model tracks the actual series quite closely and that no major turning points have been missed. Some minor turning points, however, have not been captured, especially in Figure 4.2.

Intrasample simulation of other endogenous variables in the model

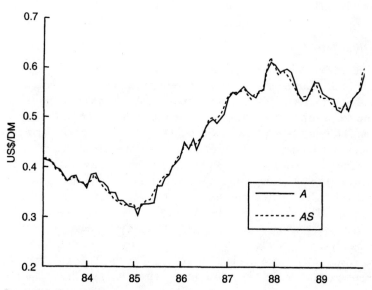

Figure 4.1 Spot price: intrasample simulation.

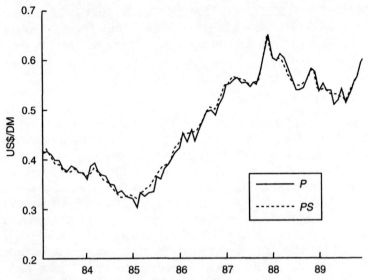

Figure 4.2 Futures price: intrasample simulation.

(not reported here) is less accurate, although this is not a major cause of concern because the spot and futures exchange rates are the focal points of this model.

Diagnostic tests

The Durbin–Watson (DW) statistics in Table 4.4 do not suggest the presence of any remaining serial correlation in the residuals of equations 4.2, 4.3 or 4.5 at the 5% level. The critical values of this statistic, however, are not invariant to the use of non-linear least squares and instrumental variable estimation compared with estimation by OLS. The DW statistics in Table 4.4, therefore, are subject to informal interpretation only.

The Ljung–Box Q statistic, which is valid under non-linear least squares and IV estimation, is used to test the null hypothesis that all autocorrelation coefficients are zero, up to lag twenty-four months in this case. The test statistic is distributed $\chi^2_{v=24}$, and suggests marginally, at the 5% level, that there is autocorrelation in the residuals of equation 4.3 only (see Appendix 4.1).

Stationarity of the residuals is confirmed by the ADF and Phillips–Perron tests. This test is used here to address the hypothesis that the residuals in each equation contain a unit root, and, as Appendix 4.1 shows, this hypothesis is rejected for all equations at 5%.

The Jarque–Bera test is used to address the hypothesis that the residuals of the respective equations are normally distributed. As Appendix 4.1 shows, this test suggests that the residuals are non-normal only in the short-speculation equation 4.3 at the 5% level.

Finally, the ARCH LM test addresses the null hypothesis of no ARCH effects (Engle, 1982, 1983) up to a lag of ten months. This test suggests that ARCH effects are present in equations 4.1–4.4 up to a lag of ten months, but not in equation 4.5. Subsequent attempts to model the conditional variance of the error terms in these equations as ARCH (P) processes, however, confirmed the presence of significant ARCH effects in equations 4.1 and 4.4 only, and these were represented as ARCH (1) and ARCH (2) respectively (see *Estimation* and Table 4.4).

Post-sample results

Post-sample simulations of spot and futures exchange rates, two months ahead,[5] for the period 1990 (02) to 1992 (11) (34 observations) are summarised in Table 4.6 and illustrated in Figures 4.3 and 4.4. Concentrating on the per cent RMSE criterion, it can be seen that both simulations have improved compared with those of the intrasample period and that each is less than 1%; the forecast of the futures rate is now slightly better than that of the spot rate. Professional interest, however, is likely to focus on forecasts of the spot rate and Table 4.7 compares the forecast of the spot rate by the model (AS is the same as A in Table 4.6) with forecasts by a naive random walk model, two months ahead, (ANAIVE) and by a futures rate lagged two periods (P_{t-2}). It can be seen, first, that the forecast of the spot rate by this model significantly outperforms the random walk forecast according to all three criteria. Second, the model forecast of the spot rate clearly surpasses the forecast of the spot rate implicit in the lagged futures rate. This last comparison provides evidence against the semistrong efficient markets hypothesis (EMH) because the model evidently contains information that is not reflected in the futures rate. The EMH should not be rejected, however,

Table 4.6 Post-sample simulation of exchange rates

Variable	Correlation coefficient	Theil's IC	% RMSE
A	0.9881	0.0047	0.945
P	0.9927	0.0038	0.785

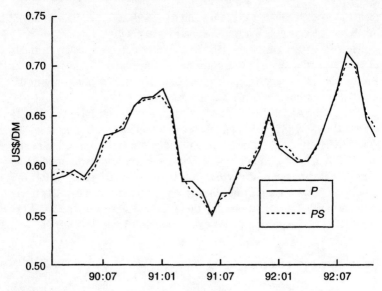

Figure 4.3 Futures price: post-sample simulation.

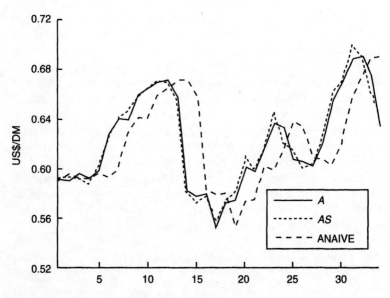

Figure 4.4 Spot price forecasts: post-sample.

Bilson, J.F.O. (1981) 'The "speculative efficiency" hypothesis', *Journal of Business* 54: 435–51.

Blume, L.E., Bray, M.M. and Easley, D. (1982) 'Introduction to the stability of rational expectations equilibrium', *Journal of Economic Theory* 26: 313–17.

Bray, M.M. and Savin, N.E. (1986) 'Rational expectations equilibria, learning and model specification', *Econometrica* 54: 1129–60.

Brennan, M.J. (1958) 'The supply of storage', *American Economic Review* 48: 50–72.

CFTC (Commodity Futures Trading Commission) (1983–92) *Commitments of Traders*, Washington, DC: CFTC.

Cumby, R.E., Huizinga, J. and Obstfeld, M. (1983) 'Two-step two-stage least squares estimation in models with rational expectations', *Journal of Econometrics* 21: 333–55.

Deutsche Bundesbank (1983–92) *Statistical Supplements to the Monthly Reports of the Deutsche Bundesbank*, series 3–5, Frankfurt am Main: Deutsche Bundesbank.

Dickey, D.A. and Fuller, W.A. (1979) 'Distribution of the estimators for autoregressive time series with a unit root', *Journal of the American Statistical Association* 74: 327–31.

Dickey, D.A. and Fuller, W.A. (1981) 'Likelihood ratio statistics for autoregressive time series with a unit root', *Econometrica* 49: 1057–72.

Ederington, L.J. (1979) 'The hedging performance of the new futures markets', *Journal of Finance* 34: 157–70.

Engle, R.F. (1982) 'Autoregressive conditional heteroskedasticity with estimates of the variance of UK inflation', *Econometrica* 50: 987–1008.

Engle, R.F. (1983) 'Estimates of the variance of US inflation based on the ARCH model', *Journal of Money Credit and Banking* 15: 286–301.

Evans, G.B.A. and Savin, N.E. (1981) 'Testing for unit roots: 1', *Econometrica*, 49: 753–79.

Flood, R.P. and Garber, P.M. (1980) 'A pitfall in estimation of models with rational expectations', *Journal of Monetary Economics* 6: 433–5.

Friedman, D., Harrison, G.W. and Salmon, J.W. (1983) 'The informational role of futures markets: some experimental evidence', in Streit, M.E. (ed.) *Futures Markets: Modelling, Managing and Monitoring Futures Trading*, Oxford: Basil Blackwell, Chapter 6.

Frydman, R. (1983) 'Individual rationality, decentralization and the rational expectations hypothesis', in Frydman, R. and Phelps, E.S. (eds) *Individual Forecasting and Aggregate Outcomes*, Cambridge: Cambridge University Press, Chapter 5.

Geweke, J. and Feige, E. (1979) 'Some joint tests of the efficiency of markets for forward foreign exchange', *Review of Economics and Statistics* 61: 334–41.

Giles, D.E.A., Goss, B.A. and Chin, O.P.L. (1985) 'Intertemporal allocation in the corn and soybeans markets with rational expectations', *American Journal of Agricultural Economics* 67: 749–60.

Table 4.7 Post-sample forecasts of spot exchange rate

Forecast model	Correlation coefficient	Theil's IC	% RMSE
AS	0.9881	0.0047	0.945
ANAIVE	0.6115	0.0262	5.414
P_{t-2}	0.5912	0.0279	5.748

unless a trading programme, based on this model, can be used to produce significant risk-adjusted profits (see Leuthold and Garcia, 1992, pp. 65–71). A further implication of this comparison is that agents evidently do not form fully rational expectations in the sense of Muth (1961), but are still learning the economic model that is driving the economy. A concept such as Stein's (1986, pp. 150–1) asymptotically rational expectations (ARE) may be relevant here.[6] With ARE, the subjective distributions of agents converge to the objective distribution of the system, with repeated sampling of information.

Conclusions

Critics have emphasised the poor performance of traditional economic models in explaining exchange rate changes, and especially in explaining post-sample forecasting of exchange rates. Deficiencies in the traditional approach to which attention has been drawn include undue reliance on single equation methods and inadequate representation of expectations. In addressing these issues, this chapter develops a simultaneous model of the US dollar/Deutschmark spot and futures markets, which includes behavioural relationships for short and long hedgers, short and long speculators in futures, and unhedged spot market commitments.

Augmented Dickey–Fuller and Phillips–Perron tests for unit roots were executed, and, where there was a difference in outcome, the latter were taken as definitive because of their generally greater power. These tests indicate that only the spot and futures exchange rates and their expectations, and the nominal interest differential, are $I(1)$, all other variables being stationary. Johansen co-integration tests suggest that these $I(1)$ variables are co-integrated in the respective equations.

Expectations are represented by fitted values on an information set comprising all predetermined variables in the model. Structural parameters are estimated by non-linear least squares for equations in which a correction for autocorrelation is necessary, and by instrumental variables in which there is no such serial correlation. There is evidence of low-order ARCH effects in the short hedging and long speculation equations, and these relationships were estimated by maximum likelihood with the conditional variance modelled as ARCH (1) and ARCH (2) processes respectively.

Although the estimates of the coefficients of all price and expected price variables are significant, this is not necessarily an indication that agents form rational expectations in the sense of Muth (1961) (MRE), for this outcome is consistent with both MRE and a situation where agents are still learning the true model that is driving the economy. Parameter estimates also are consistent with Working's (1953a) selective hedging hypothesis for short hedgers, and with his (Working, 1953b) operational hedging hypothesis for long hedgers; there is also support for the traditional view of the risk premium as analysed by Kaldor (1960). Unhedged commitments in spot Deutschmarks are negatively related to the US-German nominal interest differential.

Intrasample, this model simulates spot and futures exchange rates with per cent RMSEs of 1.7% and 2.1%, respectively, and post-sample these statistics decline to 0.8% and 0.7%, respectively, for two-month-ahead forecasts. Post-sample, the model forecast of the spot rate significantly outperforms the forecast of a naive random walk model (% RMSE = 5.4%), and that of a lagged futures rate (% RMSE = 5.7%). This last comparison provides evidence against the semistrong efficient markets hypothesis and suggests that agents do not form fully rational expectations but are still learning the true model that is driving the economy.

Acknowledgements

Research reported in this paper was supported by a grant from the Australian Research Council. The authors are indebted to Dietrich Fausten for assistance with data, to Jane Fry for research assistance, and to Brett Inder, Keith McLaren, Ray Leuthold and Jerome Stein for helpful comments. The usual disclaimer applies. A draft of this paper was prepared while the first author had a visiting appointment at Nomisma SpA, Bologna, Italy, during October 1997. Thanks are due to colleagues at that institute for their hospitality, especially to Fabio Gobbo and Patrizio Bianchi

Endnotes

1 The covered interest parity (CIP) hypothesis implies that the difference between the nominal US and German interest rates is approximately equal to the difference between the log of the forward rate and the log of the spot rate. The uncovered interest parity (UIP) hypothesis implies that the

difference between the nominal US and German interest rates is eq the expected change in the log of the spot rate between t and $(t+1)$. Tog CIP and UIP imply that the log of the forward rate is equal to the log expected spot rate. Empirical evidence has been more favourable CIP hypothesis than to the implication of unbiased prediction of UI Taylor, 1995, pp. 14–15, 19; Isard 1995, pp. 78–83; Baillie and McM 1989, chapters 5 and 6).

2 The Deutschmark (DM) contract at the Chicago Mercantile Exchange calls for delivery of DM125,000 in the months of March, June, Sept and December. Futures rate quotations were selected according following rule:
when the month is January, February, the future is March;
when the month is March, April, May, the future is June;
when the month is June, July, August, the future is September;
when the month is September, October, November, the future is Dece
when the month is December, the future is March.

3 In treating the risk premium as the difference between private and sector rates of return, it has been assumed implicitly that the return re for uncertainty about private sector securities is the same as that re for uncertainty about speculation in foreign exchange (cf. Stein, 1? 39, who regards the risk premium as a variable capable of obj observation, rather than as the residual between expected spot and f prices). GKI has been retained in the information set, along with Al

4 The presence of serially correlated error terms in equations 4.1, 4.3 ε is not necessarily evidence against the REH because this serial corr may be the result of the behaviour of other regressors in the resp equations or to specification errors.

5 The forecast horizon was set at two months because futures rates average two months from maturity.

6 This implies that the test of the semistrong REH in the *Post-sample* is a more powerful test than the significance tests in the *Results: intra. period.*

References

Asian Wall Street Journal (1990–2).

Bailey, R.W., Baillie, R.T. and McMahon, P.C. (1984) 'Interpreting econc evidence on efficiency in the foreign exchange market', *Oxford Ec Papers* 36: 67–85.

Baillie, R.T. and McMahon, P.C. (1989) *The Foreign Exchange Market: and Econometric Evidence*, Cambridge: Cambridge University Press

Baillie, R.T., Lippens, R.E. and McMahon, P.C. (1983) 'Testing r expectations and efficiency in the foreign exchange market'. *Econor* 51: 553–63.

Banerjee, A., Dolado, J.J., Galbraith, J.W. and Hendry, D.F. (199 *Integration, Error Correction, and the Econometric Analysis o Stationary Data*, Oxford: Oxford University Press.

Goss, B.A. and Avsar, S.G. (1996) 'A simultaneous, rational expectations model of the Australian dollar/US dollar market', *Applied Financial Economics* 6: 163–74.

Goss, B.A., Avsar, S.G. and Chan, S-C. (1992) 'Rational expectations and price determination in the US oats market', in Stein, J.L. and Goss B.A. (eds) *Economic Record: Special Issue on Futures Markets*, pp. 16–26.

Hansen, L.P. and Hodrick, R.J. (1980) 'Forward exchange rates as optimal predictors of future spot rates: an economic analysis', *Journal of Political Economy* 88: 829–53.

Harrison, G.W. (1992) 'Market dynamics, programmed traders and futures markets: beginning the laboratory search for a smoking gun', in Stein, J.L. and Goss B.A. (eds) *Economic Record: Special Issue on Futures Markets* pp. 46–62.

Hodrick, R.J. (1987) *The Empirical Evidence on the Efficiency of Forward and Futures Foreign Exchange Markets*, Chur: Harwood.

Hodrick, R.J. and Srivastava, S. (1984) 'An investigation of risk and return in forward foreign exchange', *Journal of International Money and Finance* 3: 1–29.

Hodrick, R.J. and Srivastava, S. (1987) 'Foreign currency futures', *Journal of International Economics* 22: 1–24.

IMM (International Monetary Market) (1983–9) *Yearbook*, Chicago: Chicago Mercantile Exchange.

Isard, P. (1987) 'Lessons from empirical models of exchange rates', *International Monetary Fund Staff Papers* 34: 1–28.

Isard, P. (1995) *Exchange Rate Economics*, Cambridge: Cambridge University Press.

Johansen, S. (1988) 'Statistical analysis of cointegration vectors', *Journal of Economic Dynamics and Control* 12: 231–54.

Johansen, S. and Juselius, K. (1990) 'Maximum likelihood estimation and inference on cointegration – with applications to the demand for money', *Oxford Bulletin of Economics and Statistics* 52: 169–210.

Kahl, K.H. (1983) 'Determination of the recommended hedging ratio', *American Journal of Agricultural Economics* 65: 603–5.

Kaldor, N. (1960) 'Speculation and economic stability', in *Essays on Economic Stability and Growth*, London: Duckworth, pp. 17–58.

Leuthold, R.M. and Garcia, P. (1992) 'Assessing market performance: an examination of livestock futures markets', in Goss, B.A. (ed.) *Rational Expectations and Efficiency in Futures Markets*, London: Routledge, pp. 52–77.

Lilien, D.M., Startz, R., Ellsworth, S., Noh, J. and Engle, R. (1995) EVIEWS, version 2.0, Irvine, CA: Quantitative Micro Software.

McCallum, B.T. (1979) 'Topics concerning the formulation, estimation and use of macroeconomic models with rational expectations', *Proceedings of the*

Business and Economic Statistics Section, Washington, DC: American Statistical Association, pp. 65–72.

McKenzie, M.D. and Brooks, R.D. (1997) 'The impact of exchange rate volatility on German–US trade flows', *Journal of International Financial Markets, Institutions and Money* 7: 73–87.

MacKinnon, J.G. (1991) 'Critical values for cointegration tests', in Engle' R.F. and Granger, C.W.J. (eds) *Long-Run Economic Relationships: Readings in Cointegration*, Oxford: Oxford University Press, pp. 267–76.

Maddala, G.S. and Kim, I-M. (1998) *Unit Roots, Cointegration and Structural Change*, Cambridge: Cambridge University Press.

Maddock, R. and Carter, M. (1982) 'A child's guide to rational expectations', *Journal of Economic Literature* 20: 39–51.

Meese, R. (1990) 'Currency fluctuations in the post-Bretton Woods era', *Journal of Economic Perspectives* 4: 117–34.

Minford, P. and Peel, D. (1986) *Rational Expectations and the New Macroeconomics*, Oxford: Basil Blackwell.

Muth, J. (1961) 'Rational expectations and the theory of price movements', *Econometrica* 29: 315–35.

OECD (Organisation for Economic Cooperation and Development) (1983–92) *Main Economic Indicators*, Paris: OECD.

Peck, A.E. (1982) 'Estimations of hedging and speculative positions in futures markets revisited', *Food Research Institute Studies* 18: 181–95.

Pesaran, M.H. (1987) *The Limits to Rational Expectations*, Oxford: Basil Blackwell, (corrected edn 1989).

Peston, M.H. and Yamey, B.S. (1960) 'Intertemporal price relationships with forward markets: a method of analysis', *Economica* 27: 355–67.

Phillips, P.C.B. and Perron, P. (1988) 'Testing for a unit root in time series regression', *Biometrika* 75: 335–46.

Pindyck, R.S. and Rubinfeld, D.L. (1981) *Econometric Models and Economic Forecasts*, 2nd. edn, Singapore: McGraw-Hill.

Plott, C.R. and Sunder, S. (1982) 'Efficiency of experimental security markets with insider information: an application of rational expectations models', *Journal of Political Economy* 90: 663–98.

Said, S.E. and Dickey, D.A. (1984) 'Testing for unit roots in autoregressive-moving average models of unknown order', *Biometrika* 71: 599–607.

Sheffrin, S.M. (1985) *Rational Expectations*, Cambridge: Cambridge University Press.

Stein, J.L. (1986) *The Economics of Futures Markets*, Oxford: Basil Blackwell.

Stein, J.L. (1991) *International Financial Markets*, Oxford: Basil Blackwell.

Stein, J.L., Polly Reynolds Allen and Associates (1995) *Fundamental Determinants of Exchange Rates*, Oxford: Oxford University Press.

Taylor, M.P. (1995) 'The economics of exchange rates', *Journal of Economic Literature* 33: March, 13–47.

Taylor, S.J. (1992) 'Rewards available to currency futures speculators: compensation for risk or evidence of inefficient pricing', in Stein, J.L. and

Goss B.A. (eds) *Economic Record: Special Issue on Futures Markets*, pp. 105–16.

Working, H. (1953a) 'Futures trading and hedging', *American Economic Review* 43: 313–43.

Working, H. (1953b) 'Hedging reconsidered', *Journal of Farm Economics* 35: 544–61.

Working, H. (1962) 'New concepts concerning futures markets and prices', *American Economic Review* 52: 431–59.

Wymer, C.R. (1977) 'Computer programs: TRANSF manual', Mimeograph, Washington DC: International Monetary Fund.

Yamey, B.S. (1971) 'Short hedging and long hedging in futures markets', *Journal of Law and Economics* 14: 413–34.

Appendix 4.1 Diagnostic tests on residuals

| Test | Equation | | | | |
	4.1 (SH)	4.2 (LH)	4.3 (SS)	4.4 (LS)	4.5 (U)
Ljung–Box Q statistic					
Calculated χ^2_{24}	20.793	33.692	36.730	20.030	19.873
Critical χ^2_{24} (0.05) = 36.415					
ADF test					
Calculated test statistic	−3.2857	−3.6005	−4.8306	−2.9652	−4.5582
5% Critical value	−2.8972	−2.8991	−2.8976	−2.8986	−2.8986
Phillips–Perron test					
Calculated test statistic	−6.6469	−9.5868	−8.5559	−3.2685	−8.1541
5% Critical value	−2.8967	−2.8981	−2.8972	−2.8967	−2.8972
Jarque–Bera test					
Calculated test statistic	1.1625	0.0270	16.1422	2.6169	0.3670
Probability value	0.5592	0.9866	0.0003	0.2702	0.8323

Chapter 5

Noise trader sentiment in futures markets

Dwight R. Sanders, Scott H. Irwin
and Raymond M. Leuthold

Introduction

> I analyze the gold market by using monthly, weekly, and daily charts.
> I then look at what the moving averages are doing with stochastic
> studies and either window envelopes or Bollinger Bands…The 18
> day moving average…is my 'Bell Weather' moving average. When
> the market is above it, I am bullish, when the market is below it, I
> am bearish… Fibonacci retracement levels are taken from finding a
> high to a low point, or a low to a high point and then dividing the
> market into quadrants. I use those quadrants to find support and
> resistance lines in the markets. History shows that this type of analysis
> has merit. When all of this is put together an analysis is made.
>
> Ira Epstein (1994)

Do traders, such as Mr Epstein, who trade on non-fundamental
information affect the behaviour of futures prices? This question is central
to our understanding of futures markets and, consequently, for effective
market participation and regulation. The following research, couched
within the noise trader paradigm, provides empirical insight into noise
traders, market sentiment and the subsequent behaviour of futures prices.

Black (1986) defines 'noise' as non-information and 'noise trading'
as trading on noise as if it were information. He asserts that noise traders
may not be eliminated from the market because rational arbitrage against
them is costly and, thus, limited. Noise traders are not rational Bayesian
forecasters; thus, they may make markets less efficient. Yet, noise traders
are also beneficial because they inadvertently provide market liquidity.
The topic of irrational speculation is not new, early economists debated
the effects of noise traders on asset prices. For instance, traditional
neoclassical economists (see, for example, Working, 1949; Friedman,

Table 4.7 Post-sample forecasts of spot exchange rate

Forecast model	Correlation coefficient	Theil's IC	% RMSE
AS	0.9881	0.0047	0.945
ANAIVE	0.6115	0.0262	5.414
P_{t-2}	0.5912	0.0279	5.748

unless a trading programme, based on this model, can be used to produce significant risk-adjusted profits (see Leuthold and Garcia, 1992, pp. 65–71). A further implication of this comparison is that agents evidently do not form fully rational expectations in the sense of Muth (1961), but are still learning the economic model that is driving the economy. A concept such as Stein's (1986, pp. 150–1) asymptotically rational expectations (ARE) may be relevant here.[6] With ARE, the subjective distributions of agents converge to the objective distribution of the system, with repeated sampling of information.

Conclusions

Critics have emphasised the poor performance of traditional economic models in explaining exchange rate changes, and especially in explaining post-sample forecasting of exchange rates. Deficiencies in the traditional approach to which attention has been drawn include undue reliance on single equation methods and inadequate representation of expectations. In addressing these issues, this chapter develops a simultaneous model of the US dollar/Deutschmark spot and futures markets, which includes behavioural relationships for short and long hedgers, short and long speculators in futures, and unhedged spot market commitments.

Augmented Dickey–Fuller and Phillips–Perron tests for unit roots were executed, and, where there was a difference in outcome, the latter were taken as definitive because of their generally greater power. These tests indicate that only the spot and futures exchange rates and their expectations, and the nominal interest differential, are $I(1)$, all other variables being stationary. Johansen co-integration tests suggest that these $I(1)$ variables are co-integrated in the respective equations.

Expectations are represented by fitted values on an information set comprising all predetermined variables in the model. Structural parameters are estimated by non-linear least squares for equations in which a correction for autocorrelation is necessary, and by instrumental variables in which there is no such serial correlation. There is evidence of low-order ARCH effects in the short hedging and long speculation equations, and these relationships were estimated by maximum likelihood with the conditional variance modelled as ARCH (1) and ARCH (2) processes respectively.

Although the estimates of the coefficients of all price and expected price variables are significant, this is not necessarily an indication that agents form rational expectations in the sense of Muth (1961) (MRE), for this outcome is consistent with both MRE and a situation where agents are still learning the true model that is driving the economy. Parameter estimates also are consistent with Working's (1953a) selective hedging hypothesis for short hedgers, and with his (Working, 1953b) operational hedging hypothesis for long hedgers; there is also support for the traditional view of the risk premium as analysed by Kaldor (1960). Unhedged commitments in spot Deutschmarks are negatively related to the US-German nominal interest differential.

Intrasample, this model simulates spot and futures exchange rates with per cent RMSEs of 1.7% and 2.1%, respectively, and post-sample these statistics decline to 0.8% and 0.7%, respectively, for two-month-ahead forecasts. Post-sample, the model forecast of the spot rate significantly outperforms the forecast of a naive random walk model (% RMSE = 5.4%), and that of a lagged futures rate (% RMSE = 5.7%). This last comparison provides evidence against the semistrong efficient markets hypothesis and suggests that agents do not form fully rational expectations but are still learning the true model that is driving the economy.

Acknowledgements

Research reported in this paper was supported by a grant from the Australian Research Council. The authors are indebted to Dietrich Fausten for assistance with data, to Jane Fry for research assistance, and to Brett Inder, Keith McLaren, Ray Leuthold and Jerome Stein for helpful comments. The usual disclaimer applies. A draft of this paper was prepared while the first author had a visiting appointment at Nomisma SpA, Bologna, Italy, during October 1997. Thanks are due to colleagues at that institute for their hospitality, especially to Fabio Gobbo and Patrizio Bianchi

Endnotes

1   The covered interest parity (CIP) hypothesis implies that the difference between the nominal US and German interest rates is approximately equal to the difference between the log of the forward rate and the log of the spot rate. The uncovered interest parity (UIP) hypothesis implies that the

difference between the nominal US and German interest rates is equal to the expected change in the log of the spot rate between t and $(t+1)$. Together, CIP and UIP imply that the log of the forward rate is equal to the log of the expected spot rate. Empirical evidence has been more favourable to the CIP hypothesis than to the implication of unbiased prediction of UIP (see Taylor, 1995, pp. 14–15, 19; Isard 1995, pp. 78–83; Baillie and McMahon, 1989, chapters 5 and 6).

2 The Deutschmark (DM) contract at the Chicago Mercantile Exchange IMM calls for delivery of DM125,000 in the months of March, June, September and December. Futures rate quotations were selected according to the following rule:

when the month is January, February, the future is March;

when the month is March, April, May, the future is June;

when the month is June, July, August, the future is September;

when the month is September, October, November, the future is December;

when the month is December, the future is March.

3 In treating the risk premium as the difference between private and public sector rates of return, it has been assumed implicitly that the return required for uncertainty about private sector securities is the same as that required for uncertainty about speculation in foreign exchange (cf. Stein, 1991, p. 39, who regards the risk premium as a variable capable of objective observation, rather than as the residual between expected spot and forward prices). GKI has been retained in the information set, along with AKO.

4 The presence of serially correlated error terms in equations 4.1, 4.3 and 4.4 is not necessarily evidence against the REH because this serial correlation may be the result of the behaviour of other regressors in the respective equations or to specification errors.

5 The forecast horizon was set at two months because futures rates are on average two months from maturity.

6 This implies that the test of the semistrong REH in the *Post-sample results* is a more powerful test than the significance tests in the *Results: intrasample period*.

References

Asian Wall Street Journal (1990–2).

Bailey, R.W., Baillie, R.T. and McMahon, P.C. (1984) 'Interpreting econometric evidence on efficiency in the foreign exchange market', *Oxford Economic Papers* 36: 67–85.

Baillie, R.T. and McMahon, P.C. (1989) *The Foreign Exchange Market: Theory and Econometric Evidence*, Cambridge: Cambridge University Press.

Baillie, R.T., Lippens, R.E. and McMahon, P.C. (1983) 'Testing rational expectations and efficiency in the foreign exchange market'. *Econometrica* 51: 553–63.

Banerjee, A., Dolado, J.J., Galbraith, J.W. and Hendry, D.F. (1993) *Co-Integration, Error Correction, and the Econometric Analysis of Non-Stationary Data*, Oxford: Oxford University Press.

Bilson, J.F.O. (1981) 'The "speculative efficiency" hypothesis', *Journal of Business* 54: 435–51.

Blume, L.E., Bray, M.M. and Easley, D. (1982) 'Introduction to the stability of rational expectations equilibrium', *Journal of Economic Theory* 26: 313–17.

Bray, M.M. and Savin, N.E. (1986) 'Rational expectations equilibria, learning and model specification', *Econometrica* 54: 1129–60.

Brennan, M.J. (1958) 'The supply of storage', *American Economic Review* 48: 50–72.

CFTC (Commodity Futures Trading Commission) (1983–92) *Commitments of Traders*, Washington, DC: CFTC.

Cumby, R.E., Huizinga, J. and Obstfeld, M. (1983) 'Two-step two-stage least squares estimation in models with rational expectations', *Journal of Econometrics* 21: 333–55.

Deutsche Bundesbank (1983–92) *Statistical Supplements to the Monthly Reports of the Deutsche Bundesbank,* series 3–5, Frankfurt am Main: Deutsche Bundesbank.

Dickey, D.A. and Fuller, W.A. (1979) 'Distribution of the estimators for autoregressive time series with a unit root', *Journal of the American Statistical Association* 74: 327–31.

Dickey, D.A. and Fuller, W.A. (1981) 'Likelihood ratio statistics for autoregressive time series with a unit root', *Econometrica* 49: 1057–72.

Ederington, L.J. (1979) 'The hedging performance of the new futures markets', *Journal of Finance* 34: 157–70.

Engle, R.F. (1982) 'Autoregressive conditional heteroskedasticity with estimates of the variance of UK inflation', *Econometrica* 50: 987–1008.

Engle, R.F. (1983) 'Estimates of the variance of US inflation based on the ARCH model', *Journal of Money Credit and Banking* 15: 286–301.

Evans, G.B.A. and Savin, N.E. (1981) 'Testing for unit roots: 1', *Econometrica*, 49: 753–79.

Flood, R.P. and Garber, P.M. (1980) 'A pitfall in estimation of models with rational expectations', *Journal of Monetary Economics* 6: 433–5.

Friedman, D., Harrison, G.W. and Salmon, J.W. (1983) 'The informational role of futures markets: some experimental evidence', in Streit, M.E. (ed.) *Futures Markets: Modelling, Managing and Monitoring Futures Trading*, Oxford: Basil Blackwell, Chapter 6.

Frydman, R. (1983) 'Individual rationality, decentralization and the rational expectations hypothesis', in Frydman, R. and Phelps, E.S. (eds) *Individual Forecasting and Aggregate Outcomes*, Cambridge: Cambridge University Press, Chapter 5.

Geweke, J. and Feige, E. (1979) 'Some joint tests of the efficiency of markets for forward foreign exchange', *Review of Economics and Statistics* 61: 334–41.

Giles, D.E.A., Goss, B.A. and Chin, O.P.L. (1985) 'Intertemporal allocation in the corn and soybeans markets with rational expectations', *American Journal of Agricultural Economics* 67: 749–60.

1953) argue that speculation is stabilising and that uninformed speculators are quickly dispatched by their rational counterparts. Other equally renowned economists (see, for example, Fisher, 1930; Keynes, 1936) argue that public speculation is a destabilising mania. Some recent theoretical advances support the possibility that irrational traders can exist and persist in markets, exerting a destabilising influence on prices (De Long et al., 1989, 1990a, 1990b, 1991; Shleifer and Summers, 1990). In this research, new empirical evidence is brought to bear on these models.

Previous empirical research concerning noise trading tends to focus on the symptoms rather than the cause. That is to say, market behaviour is examined for characteristics that suggest the presence of noise traders (for example Liu et al., 1992). For instance, autocorrelation (for example Taylor, 1985) or mean-reversion (for example, Ma et al., 1990) in futures returns can be generated by noise traders; but, they may also arise from a disequilibrium adjustment process (Beja and Goldman, 1980) or some time-varying risk premium (Bessembinder, 1992). These studies test market rationality, but they do so without a clearly defined alternative hypothesis. Researchers that do hypothesise well-defined noise trader alternatives often must rely on somewhat *ad hoc* empirical measures of noise trader sentiment (see, for example, Ma et al., 1992; Kodres, 1994). The presented research improves upon this methodology by using a measure of noise trader sentiment that reflects actual retail speculators' expectations. Consequently, noise trader effects are tested directly under clear alternative hypotheses.

In this chapter, a futures market variant of the De Long et al. (1990a) noise trader sentiment model is developed. The model provides clear alternatives to Muth's rational expectations hypothesis (Muth, 1961). The model's predictions are tested using a commercial measure of market sentiment, i.e. surveys of market participants' price outlook. Using this bullish consensus index as a proxy for noise trader sentiment, the research seeks to determine whether noise trader sentiment creates a direct and systematic price pressure effect on futures prices, in which price pressure materialises as a systematic forecast bias or in the time series predictability of returns.

A theoretical noise trader risk model for futures markets

De Long et al. (1990a) develop an overlapping generations model that provides considerable insight into the behaviour of asset prices in markets plagued by noise traders. However, the model is not directly applicable to futures markets. Most notably, the unsafe asset in the economy is fixed in supply; whereas, there is a net zero supply of futures contracts. Thus, this simple modification is made within the model to derive the impact of noise trader sentiment on zero net supply investments. The resulting model is more applicable to futures markets.[1]

De Long *et al.*'s (1990a) model is a parsimonious overlapping generations model with no labour supply decision, bequest or first period consumption.[2] There are two assets: a safe asset s, and an unsafe (risky) asset u. The safe asset is in perfectly elastic supply, pays a real dividend *r*, in every period, and has a fixed price of 1. The unsafe asset pays the same real dividend *r*, in every period as the safe asset, and it has a price of P_t. In De Long *et al.*'s model, the unsafe asset is in perfectly inelastic supply normalised at one unit. Here, in the spirit of a futures market, the unsafe asset has a net zero supply.

There are two types of two-period-lived agents: rational investors (RI), and noise traders (NT). The rational investors have rational expectations concerning the distribution of P_t and are present in measure $1 - \mu(\mu \in [0,1])$. Noise traders are present in measure μ and misperceive the distribution of P_t by an independent and identically distributed (i.i.d.) normal variable $\rho_t \sim N(\rho^*, \sigma^2_\rho)$. The mean misperception ρ^* is the average bullishness or bearishness of noise traders, and the variance σ^2_ρ is the volatility of noise trader sentiment. Market sentiment can arise from technical trading rules, extrapolation of price changes or investment fads.

Both agent types choose portfolios when young (i.e. first period of life) to maximise perceived expected utility given their beliefs about the *ex ante* distribution of u when they are old at $t + 1$. Each agent has a constant absolute risk aversion utility function: $U = -\exp^{-(2\gamma)w}$, where γ is the coefficient of absolute risk aversion. Each agent maximises the expected utility of final wealth *w*, which is equivalent in a mean-variance framework to maximising: $E(U) = \bar{w} - \gamma\sigma^2_w$.

The representative sophisticated investor rationally perceives the distribution of returns, and chooses amount λ^i_t of the risky (unsafe) asset u to maximise expected utility:

$$E(U) = c_0 + \lambda^i_t[(P_{t+1} - P_t) - r(1 - P_t)] - \gamma(\lambda^i_t)^2(\sigma^2_{Pt+1}) \qquad (5.1)$$

The first term in brackets is the expected capital gain from investing in the unsafe asset, and the second term in brackets is the effective dividend of the unsafe asset owing to purchasing it at a discount or premium to its fundamental value. The constant c_0 is a function of first period labour

income.[3,4] Following De Long *et al.* (1990a), we can rearrange equation
5.1 to get the following expression for the sophisticated investor's
expected utility:

$$E(U) = c_0 + \lambda^i_t[r + {}_tP_{t+1} - P_t(1+r)] - \gamma(\lambda^i_t)^2({}_t\sigma^2_{Pt+1}) \qquad (5.2)$$

Like the sophisticated investor, the representative noise trader chooses
the amount of the unsafe asset λ^n_t to maximise expected utility:

$$E(U) = c_0 + \lambda^n_t[r + {}_tP_{t+1} - P_t(1+r)] - \gamma(\lambda^n_t)^2(\sigma^2_{Pt+1}) + \lambda^n_t(\rho_t) \quad (5.3)$$

The difference between the two representative traders' expected utilty
is the last term in equation 5.3: the noise trader's misperception of capital
gains owing to irrational sentiment ρ_t.

The representative rational and noise traders maximise their expected
utility, resulting in demands equations 5.4 and 5.5 respectively.

$$\lambda^i_t = \frac{r + {}_tP_{t+1} - (1+r)P_t}{2\gamma({}_t\sigma^2_{P_{t+1}})} \qquad (5.4)$$

$$\lambda^i_t = \frac{r + {}_tP_{t+1} - (1+r)p_t + \rho_t}{2\gamma({}_t\sigma^2_{P_{t+1}})} \qquad (5.5)$$

$$\mu(\lambda^n_t) + (1-\mu)\lambda^i_t = 0 \qquad (5.6)$$

Demands are increasing in perceived returns and decreasing in
perceived variance.[5] The difference between equations 5.4 and 5.5 is
noise traders' sentiment ρ_t, where bullish sentiment ($\rho_t > 0$) causes an
increase in noise trader demand. Equation 5.6 is the market clearing
condition for the speculative asset in zero net supply. The three-equation
system is solved for a pricing function,

$$P_t = \frac{r + \mu\rho_t + {}_tP_{t+1}}{(1+r)} \qquad (5.7)$$

Recursively solving for the steady-state equilibria (assuming the
unconditional distribution of P_{t+1} equals the conditional distribution of
P_t), the final equilibria pricing rule is derived:

$$P_t = 1 + \frac{\mu\rho^*}{r} + \frac{\mu(\rho_t - \rho^*)}{(1+r)} \tag{5.8}$$

and

$$\sigma_{P_t}^2 = \frac{\mu^2\sigma_\rho^2}{(1+r)^2} \tag{5.9}$$

Equation 5.8 is the equilibrium pricing function and equation 5.9 is the price variance. Comparing equation 5.8 with De Long *et al.*'s (1990a) pricing rule result (De Long *et al.*'s equation 12), one difference is immediately obvious: noise traders cannot 'create their own space' in the futures market. That is to say, there is not a premium for assuming noise trader risk in futures markets. Intuitively, this stems from the fact that the futures investment is really just a side bet on price movements. It requires no net risk sharing capacity within the economy. For instance, in equation 5.8, if $\rho_t = \rho^* = 0$, then no side bets are made between noise traders and rational traders; thus, the unsafe asset u equals its fundamental value because no noise trader risk is borne.

The other general results from De Long *et al.*'s (1990a) model pertain to the futures market. Examining equation 5.9, it is clear that futures price volatility is increasing in the proportion of noise traders and in the variability of their sentiment. In equation 5.8, noise trader sentiment impacts the pricing of futures contracts. The first term of equation 5.8 indicates that the futures price equals fundamental value in the absence of noise traders. The second and third terms of equation 5.8 capture the price pressure effects of noise traders. If noise traders are on average bearish ($\rho^* < 0$), then the price is lower (on average) than fundamental value. Also, if noise traders are more bullish than average at time t ($\rho_t > \rho^*$), then they are able to push prices above fundamental value. From equation 5.8, the equilibrium pricing of futures contracts and the time series characteristics of returns can be derived.

Assuming that the futures price is equal to a fundamental value of 1 at expiration, and applying iterative expectations (see Samuelson, 1965; Kaminsky and Kumar, 1990), the pricing equation 5.8 can be rewritten to display the time series characteristics and equilibrium pricing respectively:

$$R_t = P_t - P_{t-n} = -\left[\frac{\mu\rho^*}{r} + \frac{\mu(\rho_{t-n} - \rho^*)}{1+r}\right] \tag{5.10}$$

and taking expectations,

$$E(R_t) = E(P_t - P_{t-n}) = -\frac{\mu\rho^*}{r} \qquad (5.11)$$

where R_t is the continuously compounded per cent change in the futures price over the interval n.[6]

From equation 5.10, the noise trader model suggests that the forecast error at any time t is not random, but contains a deterministic bias $-(\mu\rho^*)/r$, as well as a time-varying component $-\mu(\rho_t - \rho^*)/(1 + r)$. The pricing error at time t, i.e. the deviation from fundamental or final value, is inversely proportional to the sentiment of noise traders at time t. If noise traders are unduly bullish at time t, $(\rho_t > \rho^*)$, then the futures forecast is too high and prices will decline. Likewise, bearish time t noise traders, $(\rho_t < \rho^*)$, are associated with rising futures prices $R_t > 0$. To the extent that ρ_t is known, then the futures price violates the efficiency or orthogonality condition of traditional rational models (Muth, 1961).

Additionally, in equation 5.11, futures prices are on average biased forecasts of fundamental value, and the expected bias equals $-(\mu\rho^*)/r$. That is to say, the deterministic bias in futures prices is proportional to the average level of sentiment among noise traders. The more bearish noise traders are on average (the lower ρ^*) for a particular commodity, then the greater the downward bias in the futures price P_{t-n}. Consequently, the futures price will rise on average towards fundamental value. The predictions in equations 5.10 and 5.11 provide distinct, empirically testable alternatives to a rational expectations hypothesis. The following sections discuss two approaches to empirically testing the noise trader predictions: cross-sectional and time series testing.

Empirical methodology

Cross-sectional test for systematic forecast bias

Under the rational expectations hypothesis, the expected bias in futures prices is zero.[7] However, the systematic bias for market i under the noise trader model is expressed as a function of the model's parameters $-(\mu^i\rho^{*i})/r$. Assuming that μ^i and r are constant across commodities and time, then the noise trader model equation 5.11 predicts that the equilibrium futures return is inversely proportional to the mean noise trader sentiment in market i, ρ^{*i}. This prediction can be tested with the cross-sectional regressions of Fama and MacBeth (1973).

Let $\bar{\rho}^i$ be a sample estimate of the mean noise trader sentiment in market i. The following cross-sectional model derived from equation 5.11

$$E(R^i_t) = \alpha + \beta\rho^{*i} \tag{5.12}$$

can be empirically estimated as,

$$\overline{R}^i = \alpha + \beta\,\overline{\rho}^i + \varepsilon^i \tag{5.13}$$

The average forecast bias $\overline{R}^i$ is a function of the average level of noise trader sentiment in market i. Following the procedure set forth by Fama and MacBeth (1973), the cross-sectional regressions are estimated using *ex ante* estimates of ρ^{*i}. That is to say, $\overline{\rho}^i$ is estimated over K periods, then this *ex ante* estimate is the independent variable in explaining the average forecast bias $\overline{R}^i$ in the subsequent J periods, where J need not equal K. So, for each market i, $\overline{\rho}^i$ is calculated for the first K periods of the sample. Then, the bias $\overline{R}^i$ is calculated over the following J periods in market i. Tabulating these data for $i = 1, 2, ..., N$ markets, the regression in equation 5.13 is estimated over N cross-sectional observations. This process is repeated for each J-length non-overlapping subperiods in the entire sample.

For example, consider a sample of one hundred weekly observations on fifteen markets, and let $K = 10$ and $J = 10$. Then, for each market, $\overline{\rho}^i$ is calculated over observations 1–10, and this is the independent variable in the cross-sectional regression explaining $\overline{R}^i$, which is calculated over observations 11–20. The second cross-sectional regression for this data set would use $\overline{\rho}^i$ calculated over observations 11–20 to explain $\overline{R}^i$ calculated over observations 21–30. This procedure would be repeated through all one hundred time series observations, resulting in nine cross-sectional regressions (fifteen observations each) for the entire sample.

The individual regression results can be pooled, and inferences are drawn from the M separate OLS cross-sectional regression equations using the Fama and MacBeth (1973) procedure.

$$\overline{\beta} = \frac{1}{M}\sum_{m=1}^{M}\beta_m; \qquad \text{st.err.}\,(\overline{\beta}) = \frac{\sigma_{\overline{\beta}}}{\sqrt{M}} \tag{5.14}$$

Using the distribution of the average slope coefficient $\overline{\beta}$, the null rational hypothesis of no predictable bias across markets $\beta = 0$ can be tested against the noise trader alternative $\beta \neq 0$, using a two-tailed t-test calculated with the average slope estimate its standard error in equation 5.14.[8]

Time series tests for orthogonality of forecast error

The rational expectations hypothesis posits that the futures' forecast error is orthogonal to the available information set. Consequently, the futures return R_t is random, and the forecast is efficient with respect to available information. In contrast, the noise trader model in equation 5.10 indicates that the forecast error, and subsequently R_t, is not orthogonal to all information. Rather, R_t is correlated with and can be predicted by noise trader sentiment at time $t - n$, ρ_{t-n}. Specifically, if noise traders are bullish (bearish), then the futures' forecast is overly optimistic (pessimistic) and the subsequent return is predicted to be negative (positive). The first test of return predictability is a relatively simple specification of market timing developed by Cumby and Modest (1987), and the second is a more general specification of predictability associated with Granger (1969).

The Cumby–Modest test

The usefulness of sentiment in predicting price changes can be evaluated in the market timing framework (C–M test) proposed by Cumby and Modest (1987). Empirically, sentiment provides market signals through extremely high levels K_H and low levels K_L. The C–M test evaluates the ability to be on the correct side of major price changes with the following OLS regression:

$$R_t = \alpha + \beta_1 HI_{t-1} + \beta_2 LO_{t-1} + \varepsilon_t \qquad (5.15)$$

where $HI_{t-1} = 1$ if $\rho_{t-1} > K_H$, and equals 0 otherwise, and $LO_{t-1} = 1$ if $\rho_{t-1} < K_L$, and equals 0 otherwise. If the mean return conditioned on extreme optimism $(\alpha + \beta_1)$ or pessimism $(\alpha + \beta_2)$ is different from the unconditional mean (α), then timing ability is demonstrated. The null hypothesis of no timing ability, H_0: $\beta_1 = \beta_2 = 0$, is tested against the alternative of significant timing ability H_A: $\beta_1 \neq 0$ or $\beta_2 \neq 0$. Specifically, the noise trader model suggests that $\beta_1 < 0$ or $\beta_2 > 0$, indicating that sentiment has a negative impact on returns.

Causality tests

Solt and Statman (1988) as well as De Bondt (1993) document that retail stock market speculators exhibit extrapolative expectations – becoming more bullish after recent market increases. They demonstrate this with simple OLS regressions of sentiment on past stock market returns. Here, that methodology is replicated and refined. A general method of exploring the linear linkages between price and sentiment is to test for 'Granger causality'. Hamilton (1994) suggests the following direct or bivariate Granger test:[9]

$$\rho_t = c_0 + \sum_{i=1}^{p} a_i \rho_{t-i} + \sum_{j=1}^{q} b_j R_{t-j} + e_t \qquad (5.16)$$

and

$$R_t = k_0 + \sum_{i=1}^{m} \alpha_i R_{t-i} + \sum_{j=1}^{n} \beta_j \rho_{t-j} + \varepsilon_t \qquad (5.17)$$

where ρ_t and R_t are noise trader sentiment and futures returns, respectively, and ε_t, e_t are white noise error terms. Sentiment leads returns in equation 5.17 if market sentiment is useful in predicting returns, and it is tested under the null of $\beta_j = 0 \ \forall \ j$. Furthermore, the theoretical model suggests that $\sum \beta_j < 0$. That is to say, high sentiment portends low returns as prices decline to fundamental value. Rational expectations are also tested under the full orthogonality condition: $\beta_j = \alpha_i = 0 \ \forall \ i,j$. Similarly, causality from returns to sentiment in equation 5.16, i.e. extrapolative expectations, is tested under the null of $b_j = 0 \ \forall \ j$. Moreover, if $\sum b_j > 0$, then the aggregate impact of returns on sentiment is positive, i.e. noise traders are positive feedback traders.

Recognising the low statistical power of these tests against the null hypothesis (see Summers, 1986), the power of the tests is increased by also estimating them over pooled cross-sectional time series data. That is to say, individual markets are designated into related commodity groups (for example, grains), and the empirical models equations 5.15–5.17 are estimated with time series data pooled across the related markets. Pooling time series data across markets not only increases the power of the tests but also provides a concise way of presenting and testing for common noise trader effects in similar markets.

Choosing the appropriate lag lengths (p, q, m and n) is of practical significance in performing the causality test (see Jones, 1989). As suggested by Beveridge and Oickle (1994), the order of an autoregressive system may best be determined by searching all possible lags for the combination that minimises a model selection criterion. For example, in equation 5.17, the model is estimated by varying the own-lag length of R_t from $m = 1, 2, ..., m^{max}$ and the lag length of ρ_t from $n = 1, 2, ..., n^{max}$, such that a total of ($m^{max} \times n^{max}$) regressions are estimated. The m, n lag length combination that minimises Akaike's information criterion (AIC) is chosen as the final model specification. This search procedure is conducted for equations 5.16 and 5.17 for each individual market to choose optimal lag lengths for individual models. For the pooled regressions, the lag lengths are specified by choosing the maximum m and the maximum n from among the individual market specifications within a group. For instance, in the grain group, the maximum m is 6 (for the wheat and soybean models) and the maximum n is 4 (for the wheat and soybean meal models); therefore, the pooled grain model's lag structure is 6,4. This specification procedure may overspecify lag structures at the expense of statistical power, but it assures that the model does not suffer from an underspecification bias.[10]

Noise trader sentiment and data

Measuring noise trader sentiment

The Market Vane Corporation receives market recommendations from brokerage firms and market advisors via newsletters, hotlines and electronic transmission. From this sample of market advice, Market Vane takes a rather detailed approach in calculating a measure of aggregate market sentiment. Each market opinion (for a commodity) is weighted on a scale (B) from 0 to 8, with 0 and 8 being fully bearish and bullish respectively. Next, each market letter is weighted according to its perceived influence or following. For newsletters, hotlines and electronic bulletins, this weight (W) is proportional to the subscriber base, and for brokerage firms it is proportional to the number of brokers at the firm.[11] The Market Vane bullish sentiment index ($MVBSI_t$) at time t is:

$$MVBSI_t = \frac{\sum_{j=1}^{N} B_j W_j}{8 \sum_{j=1}^{N} W_j}$$

where B_j is the degree of bullishness on a scale from 0 to 8 for advisor j, W_j is the influence weight assigned to the advisor, and there are a total of N advisors commenting on the market. The index is compiled each Tuesday, reflecting the opinions received since the prior Tuesday. The index is released on the same Tuesday via wire and facsimile.

As a maintained hypothesis, it is assumed that the indices compiled by Market Vane reflect the sentiment of noise traders – not rational or informed market participants. That is to say, the market views subsumed within the indices are those of smaller retail speculators who are acting on non-information: technical trading rules, extrapolation or old news that is already incorporated into the market price. This maintained hypothesis is supported by reviewing the decision-making rules of small traders and their information sources.

Surveys by Smidt (1965), Canoles (1994), the Chicago Board of Trade (see Draper, 1985) and *Barron's* (see Draper, 1985) find that the average amateur futures trader is highly educated and they trade for the leverage and excitement. Furthermore, these speculators generally do not bring new information to bear on the markets; rather, they garnish much of their information from focused media sources, such as those surveyed by Market Vane (*Market Vane's Bullish Consensus*, 1983–94). Market advisors, brokers and newsletters provide decision-making information for retail futures speculators; but, are they providing real information or simply relaying old news and technical comments? Excerpts of market commentary presented in *Consensus: National Futures and Financial Weekly* (1995), such as in the introduction to this chapter, indicate that market advisors rely heavily on technical indicators for decision-making and simply pass along this information to their retail subscribers. A minority of newsletters are fundamental in nature, relaying government reports, seasonal tendencies and pertinent cash market conditions. Although these newsletters often contain detailed interpretations of relevant supply and demand factors, the fundamental analysis tends to reiterate public information, and it provides rather vague price predictions.

The non-informational nature of the market newsletters, coupled with the evidence that retail investors rely on this advice in making decisions, supports the maintained hypothesis: the sentiment indices are good proxies for noise trader sentiment. To the extent that 'systems' and pseudosignals are correlated across the advisors, then this group of noise traders will act in concert and can potentially impact market prices.

Futures data and markets

Weekly futures returns are calculated for the closest to expiration contract, where the maturity month has not been entered. To correspond with the release of the sentiment index, returns are calculated Tuesday–Tuesday, using closing prices. Returns R_t are calculated as the log-relative change in closing prices $\ln(P_t/P_{t-1})$.

A cross-section of twenty-eight futures markets is examined to strengthen general conclusions and to avoid erroneous implications based on the nuances of a particular market. Markets are chosen based on the availability of the futures and sentiment data. For pooled estimation purposes and to facilitate the presentation of results, related markets are designated into commodity groups. Group classification is based on common production/consumption patterns and expectations concerning the correlation of returns and sentiment among the markets. The five commodity groups include: grain, livestock, food/fibre, financial and metal/energy. A complete listing of groups and markets is presented in Table 5.1. MVBSI data are available weekly from January 1983 to September 1994.

Table 5.1 Markets and contract months

Market	Contract months
Grain	
Corn	Mar, May, Jul, Sep, Dec
Wheat	Mar, May, Jul, Sep, Dec
Soybeans	Jan, Mar, May, Jul, Aug, Sep, Nov
Soybean meal	Jan, Mar, May, Jul, Aug, Sep, Oct, Dec
Soybean oil	Jan, Mar, May, Jul, Aug, Sep, Oct, Dec
Livestock	
Live cattle	Feb, Apr, Jun, Aug, Oct, Dec
Feeder cattle	Jan, Mar, Apr, May, Aug, Sep, Oct, Nov
Live hogs	Feb, Apr, Jun, Jul, Aug, Oct, Dec
Pork bellies	Feb, Mar, May, Jul, Aug
Food/fibre	
Coffee	Mar, May, Jul, Sep, Dec
Sugar	Mar, May, Jul, Oct
Cocoa	Mar, May, Jul, Sep, Dec
Orange juice	Mar, May, Jul, Sep, Nov
Cotton	Mar, May, Jul, Oct, Dec
Timber	Jan, Mar, May, Jul, Sep, Nov
Financial	
Deutschmark	Mar, Jun, Sep, Dec
British pound	Mar, Jun, Sep, Dec
Swiss franc	Mar, Jun, Sep, Dec
Canadian dollar	Mar, Jun, Sep, Dec
Japanese yen	Mar, Jun, Sep, Dec
Treasury bills	Mar, Jun, Sep, Dec
Treasury bonds	Mar, Jun, Sep, Dec
Metal/energy	
Gold	Feb, Mar, Apr, Jun, Aug, Oct, Dec
Silver	Mar, May, Jul, Sep, Dec
Platinum	Jan, Apr, Jul, Oct
Heating oil	Jan–Dec
Crude oil	Jan–Dec
Petrol	Jan–Dec

Summary statistics

The general characteristics of sentiment are explored with simple summary statistics presented in Table 5.2. The mean sentiment level (% bullish) tends to be a fairly neutral 50. Of the twenty-eight markets, thirteen have a mean MVBSI statistically > 50 at the 1% level, and one market, frozen pork bellies, is statistically < 50 at the 1% level. Yet, the mean sentiment levels are in a rather narrow range from 47.1 for frozen pork bellies to a high of 55.3 for sugar. Additionally, sentiment is quite volatile, with large standard deviations and extremes of above 90 and below 10. The extreme values of sentiment along with its volatility suggest

Table 5.2 Summary statistics, Market Vane Bullish Sentiment Index

Market	Mean	Standard deviation	Minimum	Maximum
Corn[a]	53.286	16.343	12	89
Wheat	52.797	14.715	16	88
Soybeans	52.673	15.429	16	93
Soybean meal	51.321	15.767	12	89
Soybean oil	52.983	15.838	11	89
Live cattle	52.975	14.680	16	90
Feeder cattle	51.418	17.225	5	95
Live hogs	49.318	15.065	15	87
Pork bellies	47.146	15.018	15	91
Coffee	52.526	17.270	11	93
Sugar	55.299	16.758	15	91
Cocoa	49.550	17.481	11	91
Orange juice	51.602	19.316	5	93
Cotton	50.613	16.071	9	88
Timber	50.355	16.503	5	93
Deutschmark	53.044	15.692	15	96
Swiss franc	52.958	15.508	14	96
Japanese yen	52.526	15.186	14	95
British pound	51.051	16.283	13	95
Canadian dollar	50.689	15.628	10	97
Treasury bills	51.585	14.711	11	94
Treasury bonds	50.555	13.085	13	90
Gold	52.673	13.572	16	85
Silver	52.854	13.382	12	92
Platinum	52.029	16.263	10	97
Heating oil	50.871	16.102	10	90
Crude oil	48.876	16.737	8	95
Petrol	49.645	16.384	9	89

Note
a   All of the markets have 591 weekly observations.

that the advisors that make up the indices are reacting to correlated market signals. Although not presented here for brevity, the sentiment data also display a high level of cross-market correlation within commodity groups. For instance, the correlation between corn and soybeans is 0.72, and it is 0.78 between the Japanese yen and the German mark. These type of correlations are indicative of systematic noise trader sentiment that covaries across traders and markets.

Noise trader sentiment and extrapolative expectations

Solt and Statman (1988) as well as De Bondt (1993) document that retail stock market speculators exhibit extrapolative expectations – becoming more bullish after recent market increases. That is, their demand is an increasing function of past returns. Here, the linear linkages from returns to sentiment is tested with the bivariate Granger test in equation 5.16 under the null of $b_j = 0 \; \forall \; j$. Specifically, the causality test in equation 5.16 is first estimated using OLS for each market individually, and then estimated by pooling the time series data across the designated commodity groups. For individual markets, equation 5.16 is estimated with OLS. The model is tested for autocorrelation and heteroscedasticity using a Lagrange multiplier test and White's test respectively.[12] The pooled cross-sectional time series models are estimated using the GLS procedure of Kmenta (1986, pp. 616–35), correcting for cross-sectional correlation and heteroscedasticity. The null hypothesis that R_t does not lead ρ_t (i.e. $b_j = 0 \; \forall \; j$) is tested with a chi-squared test (Hamilton, 1994, p. 305). The aggregate sign of causality is addressed by summing the impact of lagged returns, $\Sigma \; b_j$, and testing whether it equals zero using a two-tailed t-test. If $\Sigma \; b_j > 0$, then the noise traders are also positive feedback traders or trend followers.

The models estimated for each individual market are presented in Table 5.3. The null hypothesis that returns do not lead sentiment (i.e. $b_j = 0 \; \forall \; j$) is rejected at the 1% level for every market. Furthermore, the cumulative impact of returns is positive ($\Sigma \; b_j > 0$) at the 1% level for every market except platinum. The estimation results are fairly consistent across markets, but general conclusions stem more naturally from the pooled models.

In Table 5.4, the estimated pooled models reveal sentiment characteristics that are systematic across the markets. First, across all groups, sentiment follows a fairly strong positive autoregressive process with first-order coefficients in the range of 0.511–0.622. Second, statistically significant positive extrapolation is demonstrated at one- and two-week

Table 5.3 Granger causality test, returns lead sentiment, individual markets

$$\rho_t = c_0 + \sum_{i=1}^{p} a_i \rho_{t-i} + \sum_{j=1}^{q} b_j R_{t-j} + e_t$$

The model is estimated with OLS, and the Wald chi-squared statistic tests the null $H_0: b_j = 0 \ \forall \ j$. The cumulative impact of returns is calculated $\sum b_j$ where $j = 1, 2, ..., q$, and tested against the null $H_0: \sum b_j = 0$ with a t-test.

Market	p,q	$\chi^2_{(q)}$	p-value	$\sum b_j$	t-statistic	p-value	Adjusted R^2
Corn[a]	3,2	22.16	0.000	123.7	4.16	0.000	0.576
Wheat	3,2	52.52	0.000	201.2	6.92	0.000	0.513
Soybeans	1,6	39.74	0.000	186.4	3.80	0.000	0.549
Soybean meal	2,2	54.78	0.000	145.9	5.82	0.000	0.572
Soybean oil	3,3	65.84	0.000	171.9	6.03	0.000	0.591
Live cattle	6,1	54.99	0.000	192.5	7.41	0.000	0.551
Feeder cattle	6,2	33.29	0.000	305.8	4.90	0.000	0.376
Live hogs	1,2	46.71	0.000	150.9	5.56	0.000	0.549
Pork bellies	1,2	39.41	0.000	88.5	5.18	0.000	0.463
Coffee	5,2	54.91	0.000	145.2	7.17	0.000	0.577
Sugar	2,3	54.18	0.000	54.7	3.18	0.002	0.598
Cocoa	5,1	47.18	0.000	102.1	6.86	0.000	0.529
Orange juice	2,2	64.21	0.000	172.2	7.44	0.000	0.629
Cotton	2,1	32.91	0.000	94.8	5.73	0.000	0.644
Timber	2,3	63.56	0.000	178.1	6.37	0.000	0.575
Deutschmark	1,1	54.60	0.000	181.4	7.38	0.000	0.699
Swiss franc	1,1	46.50	0.000	166.3	6.81	0.000	0.645
Japanese yen	1,3	33.25	0.000	311.5	4.86	0.000	0.635
British pound	2,1	41.83	0.000	164.3	6.46	0.000	0.693
Canadian dollar	2,1	41.10	0.000	501.5	6.41	0.000	0.597
Treasury bills	6,2	28.37	0.000	1651.0	4.82	0.000	0.610
Treasury bonds	5,4	37.60	0.000	243.3	3.42	0.001	0.601
Gold	1,1	17.84	0.000	71.8	4.22	0.000	0.637
Silver	4,5	33.19	0.000	94.1	3.01	0.002	0.538
Platinum	4,6	44.33	0.000	74.2	1.58	0.115	0.618
Heating oil	1,4	25.38	0.000	140.8	4.63	0.000	0.533
Crude oil	5,1	20.87	0.000	54.6	4.56	0.000	0.591
Petrol	1,4	38.33	0.000	169.5	5.63	0.000	0.466

Note
a All models are estimated over 558 weekly observations, except for those involving crude oil and petrol, which are estimated over 539 and 457 observations respectively.

lags for all the groups. For instance, in grains, a 1% weekly return results in sentiment increasing by 1.165% the following week, and 0.445% the week after that. For all the groups, the null that returns do not lead sentiment can be rejected at the 1% level, and the cumulative impact of

Table 5.4 Pooled causality test, returns lead sentiment

Independent variables	Grains	Livestock	Food/fibre	Financial	Metal/energy
Intercept	20.58 (17.9)[a]	19.80 (15.3)	15.77 (18.7)	13.84 (17.5)	14.62 (13.7)
ρ_{t-1}	0.518 (25.1)	0.511 (22.1)	0.552 (27.6)	0.622 (36.1)	0.567 (27.5)
ρ_{t-2}	0.024 (1.05)	0.018 (0.73)	0.090 (3.96)	0.046 (2.28)	0.032 (1.36)
ρ_{t-3}	0.063 (3.09)	0.017 (0.69)	0.044 (1.99)	0.063 (3.16)	0.054 (2.32)
ρ_{t-4}		0.044 (1.81)	−0.025 (−1.19)	−0.033 (−1.68)	0.061 (2.60)
ρ_{t-5}		−0.016 (−0.68)	0.034 (2.05)	0.023 (1.21)	0.006 (0.30)
ρ_{t-6}		0.037 (1.81)		0.009 (0.57)	
R_{t-1}	116.5 (15.5)	76.5 (9.95)	83.9 (16.1)	133.3 (12.6)	55.8 (9.52)
R_{t-2}	44.5 (5.65)	33.2 (4.24)	24.6 (4.49)	33.8 (3.14)	32.2 (5.36)
R_{t-3}	15.74 (2.04)		1.91 (0.35)	−3.19 (−0.29)	4.93 (0.82)
R_{t-4}	0.67 (0.08)			1.01 (0.09)	4.10 (0.68)
R_{t-5}	−3.85 (−0.52)				−11.4 (−1.94)
R_{t-6}	3.35 (0.47)				−6.34 (−1.09)
Σb_j	177.1 (8.35)	109.8 (9.74)	110.5 (10.7)	165.0 (7.27)	79.3 (4.98)
$\chi^2_{(p)}$	258.8[b]	112.9	264.1	164.8	111.3
Buse R^2	0.501	0.389	0.581	0.556	0.518

Notes

a t-statistics in parentheses test whether the coefficient equals zero, with degrees of freedom equal to $N*K - (p + q + 1)$, where $N = 558$ (457 for metal/energy) and $K =$ number of markets in the group.

b All the $\chi^2_{(p)}$ statistics reject that the coefficients on lagged returns are zero at the 1% level.

lagged returns is significantly positive (1% level). Sentiment's impulse response to an exogenous standard deviation return shock is illustrated in Figure 5.1 (see Harvey, 1991, p. 234).[13] Notably, the greatest initial sentiment increase occurs in the food/fibre group, and the sentiment response does not peak for two weeks in the metal/energy markets.

Collectively, the findings suggest that the traders comprising the sentiment index are positive feedback traders. Clearly, these traders respond to similar pseudomarket signals (i.e. past returns), and as a result sentiment moves in unison and takes large swings to extreme values. This empirical characterisation of sentiment is consistent with theoretical construct of noise trader sentiment (see De Long *et al.*, 1990a).

Noise traders' impact on futures prices

Cross-sectional test of bias

The cross-sectional test, equation 5.13, is estimated with OLS.[14] Initially, the $\bar{\rho}^i$ are calculated over fifty-week formation periods ($K = 50$), and the $\bar{R}^i$ are calculated over the subsequent fifty weeks ($J = 50$). The estimation results for this equation are presented in Table 5.5 for each formation and testing sample. Only in sample 6 is the slope coefficient statistically different from zero. Pooling across the samples with Fama and MacBeth's (1973) procedure shows that on average sentiment does not create a statistically meaningful bias in futures prices.

The results of the cross-sectional Fama and MacBeth (1973) tests can be sensitive to the size of both the formation (K) and testing periods (J).

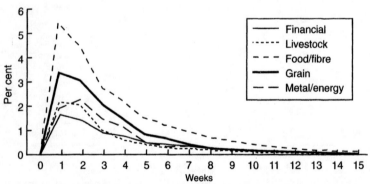

Figure 5.1 Extrapolative expectations, impulse response function and Market Vane data.

Table 5.5 Cross-sectional test.

$$\bar{R}^i = \alpha + \beta \bar{\rho}^i + \varepsilon^i$$

The model is estimated with OLS over a cross-section of twenty-eight markets. The estimate of $\bar{\rho}^i$ is made over fifty weekly observations, and the estimate of $\bar{R}^i$ over the following fifty weeks.

Sample number	$\alpha \times 10^{-2}$	$\beta \times 10^{-4}$	Adjusted R^2
1	−0.8220 (−0.775)[a]	0.9892 (0.497)	−0.031
2	−0.0806 (−0.139)	−0.0913 (−0.075)	−0.041
3	−0.4314 (−0.497)	0.8391 (0.461)	−0.030
4	0.1778 (0.303)	0.0867 (0.078)	−0.038
5	0.2330 (0.261)	−0.4272 (−0.280)	−0.035
6	1.3879 (1.940)	−2.7727 (−1.994)	0.099
7	0.7893 (1.101)	−1.1701 (−0.816)	−0.012
8	0.4773 (0.649)	−1.1315 (−0.976)	−0.001
9	0.6599 (0.675)	−1.3295 (−0.697)	−0.019
10	1.4139 (1.546)	−2.7201 (−1.503)	0.044
11	−1.2472 (−1.062)	2.4243 (1.077)	0.005
Average 1–11[b]	0.2320 (0.998)	−0.4985 (−0.951)	

Notes
a   t-statistics in parentheses test whether coefficient equals zero.
b   The average slope coefficients and their standard errors are calculated using the Fama and MacBeth (1974) procedure.

There is no strong justification for using a fifty-week period. So, to test the model's sensitivity to alternative formation and testing period lengths, the cross-sectional regressions are estimated with K,J values of 50,100; 25,25; 25,50; and 5,5.

The pooled Fama and MacBeth (1973) estimation results for various formation and testing periods are presented in Table 5.6. The results are not materially different across the alternative models. Some of the average slope coefficients are negative, but none of them is statistically different from zero at conventional levels. Generally, the null hypothesis of no systematic bias, $\beta = 0$, in futures prices cannot be rejected in favour of the noise trader alternative $\beta < 0$. This result is robust to alternative lengths of both the formation and test periods (i.e. values of K and J). The average level of noise trader sentiment has no consistently discernible ability to explain cross-sectional variation in futures market returns.

Table 5.6 Cross-sectional tests, Fama–MacBeth regressions

$$\overline{R}^i = \alpha + \beta \overline{\rho}^i + \varepsilon^i$$

The model is estimated with OLS over a cross-section of twenty-eight markets. The estimate of $\overline{\rho}^i$ is made over K weekly observations, and the estimate of $\overline{R}^i$ over the following J weeks. The M individual cross-sectional OLS models are pooled using the method of Fama and MacBeth. t-statistics in parentheses test whether the coefficient is zero.

K, J	M	$\alpha \times 10^{-2}$	$\beta \times 10^{-4}$	Average adjusted R^2
50,50	11	0.2320 (0.998)	−0.4985 (−0.951)	−0.005
50,100	5	0.0089 (0.022)	−0.3001 (−0.505)	−0.009
25,25	23	−0.1023 (−0.392)	0.1285 (0.267)	0.027
25,50	11	0.1301 (0.468)	−0.3063 (−0.586)	0.018
5,5	120	−0.0628 (0.340)	0.0947 (0.261)	0.000

Time series tests of return predictability

Cumby–Modest test

The C–M model (equation 5.15) tests whether the mean return after extremely high (K_H) or low (K_L) sentiment levels is significantly different from the unconditional mean return (i.e. when sentiment is between the extremes levels). Specifying the C–M model requires a definition of extreme sentiment. Market Vane suggests that sentiment outside the range of (25,75) indicates a market approaching extreme conditions.

Estimation results for individual markets are presented in Table 5.7. Equation 5.15 is estimated with OLS for individual markets. White's test is used to detect heteroscedasticity, and autocorrelated residuals are tested with a Lagrange multiplier test.[15] The null hypothesis $(\beta_1 = \beta_2 = 0)$ is rejected at the 10% level in seven of the twenty-eight markets, more than the three expected by chance (28×0.10). In these seven markets, all seven have $\beta_1 \geq 0$ and six of the seven have $\beta_2 \leq 0$. These results are counter the noise trader model's prediction of price reversals after extreme sentiment. Rather, the results suggest continuation: high (low) sentiment is followed by positive (negative) returns.

The C–M test is also estimated as a pooled cross-sectional time series using Kmenta's (1986) cross-sectionally correlated, heteroscedastic and time-wise autoregressive GLS estimation technique. Pooling restricts the estimated parameters to be the same for each market. In doing so, it reveals noise trader effects that are uniform and systematic across the markets. To check the results' sensitivity to varying definitions of extreme sentiment, the model is estimated with K_H and K_L defined as (25,75) and (20,80).

The pooled C–M tests with $K_H = 75$ and $K_L = 25$ are shown in Table 5.8A. None of the five market groups rejects the null of no market timing at the 10% level; although the grains and food/fibre groups have p-values of 0.115 and 0.126 respectively. In Table 5.8B, $K_H = 80$ and $K_L = 20$. When the extreme sentiment definitions are widened, the food/fibre and financial model display statistically significant timing ability at the 5% level. The financial model shows a tendency for negative returns after low sentiment, and the food/fibre group displays positive returns after extremely optimistic sentiment. This pattern of continuation $(\beta_1 > 0, \beta_2 < 0)$ is consistent with the individual market results, and it contradicts the prediction of the noise trader model.

Table 5.7 Cumby–Modest test, individual markets[a]

$$R_t = \alpha + \beta_1 HI_{t-1} + \beta_2 LO_{t-1} + \varepsilon_t$$

The model is estimated with OLS, where $HI_{t-1} = 1$ if $\rho_{t-1} > K_H$, and is equal to 0 otherwise; and $LO_{t-1} = 1$ if $\rho_{t-1} < K_L$, and is equal to 0 otherwise, and $K_H = 75$, $K_L = 25$. *t*-statistics testing that each parameter is zero are in parentheses, and the chi-squared test is a joint test of the null, H_0: $\beta_1 = \beta_2 = 0$.

Market	Extreme obs	$\alpha \times 10^{-2}$	$\beta_1 \times 10^{-2}$	$\beta_2 \times 10^{-2}$	$\chi^2_{(2)}$	p-value
Corn[a]	82	−0.1624 (−1.38)	0.5747 (1.11)	−0.2572 (−0.62)	1.66	0.435
Wheat	47	−0.0097 (−0.08)	0.0155 (0.03)	0.4154 (0.89)	0.81	0.667
Soybeans	62	−0.2517 (−2.24)	1.3192 (1.87)	1.4412 (3.17)	13.01	0.001
Soybean meal	68	−0.6232 (−0.44)	0.4064 (0.58)	−0.1686 (−0.30)	0.44	0.798
Soybean oil	73	−0.1113 (−0.75)	1.7033 (2.02)	−0.8847 (−1.36)	6.03	0.049
Live cattle	51	0.1756 (2.04)	0.2150 (0.75)	2.7969 (1.39)	2.94	0.228
Feeder cattle	81	0.0107 (1.36)	−0.2509 (−1.02)	0.3164 (0.72)	1.67	0.433
Live hogs	45	0.1414 (1.11)	0.5447 (0.91)	0.6950 (0.72)	1.29	0.525
Pork bellies	52	−0.4112 (−1.85)	0.5562 (0.81)	−0.6285 (−0.06)	0.67	0.714
Coffee	92	−0.1455 (−0.77)	0.0413 (0.05)	−0.4855 (−0.69)	0.48	0.785
Sugar	92	−0.4082 (−1.47)	0.2828 (0.29)	1.5517 (1.05)	1.16	0.561
Cocoa	95	−0.1548 (−0.85)	−0.9600 (−1.46)	0.3803 (0.60)	2.69	0.260
Orange juice	134	0.0991 (0.51)	0.5284 (1.65)	−0.6761 (−1.65)	6.61	0.036
Cotton	68	0.0838 (0.63)	0.5395 (1.09)	0.1674 (0.40)	1.33	0.514

Timber	74	−0.1160 (−0.71)	1.6291 (2.13)	−1.2540 (−1.66)	7.58	0.022
Deutschmark	71	0.0271 (0.36)	0.2510 (1.09)	−0.3791 (−0.84)	2.01	0.366
Swiss franc	69	0.0267 (0.33)	0.0577 (0.23)	−0.5663 (−1.21)	1.55	0.460
Japanese yen	68	0.1043 (1.55)	0.0812 (0.39)	−0.5411 (−2.21)	5.15	0.076
British pound	88	0.0819 (0.96)	0.1698 (0.78)	−0.7351 (−3.07)	10.90	0.004
Canadian dollar	66	0.0332 (1.28)	0.0000 (0.01)	−0.0021 (−0.93)	0.86	0.647
Treasury bills	57	0.0181 (2.01)	0.0000 (0.08)	−0.0011 (−1.58)	2.51	0.285
Treasury bonds	42	0.1137 (1.62)	0.1678 (0.58)	0.8805 (1.64)	2.99	0.224
Gold	47	−0.1871 (−2.08)	−0.1870 (−0.50)	1.4573 (0.76)	0.83	0.657
Silver	42	−0.3677 (−2.47)	−0.0879 (−0.07)	1.0533 (0.54)	0.30	0.857
Platinum	79	−0.1197 (−0.87)	−0.2466 (−0.39)	0.2598 (0.24)	0.22	0.893
Heating oil	80	0.0675 (0.35)	0.2249 (0.36)	−0.2115 (−0.44)	0.36	0.836
Crude oil	94	−0.0250 (−0.11)	0.6641 (1.13)	0.0398 (0.07)	1.27	0.528
Petrol	89	0.1381 (0.67)	1.4906 (2.21)	−0.5644 (−0.38)	4.94	0.084

Note
a All models are estimated over 558 weekly observations except for those involving crude oil and petrol, which are estimated over 539 and 457 observations respectively.

Causality from sentiment to returns

Equation 5.17 provides a general means of testing the orthogonality condition implied by the rational expectations model compared with the alternative noise trader hypothesis. The noise trader model suggests that the futures forecast error (i.e. returns) can be predicted by the level of noise trader sentiment in the market. Specifically, the model predicts

Table 5.8 Pooled Cumby–Modest test, Market Vane data, weekly[a]

$$R_t = \alpha + \beta_1 HI_{t-1} + \beta_2 LO_{t-1} + \varepsilon_t$$

The model is estimated over N cross-sections and T time series observations, where $HI_{t-1} = 1$ if $\rho_{t-1} > K_H$, and is equal to 0 otherwise; and $LO_{t-1} = 1$ if $\rho_{t-1} < K_L$, and is equal to 0 otherwise. The t-statistics in parentheses test that parameter values are zero, and the chi-squared test tests the joint null H_0: $\beta_1 = \beta_2 = 0$.

Group	$\alpha \times 10^{-2}$	$\beta_1 \times 10^{-2}$	$\beta_2 \times 10^{-2}$	$\chi^2_{(2)}$	p-value
(A) $K_H = 75$, $K_L = 25$					
Grains	−0.0287	0.2262	−0.0445	4.32	0.115
	(−0.30)	(2.05)	(−0.33)		
Livestock	0.1388	−0.0512	0.1490	0.80	0.668
	(1.86)	(−0.34)	(0.81)		
Food/fibre	−0.0667	0.4325	0.0284	4.13	0.126
	(−0.85)	(2.03)	(0.11)		
Financial	0.0113	−0.0139	0.0315	1.19	0.552
	(1.34)	(−0.58)	(0.88)		
Metal/energy	−0.0629	0.1968	0.1975	1.49	0.473
	(−0.74)	(1.07)	(0.61)		
(B) $K_H = 80$, $K_L = 20$					
Grains	0.0056	0.0025	−0.4200	2.43	0.296
	(0.06)	(0.01)	(−1.55)		
Livestock	0.1415	−0.1132	0.2421	1.19	0.550
	(1.94)	(-0.67)	(0.85)		
Food/fibre	−0.0452	0.8508	−0.3981	8.34	0.015
	(−0.61)	(2.67)	(−0.99)		
Financial	0.0126	−0.0039	−0.1776	6.24	0.044
	(1.60)	(−0.11)	(−2.49)		
Metal/energy	−0.0512	0.2101	−0.0209	0.72	0.697
	(−0.60)	(0.85)	(−0.05)		

Note
a   Each pooled regression has $N \times T$ cross-sectional time series observations, where $T = 558$ (457 for metal/energy) and N is the number of markets composing the group.

that there is a negative relationship between sentiment and returns. If this is true, it should be captured in equation 5.17 by finding that sentiment leads returns ($\beta_j \neq 0$, $\forall j$), i.e. sentiment can be used to forecast market returns, and the cumulative impact of sentiment on returns should be negative ($\Sigma \beta_j < 0$). This is tested against the rational expectations null hypothesis that forecast errors are uncorrelated with available information ($\beta_j = \alpha_i = 0 \ \forall \ i,j$).[16]

The Granger causality model is estimated and the null hypothesis tested in individual markets. For individual markets, equation 5.17 is estimated with OLS. The model is tested for autocorrelation and heteroscedasticity using a Lagrange multiplier test and White's test respectively.[17] These results are presented in Table 5.9. The null hypothesis that sentiment does not lead returns ($\beta_j = 0 \ \forall \ j$) is rejected at the 10% level in seven of twenty-eight markets. Importantly, four of these markets are currencies that, contrary to the theoretical model, show a definite tendency for continuation, i.e. $\Sigma \beta_j > 0$. The null of full orthogonality ($\beta_j = \alpha_i = 0 \ \forall \ i,j$) is soundly rejected in sixteen of the twenty-eight markets. The rejections are concentrated in the food/fibre, financial and metal/energy groups. As discussed in the following pooled model results, this stems primarily from low-level positive autocorrelation in returns.

The estimated models are presented in Table 5.10. The first chi-squared statistic (p-value in parentheses) tests the null that sentiment does not lead returns, and the second chi-squared statistic tests the full orthogonality condition. The first chi-squared test rejects the null hypothesis for the food/fibre group at the 1% level. However, the null that $\Sigma \beta_j = 0$ is not rejected in this or any of the other models (t-test, not shown). In the food/fibre model, the estimated coefficients on lagged sentiment is not consistently negative, as suggested by the theoretical model. Consistent with the individual market results, the full orthogonality null hypothesis is rejected at the 10% level in each group except livestock. The returns in general, and the food/fibre and grain groups in particular, are characterised by positive autocorrelation up to three lags. Although the autocorrelation tends to be of a small magnitude and dubious practical significance, with autocorrelation coefficients in the range of 0.01–0.09, the pooled models provide enough statistical power to consistently reject the null.

Table 5.9 Granger causality test, sentiment leads returns, weekly Market Vane data

$$R_t = k_0 + \sum_{i=1}^{m} \alpha_i R_{t-i} + \sum_{j=1}^{n} \beta_j \rho_{t-j} + \varepsilon_t$$

The model is estimated with OLS, and the first Wald chi-squared statistic tests the null, $H_0: \beta_j = 0 \; \forall \; j$. The t-statistic tests that the sum of the lagged sentiment coefficients equals zero, $\sum \beta_j = 0$. The second chi-squared statistic tests full orthogonality, $H_0: \alpha_i = 0$ and $\beta_j = 0, \; \forall \; i,j$.

Market	m,n	$\chi^2_{(n)}$	p-value	t-statistic	$\chi^2_{(m+n)}$	p-value	Adjusted R^2
Corn[a]	2,0	–	–	–	2.59	0.273	0.012
Wheat	6,4	8.63	0.071	-2.06	23.59	0.008	0.030
Soybeans	6,1	1.68	0.194	-1.29	9.31	0.230	0.022
Soybean meal	0,4	7.73	0.102	0.49	7.73	0.102	0.007
Soybean oil	5,0	–	–	–	9.57	0.088	0.015
Live cattle	0,1	0.38	0.537	-0.61	0.38	0.537	-0.001
Feeder cattle	0,1	0.67	0.409	-0.82	0.67	0.409	-0.000
Live hogs	2,0	–	–	–	4.49	0.105	0.005
Pork bellies	1,0	–	–	–	1.27	0.258	0.000
Coffee	1,2	6.32	0.042	1.29	6.70	0.082	0.008
Sugar	0,2	3.10	0.211	0.85	3.10	0.211	0.002
Cocoa	2,0	–	–	–	10.02	0.006	0.014
Orange juice	2,0	–	–	–	11.41	0.003	0.029
Cotton	6,0	–	–	–	15.77	0.015	0.017
Timber	1,0	–	–	–	9.42	0.002	0.030
Deutschmark	0,2	11.51	0.003	1.23	11.51	0.003	0.017
Swiss franc	0,2	6.75	0.034	1.45	6.75	0.034	0.008
Japanese yen	0,1	4.30	0.037	2.07	4.30	0.037	0.007
British pound	0,2	7.52	0.023	1.28	7.52	0.023	0.008
Canadian dollar	1,0	–	–	–	3.11	0.077	0.006
Treasury bills	1,2	4.51	0.104	-0.70	5.21	0.157	0.004
Treasury bonds	0,1	0.23	0.628	-0.48	0.23	0.628	-0.001
Gold	0,5	13.94	0.016	-1.48	13.94	0.016	0.018
Silver	6,0	–	–	–	15.79	0.014	0.023
Platinum	1,0	–	–	–	0.10	0.747	-0.001
Heating oil	2,0	–	–	–	5.88	0.052	0.016
Crude oil	5,0	–	–	–	7.81	0.166	0.025
Petrol	6,0	–	–	–	12.39	0.053	0.021

Note
a   The model is estimated over 558 weekly observations except for those regressions involving crude oil and petrol, which have 539 and 457 observations respectively.

Table 5.10 Pooled causality test, sentiment leads returns, weekly Market Vane data

Independent variables	Coefficient $\times 10^{-2}$				
	Grains	Livestock	Food/fibre	Financial	Metal/energy
Intercept	0.0149 (0.10)[a]	−0.0699 (−0.40)	−0.1658 (−0.83)	0.0178 (0.95)	−0.1596 (−0.99)
R_{t-1}	0.4028 (0.20)	2.4092 (1.05)	6.5781 (3.34)	−2.7300 (−1.63)	−3.7200 (−1.84)
R_{t-2}	5.6255 (2.77)	−2.438 (−1.05)	4.3187 (2.07)	3.8714 (2.29)	3.6352 (1.75)
R_{t-3}	7.2097 (3.59)	2.5207 (1.10)	2.4519 (1.17)	2.8223 (1.67)	4.6910 (2.28)
R_{t-4}	0.4432 (0.23)	−0.1779 (−0.07)	4.9758 (2.39)		1.5412 (0.75)
R_{t-5}	−2.1835 (−1.11)	−4.975 (−2.22)			−4.5359 (−2.25)
R_{t-6}		2.7824 (1.23)			−1.8822 (0.89)
p_{t-1}	−0.0005 (−0.10)	0.0012 (0.32)	−0.0135 (−2.24)	0.0001 (0.25)	0.0028 (0.89)
p_{t-2}		0.0040 (0.94)	0.0155 (2.16)	−0.0004 (−0.54)	
p_{t-3}		−0.0003 (−0.09)	−0.0099 (−1.38)	−0.0004 (−0.65)	
p_{t-4}			−0.0010 (−0.14)	0.0013 (2.13)	
p_{t-5}			0.0127 (2.32)	−0.0009 (−1.79)	
$\chi^2_{(n)}$	0.051 (0.821)[b]	2.76 (0.431)	15.08 (0.010)	5.40 (0.368)	0.80 (0.370)
$\chi^2_{(m+n)}$	22.28 (0.001)	13.75 (0.131)	35.69 (0.000)	15.26 (0.054)	19.98 (0.005)
Buse R^2	0.006	0.001	0.009	0.002	0.006

Notes

a t-statistics in parentheses test whether coefficient equals zero with degrees of freedom equal to $N*K - (m + n + 1)$, where $N = 558$ (457 for metal/energy) and K = number of markets in group.

b First (second) chi-squared statistic tests H_0: $\beta_j = 0$ (and $\alpha_i = 0$) $\forall$ i,j (p-values in parentheses).

Summary and conclusions

In this chapter, the noise trader sentiment model of De Long *et al.* (1990a) has been applied to futures markets. The theoretical results predict that overly optimistic (pessimistic) noise traders result in market prices that are greater (less) than fundamental value. Thus, returns can be predicted using the level of noise trader sentiment. Specifically, the noise trader model indicates that futures prices contain a systematic bias that is proportional to the average level of noise trader sentiment, and market returns contain a predictable time-varying component that is inversely related to the level of noise trader sentiment. These predictions pose distinct alternatives to Muth's (1961) rational expectations hypothesis.

The null rational expectations hypothesis is tested against the noise trader alternative using commercial market sentiment indices as proxies for noise trader sentiment. It is demonstrated that this index is a good proxy for noise trader sentiment, and it represents a preferred alternative to *ad hoc* measures utilised in prior research. Utilising these indices and weekly futures returns, Fama and MacBeth (1973) cross-sectional regressions test whether noise traders create a systematic bias in futures prices. The time-series predictability of futures returns using known sentiment levels is tested in a Cumby and Modest (1987) market timing framework and a more general causality specification.

The empirical results lead to the following conclusions. First, there is no evidence that noise trader sentiment creates a systematic bias in futures prices. Second, predictable market returns using noise trader sentiment is not characteristic of futures markets in general. Third, futures market returns at weekly intervals are characterised by low-order positive autocorrelation with relatively small autoregressive parameters. In those instances in which there is evidence of noise trader effects, it is at best limited to isolated markets and particular specifications. Specifically, the impact is most apparent during times of extreme optimism or pessimism in which, contrary to the theoretical model's predictions, prices tend to show momentum or continuation.

The finding that noise trader sentiment has little (or at least an inconsistent) impact on futures prices is compatible with previous research (see, for example, Kodres, 1994). Based on this limited evidence, it is unlikely that noise traders impose a large cost on society in terms of systematic pricing errors and the subsequent misallocation of resources (Stein, 1981). Thus, concerns about and attempts to curb futures market speculation, particularly trend-following fund activity, may be unfounded (see France *et al.*, 1994). However, the cost and impact of noise traders on market microstructure (see Ma *et al.*, 1992) warrants further examination; yet, it must be weighed carefully against the liquidity enhancement provided by noise traders (Black, 1986).

Endnotes

1 The other major abstraction in De Long *et al.*'s (1990a) model from a futures market is that the unsafe asset pays a real dividend *r*, whereas there are no cash flows associated with the ownership of futures contracts. This is a necessary abstraction for the overlapping generations structure of the model. If this aspect of the unsafe asset *u* is not kept, then the model does not have an equilibrium solution. That is to say, recursive model solutions can diverge in the limit.

2 See De Long *et al.* (1990a) for a detailed description and discussion of the model's assumptions.

3 Both assets u and s pay real dividend *r* in the second period. Thus, all of first period income earns *r* regardless of where invested. Thus, c_0 is total second period dividends as a function of invested first period income. The remainder of the terms adjust c_0 for capital gains and the increased (decreased) yield on u from purchasing it at a discount (premium) to fundamental value.

4 Prescripts on random variables represent expectations for the variable taken at the indicated time. For example, $_tP_{t+1}$ is the expectation at time *t* for *P* at time *t* + 1.

5 Both rational and noise traders are allowed to take short positions in u.

6 Henceforth, R_t is referred to interchangeably as the futures forecast bias or pricing error, where $R_t > 0$ implies that $P_t > P_{t-n}$ or the futures price at time *t* − *n* was below fundamental value.

7 This assumes that there is not a hedge-related risk premium.

8 Alternative methods of estimating and pooling the regression equations exist; however, the Fama and MacBeth (1973) regressions have been shown to be statistically powerful and are still widely used in the literature (see Elton and Gruber, 1984, pp. 325–49).

9 Note misspecification of equations 5.16 and 5.17 because of co-integration and an omitted error-correction term is not a problem with these data because sentiment is clearly stationary *I*(0) in levels.

10 Alternative lag-length specification procedures were utilised, but the results were nearly identical to those presented.

11 Market Vane Incorporated does not go into great detail as to the exact weighting scheme, method of calculation or the determination of weights for particular advisory services.

12 Heteroscedasticity is accounted for by re-estimating the model with White's heteroscedastic consistent covariance estimator, and autocorrelation is corrected by adding additional lags of the dependent variable (see Greene, 1993, p. 392).

13 The standard deviation of weekly returns (in parentheses) for each group is as follows: grain (0.029), livestock (0.029), food/fibre (0.042), financial (0.013) and metal/energy (0.036).

14 A battery of diagnostic tests did not reveal any significant violations of the OLS assumptions.
15 Heteroscedasticity and autocorrelation are corrected by using the Newey–West estimator (see Greene, 1993, p. 423).
16 It is implicitly assumed that all relevant information is contained in past returns and sentiment.
17 Heteroscedasticity is accounted for by re-estimating the model with White's heteroscedastic consistent covariance estimator, and autocorrelation is corrected by adding additional lags of the dependent variable (see Greene, 1993, p. 392).

References

Beja, A. and Goldman, M.B. (1980) 'On the dynamic behavior of prices in disequilibrium', *Journal of Finance* 34: 235–47.
Bessembinder, H. (1992) 'Systematic risk, hedging pressure, and risk premiums in futures markets', *Review of Financial Studies* 5: 637–67.
Beveridge, S. and Oickle, C. (1994) 'A comparison of Box-Jenkins and objective methods for determining the order of a non-seasonal ARMA model', *Journal of Forecasting* 13: 419–34.
Black, F. (1986) 'Noise', *Journal of Finance* 41: 529–43.
Canoles, B.W. (1994) 'An Analysis of the Profiles, Motivations, and Modes of Habitual Commodity Speculators', PhD dissertation, Illinois: Department of Agricultural Economics, University of Illinois.
Consensus: National Futures and Financial Weekly (1995) vol. 25, no. 7, February 17, Kansas City, MO: Consensus, Inc.
Cumby, R.E. and Modest, D.M. (1987) 'Testing for market timing ability: a framework for forecast evaluation', *Journal of Financial Economics* 19: 169–89.
De Bondt, W.F.M. (1993) 'Betting on trends: intuitive forecasts of financial risk and return', *International Journal of Forecasting* 9: 355–71.
De Long, J.B., Shleifer, A., Summers, L.H. and Waldmann, R.J. (1989) 'The size and incidence of the losses from noise trading', *Journal of Finance* 44: 681–96.
De Long, J.B., Shleifer, A., Summers, L.H. and Waldmann, R.J. (1990a) 'Noise trader risk in financial markets', *Journal of Political Economy* 98: 703–38.
De Long, J.B., Shleifer, A., Summers, L.H. and Waldmann, R.J. (1990b) 'Positive feedback investment strategies and destabilizing rational speculation', *Journal of Finance* 45: 379–95.
De Long, J.B., Shleifer, A., Summers, L.H. and Waldmann, R.J. (1991) 'The survival of noise traders in financial markets', *Journal of Business* 64: 1–19.
Draper, D.W. (1985) 'The small public trader in futures markets', in Peck, A.E. (ed.) *Futures Markets: Regulatory Issues*, Washington, DC: American Enterprise Institute for Public Policy Research.

Elton, J. and Gruber, M.J. (1984) *Modern Portfolio Theory and Investment Analysis*, New York: Wiley.

Epstein, I. (1994) 'Ira Epstein and Company Futures Market Report, 14 July 1994', in *Consensus: National Futures and Financial Weekly*, vol. 24, no. 28: 34.

Fama, E. and MacBeth, J.D. (1973) 'Risk, return and equilibrium: empirical tests', *Journal of Political Economy* 81: 607–36.

Fisher, I. (1930) *The Theory of Interest*, New York: MacMillan.

France, V.G., Kodres, L., and Moser, J.T. (1994) 'A review of regulatory mechanisms to control the volatility of prices', in *Federal Reserve Bank of Chicago's Economic Perspectives*, pp. 15–28.

Friedman, M. (1953) 'The case for flexible exchange rates', in *Essays in Positive Economics*, Chicago: University of Chicago Press, pp. 157–203.

Granger, C. (1969) 'Investigating causal relations by econometric models and cross-spectral methods', *Econometrica* 37: 24–36.

Greene, W.H. (1993) *Econometric Analysis*, New York: MacMillan.

Hamilton, J.D. (1994) *Time Series Analysis*. Princeton, NJ: Princeton University Press.

Harvey, A.C. (1991) *The Econometric Analysis of Time Series*, 2nd edn, Cambridge, MA: MIT Press.

Jones, J. (1989) 'A comparison of lag-length selection techniques in tests of Granger causality between money growth and inflation: evidence for the US, 1959–86', *Applied Economics* 24: 809–22.

Kaminsky, G. and Kumar, M. (1990) 'Efficiency in commodity futures markets', *IMF Staff Papers* 37: 670–99.

Keynes, J.M. (1936) *The General Theory of Employment Interest and Money*, New York: Harcourt, Brace and Co.

Kmenta, J. (1986) *Elements of Econometrics*, 2nd edn, New York: Macmillan.

Kodres, L.E. (1994) 'The existence and impact of destabilizing positive feedback traders: evidence from the S&P 500 Index Futures Market', working paper, Board of Governors of The Federal Reserve System.

Liu, S-M, Thompson, S. and Newbold, P. (1992) 'Impact of the price adjustment process and trading noise on return patterns of grain futures', *Journal of Futures Markets* 12: 575–85.

Ma, C.K., Dare, W.H. and Donaldson, D.R. (1990) 'Testing rationality in futures markets', *Journal of Futures Markets* 10: 137–52.

Ma, C.K., Peterson, R.L. and Sears, R.S. (1992) 'Trading noise, adverse selection, and intraday bid–ask spreads in futures markets', *Journal of Futures Markets* 12: 519–38.

Market Vane's Bullish Consensus (1983–94) Hadady Corporation, Pasadena, CA.

Muth, J.F. (1961) 'Rational expectations and the theory of price movements', *Econometrica* 29: 315–35.

Samuelson, P. (1965) 'Proof that properly anticipated prices fluctuate randomly', *Industrial Management Science* 6: 41–9.

Shleifer, A. and Summers, L.H. (1990) 'The noise trader approach to finance', *Journal of Economic Perspectives* 4: 19–33.

Smidt, S. (1965) 'Amateur speculators', in *Cornell Studies in Policy Administration*. Cornell: Cornell University.

Solt, M.E. and Statman, M. (1988) 'How useful is the sentiment index', *Financial Analysts Journal* September: 45–55.

Stein, J.L. (1981) 'Speculative price: economic welfare and the idiot of chance', *Review of Economics and Statistics* 63: 223–32.

Summers, L.H. (1986) 'Does the stock market rationally reflect fundamental values?', *Journal of Finance* 41: 591–601.

Taylor, S.J. (1985) 'The behavior of futures prices over time', *Applied Economics* 17: 713–34.

Working, H. (1949) 'The investigation of economic expectations', *American Economic Review* 39(2): 159–70.

Chapter 6

Microanalytics of price volatility in futures markets

A. G. Malliaris and Jerome L. Stein

Introduction

The stochastic paradigm of asset prices, developed from the efficient market hypothesis (EMH), states that the futures prices follow a martingale. The structural stability assumption (SSA) claims that a model is valuable or realistic only if its qualitative properties do not change with perturbations in the parameters. In this chapter, we argue that the stochastic paradigm of asset prices and the SSA may have prevented us from understanding market behaviour to such an extent that most of the variance of the pertinent economic variables is attributed to 'random shocks', i.e. the error term.

This state of events has led some researchers to investigate a key question: 'Is there a non-linear deterministic methodology, chaos, which could serve as an alternative to the stochastic approach of the EMH, which generates a time series sequence of price changes that appear random when in fact such a sequence is non-random?' With this in mind, we attempt to explain the behaviour of volatility in a non-linear dynamic system with an underlying stochastic foundation that clearly establishes the relationship of asset price volatility to speculation and Bayesian learning processes. The aims of this chapter are to show how such stochastic non-linear dynamics may clarify the relation between price variability and speculation, and to what extent the various approaches can explain the empirical studies of the time series properties of asset prices.

The next section reviews the background literature. In the following section, we suggest an economic interpretation of the Lorenz system. This is the best-known three-dimensional chaotic system whose trajectories look random when they are actually fully deterministic and converge to a strange attractor. Then, some important properties of the Lorenz system are presented. Next, we use futures data to empirically estimate the various parameters of the hypothesised Lorenz system and conclude in the last section that neither the random nor the deterministic methodologies find strong support from the data.

Background literature

Paul Samuelson (1965) developed the EMH to rationalise the random walk behaviour of futures prices, whereby the current price fully reflects all relevant information. The flow of real world information, denoted $e(t)$, is then modelled as a process of random sampling from an arbitrary space. Because sampling is random, the EMH claims that price changes are also random. In this manner, the statistical notion of a random sample of information is connected by the EMH to the economic notion of unpredictable price changes. Neither the EMH nor the numerous statistical studies about random walk investigate the analytical properties or characteristics of the information set $e(t)$.

We know that at time t the spot price of a storable commodity and the futures price of a contract maturing at time T, denoted $q(T;t)$, are linked by arbitrage to the cost of carry. Thus, it makes no difference whether we study the change in the spot price or the change in the futures price from t to $t + h$, denoted $dq(h) = q(T;t + h) - q(T - t)$.

The EMH states that $dq(h)$ results from changes in information $e(t)$, which have an expectation of zero but a finite variance. Hence, changes in futures prices are random, unpredictable and have an expectation of zero.

In other words, the stochastic approach has generally started with the equation: $q(t) = a\,q(t - 1) + e(t)$ and asked two questions: first, is $a = 1$, such that the price $q(t)$ is a martingale, or in other words is there a unit root? Second, is $e(t)$ an i.i.d. term? If not, how can one characterise its variance? This has generated a series of tests: ARCH, generalised autoregressive conditional heteroscedasticity (GARCH) and others.

There are several reasons why the purely stochastic approach should be re-evaluated. First, when researchers postulate that the futures price of an asset follows a martingale, i.e. has a unit root, then the conditional variance of the price change

$$\mathrm{var}\big[dq(h)\big] = \mathrm{var}\left[\sum_{0}^{h} e(s)\right]$$

increases with distance h. Consequently, these models are not suitable for theoretical analysis. As the influence of the postulated random shock is necessarily, theoretically speaking, unpredictable, so is the value of the price in the future. To put it differently, the influence of the postulated random shock dominates the importance of the independent variables; and because such a shock is necessarily, theoretically, unpredictable, so is the value of the dependent variable.

If price changes are induced by changes in information, can shocks in fundamental factors explain the magnitude of the observed price volatility? Or, is the variance of price changes var[d$q(h)$] due to other factors? This is the subject of the literature known as volatility tests (Shiller, 1989). This literature claims that prices are 'too volatile', and although this evidence does not reject the EMH it raises the crucial question: what factors, other than fundamental shocks, can explain the evidence of high volatility?[1]

Second, stochastic models typically discourage active economic policy or regulation designed to improve market performance. This is a consequence of the unpredictability of future shocks. Randomness does not render itself to a clear diagnosis of market behaviour or to an understanding of the relation between changes in the fundamentals and economic performance. The randomness of price changes does not render itself to a clear diagnosis of the extent to which price changes are related to changes in economic fundamentals. That is to say, there is no theory to explain what determines the characteristics of the $e(t)$ term.

Third, economic theory has accepted the structural stability assumption (SSA) as an axiom. Brock and Malliaris (1989) explain how existence, uniqueness and stability are interrelated methodological issues. The SSA, in particular, states that a model is valuable or realistic only if its qualitative properties do not change with perturbations of its parameters. The reason why the SSA is imposed is that we know that the parameters of a system cannot be measured accurately. The confidence limits of the estimated coefficients and the standard errors of the estimates are extremely large. Economists have imposed the SSA as a prior restriction to permit us to argue that, within a large range of parameter estimates and for almost any initial conditions, our qualitative results hold.

Numerous expository articles, such as Brock (1988), Baumol and Benhabib (1989) and Boldrin and Woodford (1990), have appeared using various single variable chaotic maps as a metaphor to illustrate the intellectual possibilities of the deterministic approach. We wish to go beyond these illustrations and explain the behaviour of volatility in a non-linear dynamic system that establishes a relationship of such asset volatility to speculation and to Bayesian learning processes followed by the traders. In other words, the aim of this chapter is to show how non-linear dynamics, as a complement to linear stochastic models, can clarify the relation between price variability and speculation, and at the same time explain why the empirical studies of the time series properties of asset prices are ambiguous and inconclusive.

As already mentioned in the introduction to this chapter, there is a serious critique of the chaos literature by Granger (1994) and by Allen (1995) in her review of the book by De Grauwe *et al.* (1993). Granger (1994, p. 142) argues that 'If the purpose of this research effort is to show that it is possible to produce economic theory that has chaos as an outcome then this certainly has been achieved, but it is unclear why more than one paper is required that shows this. The recent papers produce more general models but are still not realistic and are not in a form that is empirically testable in any specific fashion'. Granger (1994, p. 144) continues by saying '...as an econometrician, I would want...evidence that...[the chaos model] reproduced many features of an actual economy, not just a couple, and that it suggested and correctly predicted features that have not been previously tested'.

The empirical evidence for deterministic chaos is weak. For example, De Grauwe *et al.* (1993) examined several exchange rates. In no case, could they find a strange attractor. When they used other tests concerning the correlation dimension, they found that for a few currencies in some subperiods there was some visual evidence of chaotic behaviour. They concluded that 'The empirical analysis presented in this book can certainly not be considered as conclusive evidence of chaos in the foreign exchange market' (De Grauwe *et al.*, 1993, p. 257).

An economic theory that implies the Lorenz system

The volatility generated from a non-linear dynamic deterministic system can be contrasted with the stochastic paradigm. The deterministic system establishes a relationship between asset price volatility, speculation and Bayesian learning processes followed by the traders. We show in this section how non-linear dynamics may contribute to modelling price volatility and may provide further content to what is called randomness.

Let the price $P(t)$ of an asset depend upon the fundamentals $W(t)$ and what we refer to as the Bayesian error $E_p - E^*_p$, in equation 6.1. The Bayesian error is the difference between the true or objective expectation of the price E_p, which is a function of the fundamentals, and the subjective estimate E^*_p. The 'rational expectations' hypothesis states that there is no Bayesian error: the subjective anticipation is the same as the objective expectation:

$$P(t) = P[W(t), E_p - E^*_p] \qquad (6.1)$$

where E_p is the objective expectation of the price prevailing at a later date $(t + h)$ and E^*_p is the subjective expectation of the price prevailing at later $(t + h)$, based upon information known at time t.

The correlation coefficient between the price $P(t)$ and the fundamentals $W(t)$ is $r = \text{cov}(P,W)/\sigma(P)\sigma(W)$. Define the excess volatility, denoted by $x(t)$, of a given financial variable as the volatility of the price of an asset less the volatility owing to the fundamentals:

$$x(t) = (1 - r^2)\, \text{var}(P) \qquad (6.2)$$

It is clear from equation 6.1 that excess volatility $x(t)$ depends upon the variance of the Bayesian error: $y(t) = \text{var}(E_p - E^*_p)$, and the covariance with the fundamentals. A Bayesian error exists as long as the market participants are learning what are the fundamentals and how they affect the price. The convergence of a system to a rational expectations equilibrium requires that the expectation and variance of the Bayesian error go to zero.

The market participants sample from the information set to learn what are the fundamentals. It has been proved[2] that the Bayesian error depends upon the noisiness of the system and the average costs of sampling by the market participants. There are many different types of participants in the market with different costs of sampling and, hence, different Bayesian errors. Thus, $x(t)$ depends upon the variance of the Bayesian errors, and the latter depends upon the types of agents in the market.

We consider three key variables: excess price volatility, speculation and Bayesian errors made by traders. We propose a model[3] of three differential equations that relate these three variables. The mathematical form of this model is known in the dynamical systems literature as the Lorenz equations. This system is perhaps the most famous chaotic map in the mathematical literature of dynamical systems and has been extensively studied[4] for its remarkable properties.

Equation 6.3 states that, given the variance of the Bayesian errors $y(t)$, the excess volatility will converge to the variance of the Bayesian error. This is an eminently sensible implication from equations 6.1 and 6.2. The speed of convergence is given by coefficient $s > 0$.

$$dx/dt = -sx + sy \qquad (6.3)$$

Equation 6.4 describes the dynamics of the Bayesian error.[5] This is precisely the theory concerning the speed of convergence to rational expectations[6] – a situation where there is no Bayesian error. There are three variables (x, y, z) that determine the rate of change of the Bayesian error: dy/dt.

$$dy/dt = x(r - z) - y \qquad (6.4)$$

The first determinant is the level $y(t)$ of the Bayesian error. Think of the market Bayesian error as a weighted average of sampling errors. Each set of participants takes a sample from the information set. The sample mean is the participant's expected price. The average of the sample means is the market's estimate E^*_p of the price. The sample means have a distribution based upon the variance of the information set and the sample size. The costs of sampling determine the optimal sample size.

It follows that the Bayesian error depends upon the noisiness of the system and the average costs of sampling from the information set concerning the fundamentals. Different market participants have different costs of sampling and, hence, have different Bayesian errors. The average costs of sampling depends upon the types of people attracted to the market. If the system were not too noisy, then people would learn quickly. The Bayesian error would go towards zero because the cumulative sample size had increased. This is equivalent to the central limit theorem, i.e. if $x(r - z) = 0$, then $y(t)$ converges close to zero.

The second determinant of dy/dt is the excess volatility $x(t)$, the noisiness of the system. The third determinant is a measure of informed speculation $z(t)$. We shall measure it as the volume generated by large speculators relative to the open interest.

The market Bayesian error is produced by differential costs of information. Small traders have higher marginal costs of information than large traders, especially the large commercials. The large commercials have the lowest marginal cost of information because their activities are widespread over many markets.[7] Think of small traders as noise traders. Insofar as there is an entry of more small traders who have high marginal costs of information, z will decline. The activities of noise traders will increase the variance of the Bayesian error and the price variance will rise. When z rises as a result of the entrance of more large commercial and non-commercial traders, then the variance of the Bayesian error will decline, and price variance will decrease.

Equation 6.4 involves a parameter r and two variables x and z. Variable z is a measure of informed speculation. Equation 6.4 states that the effect of a change in excess volatility upon the rate of change of the Bayesian error $\delta(dy/dt)/\delta x = (r - z)$. Parameter r denotes the critical amount of speculation. The hypothesis described by the first term $x(r-z)$ is that the noisiness of the system $x(t)$ increases price variance in thin markets where there is a small amount of informed speculation $(r > z)$. As speculation increases above the critical level $(z > r)$, the variance of the Bayesian error decreases. When there are many informed speculators $(z > r)$ who take large samples from the information set, as described in Stein (1992a), then the variance of the sample mean E^*_p around the population mean E_p (concerning the fundamentals) is low and the market on average is better informed. This is the rationale of the term $\delta(dy/dt)/\delta x = (r - z)$.

Equation 6.5 states again that the measure of speculation z tends to converge. Given the noisiness of the system and the Bayesian error, the index of speculation converges to xy/b. The economic hypothesis is that: (i) the greater the noisiness of the system the greater is the diversity of views, (ii) profits are generated by a diversity of views, and (iii) speculation is induced by profits to speculators. The profits of speculators converge, given xy, and are driven to zero when $xy = 0$.

$$dz/dt = -bz + xy \qquad (6.5)$$

This is an extremely rich system in its implications for the time series of price changes and index of speculation. There are three crucial parameters b, s and r, where r is the most important. Parameter b reflects the speed of convergence of excess speculation to zero. Hence, b reflects how speculation affects profits or losses, which in turn induce entry or exit of non-commercials into speculative markets. Parameter s reflects the speed of convergence of the volatility to a constant if the Bayesian errors are given.

Analysis of the Lorenz system

The dynamics of the system depend upon the critical amount of speculation r relative to the speeds of convergence b,s. Almost anything is possible in this system, depending upon the specification of the parameters. There may be a strange attractor as a special case of chaotic dynamics. A strange attractor is a closed simply connected region containing an equilibrium point, such that the vector field is directed everywhere inwards on the boundary. Chaotic dynamics with a strange attractor are produced from equations 6.3–6.5 when:

$$r > r^* = s(s + b + 3)/(s - b - 1) > 0; \text{ where } (s > 1 + b) \qquad (6.6)$$

This system cannot be solved analytically. One cannot express variables (x,y,z) as functions of time and initial conditions. The system can only be solved on a computer. It is difficult to have the intuition for the strange attractor, but we shall try to convey it as follows.

A rise in the noisiness of the system $x(t)$ changes the variance of the Bayesian error by $(r - z)$. The value of r is equal to $\delta(dy/dt)/\delta x$ when $z = 0$. If z exceeds the value r, then the variance of the Bayesian error declines, and price volatility is reduced. However, the reduction in price volatility reduces the index of speculation z. This reduction in z tends to raise $(r - z)$, which raises the variance of the Bayesian error. Thereby, the movement in price volatility is reversed. But it does not produce the usual cyclical behaviour. The three variables (x,y,z) interact. In this highly complicated system, there is a critical value of $r = r^*$, given above. If $r > r^*$, then the three variables interact in a chaotic way, such that the system is driven into a 'strange attractor'.

Anything can happen in this system, depending upon the parameter values. For example, in Table 6.1, column (1) is a set of parameters that yield a strange attractor, and columns (2) and (3) produce asymptotic stability.

There are important economic implications of this analysis for the questions and issues raised in the introduction to this chapter. First, if the economic model were as described by equations 6.3–6.5, then the pattern of the variables would change qualitatively as a result of 'slight' changes in parameter values. *The structural stability condition is not valid.* Compare column (1) with the other two columns. Second, when the parameters satisfy equation 6.6 above, the variables do not follow random walks, but are constrained by the strange attractor. This is a pleasing result to the economist who does not like the random walk conclusion that the variable could end up anywhere. Within the strange attractor, the behaviour of the variables seems random. Third, the behaviour of the variables within the strange attractor is qualitatively dependent upon the initial conditions. Each set of initial conditions will generate a different trajectory within the strange attractor. Therefore, without perfect

Table 6.1 Interaction of variables

Parameters	Strange attractor (1)	Asymptotic stability (2)	(3)
b	1	1	4
r	5	5	5
s	15	14	15

knowledge of the system, it is impossible to predict the movement of the variables, except to say that it lies within the strange attractor SA*. Instead of the old concept of equilibrium as a point, we may have a different concept: the equilibrium as a set SA*. The solution stays within the set SA*, but its behaviour in that set is unpredictable without perfect knowledge of initial conditions; and its behaviour with the equilibrium SA* seems almost indistinguishable from random.

Empirical tests

This part of the chapter is concerned with the question of which set of parameters is consistent with the evidence. Do the empirical results lead us to accept or reject parameter values that imply a strange attractor? There is a phenomenological approach to the analysis of data developed for physical sciences by Takens (1981) and others. This approach attempts to imply the multidimensional attractor underlying the observed time series without any prior specification of the underlying mechanism. Although this approach may be fruitful, it requires extremely long runs of data, which limits its usefulness to economists. Our approach is hypothesis testing, rather than the phenomenological time series analysis because we want to understand the economic interrelationships that generate price volatility.

Price volatility, Bayesian errors and speculation are dynamically interrelated in the system of equations 6.3–6.5. This is a general system with both a linear part and a non-linear part. The Lorenz specification may be viewed as a special case and one could generalise the interrelationships among price volatility, Bayesian errors and speculation.

Our estimates of the variables (x,y,z) are as follows. We have weekly data for corn and soybean futures contracts traded at the Chicago Board of Trade from January 1993 to December 1994. Price volatility, denoted by x_t, is computed by the Chicago Board of Trade using an average of implied volatilities from several options using the Black–Scholes model.[8] The Bayesian error, denoted y_t, is the absolute value of the difference between the futures price at time t and the futures price at the expiration of the nearby contract.[9] Speculation, denoted by z_t, is the ratio of the number of contracts bought by large speculators divided by the open interest, i.e. divided by all outstanding futures contracts. Figures 6.1 and 6.2 plot the three variables for corn and soybeans.

Our dynamic system in equations 6.3–6.5 above is estimated by equations 6.7–6.9 below. The different c_i are the coefficients to be estimated. Because our system is non-linear, the residuals are recalculated

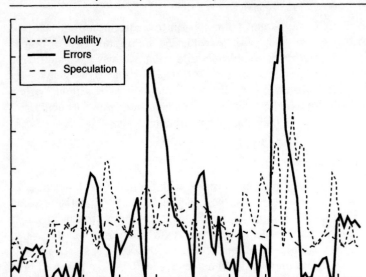

Figure 6.1 Time series of volatility, errors and speculation for corn. Weekly sample data from January 1993 to December 1994.

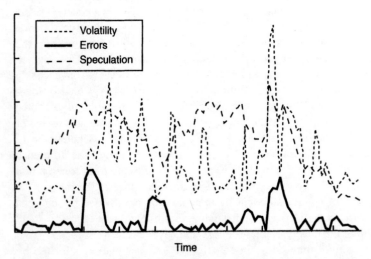

Figure 6.2 Time series of volatility, errors and speculation for soybeans. Weekly sample data from January 1993 to December 1994.

and the residual covariance matrix is updated. We use a seemingly unrelated regression system estimation method. Estimation is repeated until convergence is achieved. This technique is asymptotically full information maximum likelihood. The system in equations 6.7–6.9 is estimated for three sample periods for each of the two commodities (corn and soybeans). First, it is estimated for the entire sample period January 1993 to December 1994, and then twice for a one-year subperiod. The error term is i.i.d. with a zero expectation.

General unrestricted formulation

$$x_t = c_1 x_{t-1} + c_2 y_{t-1} + \varepsilon_{1t} \tag{6.7}$$

$$y_t = c_3 x_{t-1} - c_4 x_{t-1} z_{t-1} + c_5 y_{t-1} + \varepsilon_{2t} \tag{6.8}$$

$$z_t = c_6 z_{t-1} + c_7 x_{t-1} y_{t-1} + \varepsilon_{3t} \tag{6.9}$$

In Table 6.2, based upon equations 6.7–6.9, we present estimates of the unrestricted general model without the restrictions on coefficients imposed by any one of the specific models implied by the general analysis in *An economic theory that implies the Lorenz system*. Table 6.3 examines the hypotheses contained in various subsets of restrictions, i.e. equations 6.1–6.6.

The aim of this chapter is to evaluate which model of asset pricing is consistent with the data. The Lorenz equations are differential equations which arise from a specific form of the non-linear part. We shall consider several specifications. In Table 6.3, we show the results of Wald tests designed to test which formulation is consistent with the evidence.

The pure random walk hypothesis is that the price volatility is unexplained Brownian motion. This hypothesis implies restriction 1 in Table 6.3: $c_1 = 1$, $c_2 = 0$.

$$x(t) = x(t-1) + \varepsilon(t) \qquad \text{restriction 1}$$

For the entire period, restriction 1 is rejected by both commodities. The results for the subperiods are mixed.

Restriction 6 is a generalisation that claims that all of the three variables are martingales. It states that in Table 6.3 coefficients $c_1 = 1$, $c_5 = 1$, $c_6 = 1$, and all others $c_i = 0$, where $i = 2,3,4,7$.

$$Ex(t) = x(t-1), \; Ey(t) = y(t-1), \; Ez(t) = z(t-1) \qquad \text{restriction 6}$$

Table 6.2 Values of coefficients from system estimation: model 2

$$x_t = c_1 x_{t-1} + c_2 y_{t-1} + \varepsilon_1$$

$$y_t = c_3 x_{t-1} - c_4 x_{t-1} z_{t-1} + c_5 y_{t-1} + \varepsilon_2$$

$$z_t = c_6 z_{t-1} + c_7 x_{t-1} y_{t-1} + \varepsilon_3$$

Commodity	Period	c_1	c_2	c_3	c_4	c_5	c_6	c_7
Corn	Jan 1993–Dec 1994	0.871886[a] (18.32261)	0.086754[b] (2.029803)	-0.105118 (-0.509720)	-0.027477[b] (-1.768015)	0.692318[a] (10.17364)	0.996669[a] (68.19037)	-0.0000889 (-0.224902)
Corn	Jan 1993–Dec 1993	0.932341[a] (17.21280)	0.031155 (0.700313)	0.434205 (1.210064)	0.007542 (0.334792)	0.707621[a] (7.756978)	0.991582[a] (39.86482)	0.000889 (0.3556)
Corn	Jan 1994–Dec 1994	0.825401[a] (11.01738)	0.135264[b] (1.872283)	-0.628648[b] (2.084178)	-0.073650[a] (-2.736716)	0.632155[a] (6.333528)	0.984880[a] (65.20979)	-0.000307 (-0.972821)
Soybeans	Jan 1993–Dec 1994	0.852024[a] (17.28032)	0.429578[b] (2.163062)	-0.002310 (-0.047218)	-0.001493 (-0.752885)	0.775010[a] (11.84851)	1.001594[a] (71.45370)	-0.005547[b] (-1.775370)
Soybeans	Jan 1993–Dec 1993	0.862833[a] (16.30281)	0.475209[a] (2.598100)	0.046012 (0.401926)	0.001228 (0.256321)	0.842916[a] (10.35966)	1.014184[a] (52.42731)	-0.004281 (-0.775628)
Soybeans	Jan 1994–Dec 1994	0.864158[a] (8.862383)	0.267857 (0.573671)	0.012756 (0.285637)	-0.002701 (-1.516465)	0.535107[a] (4.887126)	0.994622[b] (50.84558)	-0.006958[b] (-1.885839)

Note
a and b indicate that the coefficient is significant at the 1% and 10% confidence levels respectively. The t-statistics are given in parentheses.

Table 6.3 Wald coefficient tests: model 2

$$x_t = c_1 x_{t-1} + c_2 y_{t-1} + \varepsilon_1$$

$$y_t = c_3 x_{t-1} - c_4 x_{t-1} z_{t-1} + c_5 y_{t-1} + \varepsilon_2$$

$$z_t = c_6 z_{t-1} + c_7 x_{t-1} y_{t-1} + \varepsilon_3$$

Parameter restriction/ null hypotheses	Commodity	Jan 1993–Dec 1994		Jan 1993–Dec 1993		Jan 1994–Dec 1994	
		χ^2	Probability	χ^2	Probability	χ^2	Probability
Restriction 1: $c_1 = 1, c_2 = 0$	Corn	7.317363	0.025766	1.590846	0.451390	5.557753	0.062108
	Soybeans	9.069919	0.010727	8.684261	0.013009	2.733767	0.254900
Restriction 2: $c_3 = 0, c_4 = 0, c_5 = 0$	Corn	354.0297	0.000000	185.9297	0.000000	193.8882	0.000000
	Soybeans	325.1237	0.000000	167.3906	0.000000	181.1952	0.000000
Restriction 3: $c_3 = 0, c_4 = 0, c_5 = 1$	Corn	20.92695	0.000109	11.54009	0.009137	14.66806	0.002123
	Soybeans	11.96054	0.007520	4.067382	0.254279	18.24999	0.000391
Restriction 4: $c_6 = 0, c_7 = 0$	Corn	7172.763	0.000000	3112.694	0.000000	5947.188	0.000000
	Soybeans	7436.462	0.000000	4214.733	0.000000	3531.458	0.000000
Restriction 5: $c_6 = 1, c_7 = 0$	Corn	0.253217	0.881078	1.028678	0.597896	4.276984	0.117832
	Soybeans	4.393699	0.111153	0.713924	0.699799	5.965239	0.050660
Restriction 6: $c_1 = 1, c_2 = 0, c_3 = 0,$ $c_4 = 0, c_5 = 1, c_6 = 1,$ $c_7 = 0$	Corn	26.37768	0.000431	13.75545	0.055706	23.78946	0.001241
	Soybeans	25.21629	0.000695	12.40919	0.087880	26.74112	0.000371

Table 6.3 shows that restriction 6 is rejected at the 1% and 5% levels for both corn and soybeans over the entire period January 1993 to December 1994, and at the 5% for subperiods.

The rejection of restrictions 1 and 6 then leads to the next and most important set of questions.

1 Is the system linear or non-linear, and what precisely are the interrelations among the variables? The non-linear terms are associated with coefficients c_4 and c_7.
2 Is the price variance affected by the Bayesian error in the manner developed in *An economic theory that implies the Lorenz system* above?

To answer question (1), consider the t-statistics for c_4 and c_7 – the non-linear terms – in Table 6.2. The evidence that these are significant is mixed over the entire period, but something shows up for subperiods.

Question (2) is addressed in restrictions 2 and 3. Restriction 2 states that the Bayesian error $y(t)$ is purely random. This is the rational expectations hypothesis (REH).

$$y(t) = \varepsilon(t) \qquad \text{restriction 2}$$

where e is i.i.d. with a zero mean. Table 6.3 shows that restriction 2, the REH, is rejected: the Bayesian error, or forecast error, is not a random variable. Restriction 3 states that the Bayesian error is a martingale. Table 6.3 shows that this too is rejected.

$$Ey(t) = y(t-1) \qquad \text{restriction 3}$$

Restrictions 4 and 5 concern the speculation variables. Restriction 4 states that speculation is a random variable $\varepsilon(t)$ which is i.i.d. with a zero mean. This hypothesis is rejected. Restriction 5, which states that it is a martingale, is not rejected.

$$z(t) = \varepsilon(t) \qquad \text{restriction 4}$$

$$Ez(t) = z(t-1) \qquad \text{restriction 5}$$

Our interpretation of the significant values of the coefficients in Tables 6.2 and 6.3 is that the system is linear as described by equations 6.10–6.12. This interpretation is most consistent with the theoretical analysis in *An economic theory that implies the Lorenz system*.

$$x(t) = c_1 x(t-1) + c_2 y(t-1) \qquad\qquad + e_1(t) \qquad\qquad (6.10)$$

$$y(t) = \qquad\qquad c_5 y(t-1) \qquad\qquad + e_2(t) \qquad\qquad (6.11)$$

$$z(t) = \qquad\qquad\qquad c_6 z(t-1) + e_3(t) \qquad\qquad (6.12)$$

This is a decomposable and recursive linear system. Speculation is a random walk $c_6 = 1$, so its effect may simply be contained in the error terms in equations 6.10 and 6.11. However, there is a dynamic interaction between price volatility and the Bayesian errors, exactly as described in *An economic theory that implies the Lorenz system* above.

This is an important result. The analysis claims that the price variance is the sum of the variance of the fundamentals and that of the Bayesian errors. The analysis has a structure, such that if the variance of the fundamentals is given the variance of the Bayesian error converges to zero. This is very different from the REH, and was called asymptotically rational expectations (Stein, 1986, Chapter 3). The economic dynamics of the Bayesian error involve both a learning process and the entry of different types of speculators (Stein, 1986, Chapter 5). Unlike the REH, the general formulation implies that there is a positive relation between price volatility and trading volume. This is a well-established empirical relation. See Rutledge (1986), Bhar and Malliaris (1998) and Malliaris and Urrutia (1998).

The linear differential equation system in (x,y,z), based upon the results in Table 6.3, has the following characteristics. It seems that speculation is a martingale. The system in (x,y), the price volatility and Bayesian error, is dynamically stable. The eigenvalues $\lambda = (c_1, c_5)$ are both less than unity in absolute value. For both of the commodities, over the entire period: $\lambda = (0.8, 0.5) < |1|$. Hence, the system is stable and converges to the equilibrium $(x^*, y^*) = 0$, although speculation is a martingale $c_6 = 1$.

Conclusion

We analyse the theoretical foundations of the efficient market hypothesis by stressing the efficient use of information and its effect upon price volatility. The 'random walk' hypothesis assumes that price volatility is exogenous and unexplained. Randomness means that a knowledge of the past is not helpful in predicting the future. We believe that randomness appears because information is incomplete. An analogy with a coin tossing or dice rolling experiment can be made. If we knew the spin and velocity of a coin or a die, we could predict the outcome. However, that information is unavailable. The global reality is deterministic, but human beings can only know a small subset. The larger the subset available and known, the less emphasis one must place upon the generic term randomness.[10]

Our contribution is to provide an economic interpretation to a well-known three-dimensional chaotic model. Our analysis is used to explain the learning process and the efficient use of information. The Bayesian error is the difference between the objective and subjective expectations of the specified fundamentals. The objective expectation is not known because it depends upon information that is not available to the observer. It is generated by a global deterministic system. The subjective estimate is arrived at via Bayesian learning, taking into account the costs and benefits of further sampling from a multidimensional space. We derive the determinants of the dynamics of the Bayesian error. Thus, we expand the information set or further specify a component of what is generically attributed to 'randomness'.

We show that the resulting system is of third order in price variability, Bayesian error and speculation. One very specific possibility is that the system is chaotic and moves into a strange attractor, wherein the resulting movements of price variability can be described statistically as random. In that case, randomness is chaotic.

We then estimate a general unrestricted system to see which specifications we can reject. Both the pure 'random walk' and the non-linear system, which could generate chaotic randomness, are rejected. What emerges is that a system very close to our original model is consistent with the evidence. Price variability is a serially correlated variable that is affected by the Bayesian error. Putting the two together, we obtain an equation for price volatility which looks a lot like the GARCH equation. The price variability is a serially correlated variable which is affected by the Bayesian error, and the latter is a serially correlated variable. The third order system is linear and dynamically stable. Our conclusion is that we have shown that price variability is consistent with the efficient use of information, and that part of price variability is derived from the dynamics of the Bayesian error.

Acknowledgements

We are thankful to Henry Wen-herng King, Dimitrios Bouroudzoglou, Raffaella Cremonesi and Caglar Alkan for extensive computations. Earlier versions of this chapter were presented at the European Working Group on Financial Modelling, 1–3 June 1995, the Allied Social Science Association Meeting in San Francisco, 5–7 January 1996, and The Chicago Risk Management Workshop, 8 October 1997.

Endnotes

1 Among such factors, speculation has received special attention. The topic of speculation and price volatility has been studied at both the theoretical and the empirical level. In an efficient market, as price changes are unpredictable, speculation should not be profitable. Friedman (1953) argued that profitable speculation reduces the price variance. This insight has generated many empirical papers which examined the profitability of speculation. However, it was shown in many theoretical articles, such as in Hart and Kreps (1986), that his conclusion only applies under special conditions, and that plausible models can be developed explaining excess volatility by the speculative behaviour of noise traders.

2 Stein (1986, pp. 62–76; 1992a).

3 Malliaris and Stein (1998)

4 See, for example, Sparrow (1982).

5 Stein (1992a, p. 39) derived the formula for the variance of the Bayesian error: $y(t) = \mathrm{var}\,(E^*P - EP) = (2gc/k^2t^2)^{1/3}$, where g reflects the convexity of the costs of information; $(1/k)$ is the noisiness of the system – think of it as the variance of the fundamentals; and t is time.

6 This is the subject of Stein (1992b).

7 Stein (1986, Chapter 5)

8 In the model, $x(t)$ was excess volatility relative to the fundamentals. In our empirical work, we are using actual volatility implied by the Black–Scholes options pricing model.

9 The $y(t)$ in the model was the variance of the Bayesian error. Empirically, we are using the absolute value of the Bayesian error. It has been proved (Stein, 1986, pp. 72–6, 92–3) that both have similar shapes as functions of time.

10 We derived great benefit from the book by Ekeland (1988) in understanding the relation between randomness and deterministic chaos.

References

Allen, P.R. (1995) 'Review of De Grauwe *et al*. Exchange rate theory: chaotic models of foreign exchange', *Journal of Economic Literature* 33: 224–5.

Baumol, W. and Benhabib, J. (1989) 'Chaos: significance, mechanism and economic applications', *Journal of Economic Perspectives* 3: 77–105.

Bhar, R. and Malliaris, A.G. (1998) 'Volume and volatility in foreign currency futures markets', *Review of Quantitative Finance and Accounting* 10: 228–98.

Boldrin, M. and Woodford, M. (1990) Equilibrium models displaying endogenous fluctuations and chaos', *Journal of Monetary Economics* 25: 189–222.

Brock, W. (1988) 'Nonlinearity and complex dynamics in economics and finance', in *The Economy as an Evolving Complex System*, SFI Studies in the Sciences of Complexity, Madison, WI: Addison-Wesley.

Brock, W. and Malliaris, A.G. (1989) *Differential Equations, Stability and Chaos in Dynamic Economics*, Amsterdam: North-Holland Publishing.

De Grauwe P., Dewachter H. and Embrechts M. (1993) *Exchange Rate Theory: Chaotic Models and Foreign Exchange*, Oxford: Blackwell.

Ekeland, I. (1988) *Mathematics and the Unexpected*, Chicago: University of Chicago Press.

Friedman, M. (1953) 'The case for flexible exchange rates', in *Essays in Positive Economics*, Chicago: University of Chicago Press.

Granger, C. (1994) 'Is chaotic economic theory relevant for economics?', *Journal of International and Comparative Economics* 3: 139–45.

Hart, O and Kreps, D. (1986) 'Price destabilizing speculation', *Journal of Political Economy* 94: 927–52.

Malliaris A.G. and Stein, J.L. (1999) 'Methodological issues in asset pricing: random walks or chaotic dynamics', *Journal of Banking and Finance*, 223: 1605–35.

Malliaris, A.G. and Urrutia J. (1998) 'Volume and price relationships: hypotheses and testing for agricultural futures', *Journal of Futures Markets* 18: 53–72.

Rutledge, D. (1986) 'Trading volume and price variability', in Goss, B.A. (ed.) *Futures Markets*, London: Croom Helm.

Samuelson, P. (1965) 'Proof that properly anticipated prices fluctuate randomly', *Industrial Management Review* 6: 41–9.

Shiller, R. (1989) *Market Volatility*, Cambridge, MA: The MIT Press.

Sparrow, C. (1982) *The Lorenz Equations: Bifurcations, Chaos and Strange Attractors*, New York: Springer-Verlag.

Stein, J. (1986) *The Economics of Futures Markets*, Oxford: Blackwell.

—— (1992a) 'Cobwebs, rational expectations and futures markets', *Review of Economics and Statistics* 74 127–34.

—— (1992b) 'Price discovery processes', in Stein, J.L. and Goss, B. (eds) *Economic Record: Special Issue on Futures Markets*.

Takens, F. (1980) 'Detecting strange attractors in turbulence', in Rand, D.A. and Young, L.-S. (eds) *Springer Lecture Notes in Mathematics*, Vol. 898, New York: Springer, pp. 366–81.

Chapter 7

The integrity of futures markets

The impact of price limits on futures prices

Anthony D. Hall, Paul Kofman
and Anthony Siouclis

Introduction

Defaulting traders, market crashes and asymmetric information problems attract negative attention to the integrity of derivatives exchanges. As a result, calls for further regulation arise with almost every large realignment of market values. Regulation clearly responds to the trading behaviour of market participants. Whether or not trading behaviour is also affected by regulation has so far largely been neglected.[1] When traders are confronted with market impediments, they will revise their expectations accordingly. This affects their order flow and, hence, the volatility of prices. Evaluations of the impact of market regulations on the price discovery process that consider the trading process exogenous ignore these dynamic adjustments. If trades are diverted to other outlets (such as non-regulated options or the cash market), this may lead to increased volatility and a reduction in order flow. Thus, the 'integrity' of the exchange can even be further endangered as a result of the trading impediments invoked by regulation. A proper cost–benefit analysis of the imposition of regulatory tools therefore needs to assess trading behaviour dynamics. Before elaborating on our approach, it seems worthwhile to first define the type of regulation on which we will focus.

To prevent excessive trading reactions in the case of large unexpected price changes, a set of protective (market driven and regulatory) tools operates at futures markets. Market-makers quote bid–ask spreads to be compensated for temporarily holding open positions. The size of these spreads typically varies with the liquidity of the market and its price volatility over the expected holding period. Despite these spreads, large sudden price changes can still lead to excessive losses and, potentially, defaulting exchange members. To protect the integrity of exchanges against such defaults, clearing houses levy margins that have to be maintained on a daily basis. The possibility of intraday margin calls even further 'smooths' the absorption of price losses. High volatility periods such as the 1987 and 1989 stock market crashes illustrated that these measures may still prove insufficient to smooth large pieces of information into an orderly price adjustment process. Whereas the market's integrity is usually well preserved, small traders turn out to be very vulnerable to these extreme price changes. A series of investigations (led by the Presidential Task Force on Market Mechanisms, 1988) has since led to the introduction of new regulatory tools, e.g. the circuit breaker that temporarily suspends trading after large price changes. These impediments aim at providing traders with sufficient time to reconsider and rearrange their positions in line with readjusted price expectations. Circuit breakers operate in a similar fashion to price limits that have been active for quite a long time in most futures markets. Unlike circuit breakers that effectively suspend trading for a preset time interval, price limits allow trading as long as the transaction price does not move outside these limits. On the negative side, these limits are rather rigid tools because they are not progressively stretched after some time period has elapsed. This implies that if a price limit is hit at the market's opening it will act as a one-day circuit breaker if there is a strong drift pushing the fundamental price beyond the limit. Discrimination between the two types of trading suspension then depends on the informational content of the price change. If the change is owing to an overreaction to news, a limit would possibly realign expectations best, whereas if the change truly reflects new information the shorter the suspension the better and a circuit breaker would be preferable. However, before reaching this conclusion, a proper understanding of price limits requires us to consider trading as a dynamic process.

This chapter focuses on price limit regulation and investigates how it affects the trading behaviour of market participants. Technical (i.e. statistical) consequences of price limits have been investigated in a number of papers. For example, as Roll (1984) correctly notes, the use of possibly stale prices implied by limit moves will inevitably affect any informational efficiency study. A second study that carefully accounts for the possibility of limit moves is Kodres (1988, 1993), who analyses the impact of price limits on tests of the unbiasedness hypothesis in foreign exchange futures markets. Both studies, however, restrict the impact of limits to actual limit move occurrences and thereby ignore any 'intra' limit dynamics. There are also a number of studies more directly focusing on the impact of price limits, in particular on measures of intraday volatility. Most of them perform this analysis in an event–study context. Ma et al. (1989), Greenwald and Stein (1991) and Kodres and O'Brien

(1994) claim that trading halts mitigate price risk and enhance informational efficiency. Others, however, argue that limits obstruct informational efficiency, and in the process tend to inflate volatility excessively (see, among others, McMillan, 1991; Lee *et al.*, 1994; Subrahmanyam, 1994, 1995). So far, there has been no attempt to encompass the two conflicting models.

Our modelling framework offers a tool to properly interpret (and discriminate among) these conflicting findings. Underlying our model is the notion that *ex ante* trading decisions incorporate the existence of bounded trading zones, i.e. bounded by the price limits. For example, market-makers may try to avoid or at least postpone the price hitting the boundaries because that would imply interrupted trading, and hence a loss of earnings/profits. Kuserk and Locke (1996) investigate the impact of price limits on market-making profitability and conclude that on average market-makers profit from trading halts. This finding contrasts with Roll's (1984) remark that limits do create informational inefficiencies, but not a profit opportunity. Kuserk and Locke (1996) focus on market-maker behaviour immediately before and after limit moves and thereby also ignore potential impacts further away from those limits. Similarly, informed traders will try to smooth their planned trading volume before the price hits the limits, after which the risk of a dissipation of their private information increases. Market-makers protect themselves against these actions by increasing the bid–ask spread upwards when the market moves towards the limits. This may 'exaggerate' volatility and lead to wrong conclusions from observing increased volatility near the limits. The last argument has been extensively used by the gravitation or magnet proponents. These gravitationists argue that limits are self-exciting because they induce a strong drift in prices. Traders, allegedly, increase this drift by unwinding positions whenever the price gets close to the limits. Empirical work in this area is rather extensive, examples of which are McMillan (1991) and Kuserk and Locke (1996). Some of these papers deal with circuit breakers, but their findings supposedly apply identically to price limits. A theoretical microstructural analysis of these (opposing) dynamic trading adjustments is given in Greenwald and Stein (1991), Kodres and O'Brien (1994) and Subrahmanyam (1994, 1995). Whereas the first two papers tend to support trade suspension rules as (second best) optimal, the last clearly rejects these rules based on an informational inefficiency that arises because of traders advancing their trades in time as in the informed trader context above. Obviously, the theoretical specification has some impact on the subsequent results.

We address the issue of how price expectations are influenced by limits, by using concepts recently developed for exchange rate target zones. The seminal paper by Krugman (1991) shows that bounded exchange rates no longer exhibit a linear relationship with the underlying fundamentals of supply and demand. If, for example, there is a fixed (and credible) upper limit and the exchange rate is close to that limit, then the probability of a further increase will be limited (the probability on exceedance is zero), whereas the probability of a decrease will be relatively larger. Thus, the probability distribution of the next price move will become increasingly skewed the closer we get to the limits. This phenomenon implies a non-linear relationship between the actually observed price and the fundamental (based on supply and demand) price. In the absence of trade 'disruptions', the relationship between the two will be linear. The presence of limits, however, implies a non-linear S-shape. The relation will be convex for prices negatively drifting towards the lower limit, and concave for prices positively drifting towards the upper limit. Thus, the effect of limits will theoretically be to stabilise prices. Shocks (demand/supply driven) in the fundamental value will have a less than proportional impact on the observed (i.e. realised) price. Our statistical specification will also allow for non-linearity of a different (opposite) type. Instead of a smoothing impact, price limits may have an exacerbating impact. Shocks in the fundamental value will then have a more than proportional impact on the observed price. Thus, we nest the two competing models of mean reversion[2] versus gravitation.

We propose to investigate the existence of similar non-linear relationships in futures markets that are regulated by price limits. The target zone is then defined by the difference between the upper and lower limit prices. In our case, the issue is not so much whether the 'band' is credible (it will always move the next day and is fully credible intraday), but whether its existence has an impact far away from the boundaries. This, in particular, distinguishes our chapter from the previous price limits literature. As suggested by Strongin (1995, p. 205), work on the impact of price limits, away from limit moves themselves, is urgently needed and we aim to address this issue. Summarising our main hypothesis:

> We postulate a non-linear relationship between the theoretical and observed futures prices.

If we reject this hypothesis, we conclude that price limits do not affect the random walk model of futures prices. If we cannot reject this hypothesis, we formulate the following subhypothesis:

This non-linear relationship is of the mean-reversion (target zone) type.

If we reject this sub-hypothesis we conclude that price limits cause gravitation behaviour. The underlying theory and its relevance for our setting will be discussed in the next section.

After developing the theoretical target zone model of price expectations, we apply it empirically to the agricultural futures contracts traded at the Chicago Board of Trade. Daily limits apply to all of these contracts and are allegedly effective in the sense that they alter trading behaviour. Our sample period, which extends from January to December 1988, was chosen because of the frequency of limit moves and hits[3] in the months of June and July 1988.

Absorbing limits: a target zone model

This chapter adapts a procedure recently developed in the exchange rate literature. We consider the existence of a non-linear relationship between fundamental (theoretical) futures prices and observed futures prices that are regulated by price limits. The main distinction with the target zone literature is the fact that futures price limits are valid for one day only. Except when the closing price is exactly the same as the opening price on a particular trading day, the next trading day will have a different target zone. Hence, the limits will not be 'credible' on an interday basis. Intraday, however, the limits are perfectly credible, so our focus is on intraday trading behaviour.

An important difference with the exchange rate target zones is that the observed futures price is regulated directly, whereas exchange rates are typically regulated indirectly by monetary authorities influencing the fundamentals (i.e. supply and demand of foreign exchange). Additionally, unlike the well-known intramarginal regulations prevailing in exchange rate target zones, futures price limit regulation only operates at the limits. The observed intraday futures price f_{t+j} is prevented from taking values outside the intraday price limits and should be treated as a censored variable,

$$
f_{t+j} = \begin{cases} \bar{f} & \text{if} \quad (f_{t+j-1} + u_{t+j}) \geq \bar{f} \\ (f_{t+j-1} + u_{t+j}) & \text{if} \quad \underline{f} < (f_{t+j-1} + u_{t+j}) < \bar{f} \\ \underline{f} & \text{if} \quad (f_{t+j-1} + u_{t+j}) \leq \underline{f} \end{cases} \tag{7.1}
$$

where $j = 1,...,N$ and $\bar{f}$, $\underline{f}$ are the upper and lower limits, respectively, on the N intraday futures prices for any particular day. The innovation u_{t+j} is the jth intraday innovation in the futures price $(f_{t+j} - f_{t+j-1})$, with f_t being the previous day's closing price (i.e. the 'target' futures price around which the limits are symmetrically specified). The u_{t+j} are conditionally distributed according to a unimodal distribution function $F(u)$ with mean zero and conditional variance $\sigma^2_{u,t+j}$.

Rose (1995) generalises this conditional distribution problem in the context of doubly censored distributions. In the case of credible reflecting barriers (what price limits are on an intraday basis), the probability of f_{t+j} exceeding the barriers will be folded inwards. Thus, $F(u)$ can hardly be expected to display normality. In fact, whereas it is likely to be unimodal, it will typically have excessive tail probability mass. Intuitively appealing estimation methods include the Tobit model by Yang and Brorsen (1995) and the limited dependent rational expectations approach advocated by Pesaran and Samiei (1992) and Pesaran and Ruge-Murcia (1996), which model time-varying volatility as an increasing function of the distance from the target price. This is the key notion that we exploit in this chapter, albeit with a different functional specification. In a commentary by Margulis (1991) on McMillan (1991):

'[the existence of trading halts] starts affecting trading decisions at some indeterminate level [well within the price limits] and it becomes stronger and stronger as the futures price approaches the limit price.'

If trading decisions are reflected in prices, we expect to observe a relationship between those prices and the distance from the boundaries on those prices, or, alternatively, the distance from the target price. According to the target zone literature (and following from equation 7.1 above), this relationship is non-linear because of the distortion in $F(.)$. Typically, the non-linear specifications following from the target zone models are estimated in continuous time, but it is notoriously difficult to capture particular empirical characteristics like fat-tailedness and time-varying volatility in those models and the assumption of normality is frequently violated. In discrete time, a simple analytical solution for this target zone problem has been suggested by Koedijk et al. (1998) that allows us to modify $F(u)$ in line with the empirical characteristics.

First, note from equation 7.1 that the conditional expectation of intraday futures price f_{t+j} is bounded,

$$E(f_{t+j} \mid f_{t+j-1}) = f_{t+j-1} + (\bar{f} - f_{t+j-1})\left[1 - F(\bar{f} - f_{t+j-1})\right] + \dots$$

$$+ (\underline{f} - f_{t+j-1})\left[F(\underline{f} - f_{t+j-1})\right] + \int_{\underline{f}-f_{t+j-1}}^{\bar{f}-f_{t+j-1}} (u_{t+j})f(u)du \qquad (7.2)$$

where $F(.)$, $f(.)$ are, respectively, the probability distribution and probability density function of the innovations u_{t+j}. Now, as we know that,

$$(\bar{f} - f_{t+j-1}) = \max\{u_{t+j}\}$$

$$(\underline{f} - f_{t+j-1}) = \min\{u_{t+j}\}$$

we find:

$$f_{t+j-1} = E[u_{t+j} \mid f_{t+j-1}] + \varepsilon_{t+j} \qquad (7.3)$$

where ε is orthogonal to the conditional expectation term. This is our regression equation, straightforwardly implied by theory. We know that for a credible target zone, $E[.]$ follows an S-shape in $(f_{t+j-1} - f_t)$ (see Koedijk et al., 1998). The first two derivatives will then satisfy:

$$\frac{\partial E[u_{t+j} \mid f_{t+j-1}]}{\partial(f_{t+j-1} - f_t)} = F(\bar{f} - f_{t+j-1}) - F(\underline{f} - f_{t+j-1}) > 0 \qquad (7.4a)$$

$$\frac{\partial^2 E[u_{t+j} \mid f_{t+j-1}]}{\partial(f_{t+j-1} - f_t)^2} = -f(\bar{f} - f_{t+j-1}) +$$

$$f(\underline{f} - f_{t+j-1}) \begin{cases} < 0 & \text{if} \quad f_{t+j-1} > f_t \\ > 0 & \text{if} \quad f_{t+j-1} < f_t \\ = 0 & \text{if} \quad f_{t+j-1} = f_t \end{cases} \qquad (7.4b)$$

and we can specify the following functional form which captures these necessary requirements for an S-shape. One approach suggested in the literature is to use a Laguerre function (as in Miller and Weller, 1991), or one can take a Taylor expansion around f_t (see Rose and Svensson, 1995; Koedijk et al., 1998), to obtain,

$$f_{t+j} - f_{t+j-1} = \delta_0 + \delta_1\left(f_{t+j-1} - f_t\right) +$$

$$\sum_{i=1}^{2} \delta_{2i}I(.)\left(f_{t+j-1} - f_t\right)^2 + \delta_3(f_t)^3 + e_{t+j} \qquad (7.5)$$

where the residual e_{t+j} consists of e_{t+j} and any omitted higher order Taylor expansion terms. The indicator variable $I(.)$ separates the positive from the negative deviations from the target futures price. The fact that the error term contains omitted higher order terms unfortunately implies that e_{t+j} is not necessarily orthogonal to the futures price change. This is a potential problem when estimating equation 7.5 that we will address below.

Having estimated equation 7.5, we can test our hypotheses. For a non-linear relationship, i.e. to establish whether the limits have an impact on the observed futures prices, we need to test whether any of the parameters δ_1, δ_{21}, δ_{22} or δ_3 is significantly different from zero. In the case of non-credible limits (a finding of insignificant parameter estimates), we expect the random walk model for futures prices to prevail. To interpret the parameters, we consider the following parameter signs that imply the theoretical S-shape. To establish a 'credible' (or mean-reverting) target zone, we need δ_1 to be negative, δ_{21} (for positive deviations from f_t) to be negative, and δ_{22} (for negative deviations from f_t) to be positive. These conditions follow directly from equations 7.4a and 7.4b. Additionally, we also expect a negative sign for parameter δ_3. Bleaney and Mizen (1996) model a target zone for exchange rates by specifying two models – a linear mean-reversion versus a cubic mean-reversion – both models being nested in equation 7.5 above, and conclude that the cubic model clearly outperforms the linear model. However, by ignoring the quadratic terms, they have a misspecified model and, by distorting the empirically desirable orthogonality of the error term in equation 7.5, this may have a pronounced effect on the outcome. We will illustrate this below in the empirical section. We do not restrict our regression model, but instead opt for a pragmatic approach. After estimating equation 7.5, we will investigate the function and conclude from its shape whether or not we can reject the mean-reversion hypothesis.

In general, the above-mentioned signs of parameters capture the mean(target)-reverting behaviour of the futures price, and any non-linearity involved in this behaviour. The third-order term in equation 7.5 is (inversely) related to the gravity variable in McMillan (1991), illustrating that the 'pull-towards-the-limits' increases at an increasing rate. A negative parameter for this variable indicates a gravitational effect; a positive parameter indicates a 'bouncing' (reflecting barrier) effect. Our parameter's interpretation is the other way around: negative implies bouncing or mean-reverting behaviour.

Next, we need to address the error term in equation 7.5. Because futures price changes are most often characterised by time-varying conditional variance and fat tails, we model the innovations according to these two characteristics. The apparent non-normality of futures price changes has been investigated by numerous authors. Typically, a fat-tailed alternative has been proposed with the evidence pointing towards the class of Student's t-distributions (see Kofman, 1994) or the stable class of distributions (see McCulloch, 1997). We allow for non-normal distributions by assuming that the innovations in equation 7.5 follow a fat-tailed distribution:

$$e_{t+j} \sim t_\nu(0, \mathrm{h}_{t+j}) \tag{7.6}$$

where e_t is assumed to follow a symmetric Student's t-distribution with mean zero, variance h and degrees of freedom ν ($\nu > 2$). The ν parameter measures the extent of fat-tailedness of the distribution because the smaller ν is then the larger the extremal probability mass. Unfortunately, the Student's t-distribution does not have the nice property of invariance under addition, so that a sum of independent (i.i.d.) t-distributed random variables with degrees of freedom ν will not necessarily be t-distributed with the same ν. In our case, this implies that after correcting for intraday anomalies intraday price changes may have different fat-tailedness from daily price changes. For the limiting case $\nu = \infty$, the Student's t-distribution converges to a normal distribution and will be sum stable. For the limiting case $\nu = 2$, the Student's t-distribution does not have a finite variance and in this case the symmetric sum stable class may be more appropriate. However, this turns out to be a problem. As $\nu = 2$ is the limit case, we cannot include the symmetric stable distribution in a straightforward likelihood ratio comparison. To resolve this issue, we adopt a two-step procedure that initially attempts to identify the class of appropriate distributions using Hill's (1975) tail test. If we cannot reject $\nu > 2$, we then proceed by assuming a Student's t-distribution.

Note that we cannot, a priori, reject the normal distribution based on observed excess kurtosis. It is possible that the fat tails are driven by time-varying conditional variance. In that case, the standardised price changes may well be normal. Given the extent of fat-tailedness, it seems unlikely that the normal will be appropriate in our setting. However, as noted in McCulloch (1996), any seasonality and/or temporal clustering of price changes can induce non-i.i.d. price changes that invalidate a proper likelihood comparison. Thus, we will allow the variance in equation 7.6 to have a time-varying specification,

$$h_{t+j} = \beta_0 + \beta_1 e^2_{t+j-1} + \beta_2 h_{t+j-1} \tag{7.7}$$

If the innovations are Student's t-distributed, i.e. we cannot reject $v > 2$, equation 7.7 reflects the well-known GARCH(1,1) variance specification. If we do reject $v > 2$, as the variance is no longer finite, we can respecify equation 7.7 as in McCulloch, in which case h is identified as the time-varying scale parameter.

Price limits in agricultural futures contracts

Having introduced our approach, we now proceed by applying our methodology to a set of agricultural futures contracts that are regulated by price limits. Our data set consists of six agricultural commodities traded at the Chicago Board of Trade for the time period January to December 1988. Contract descriptions and limit regulations for these contracts are given in Appendix 7.1. Our sample period is characterised by an unusual frequency of limit moves, in particular in the month of June. In total, in our sample period there were 147 limit move days (out of 200 in the time period January 1987 to May 1994) in the six contracts we consider. Our data set is based on the nearby futures contracts which rolls over two business days before the delivery month. This coincides with the date when the price limits are lifted. A five-minute sampling interval has been chosen based on a trade-off between minimising the number of no-trade intervals while using as much information as possible. To some extent, this choice alleviates the noise to signal problem endemic in using high-frequency data. If no price was recorded during this interval, the last previously recorded price was taken. From the futures prices f_t, we construct price changes (hereafter called returns) $R_{t+j} = f_{t+j} - f_{t+j-1}$. We omit the roll-over return and impute zero returns for empty intervals to obtain about 10,400 observations per contract for the time period 5 January to 1 December 1988 (note that three contracts terminate on 28 November 1988).

The descriptive statistics for the six contracts' five-minute returns are given in Table 7.1. The number of limit move days is given in the very last row. It is obvious that wheat forms an exception among these contracts because its limits have been hit on only five days compared with at least

Table 7.1 Descriptive statistics

This table reports a range of descriptive statistics for the returns (i.e. futures price changes) of six commodity futures contracts traded at the Chicago Board of Trade. The nearest delivery contract has been chosen and roll-over to the next-to-nearest occurs two trading days before the delivery month. The last line indicates the number of five-minute sampling intervals for 1988 for each of these contracts.

Statistics given in this table comprise the first four moments, and a set of tests for normality, serial correlation and heteroscedasticity. The Jarque–Bera test is a normality test based on skewness and excess kurtosis measures. Autocorrelation ρ gives the first-order autocorrelation coefficient estimate. The Ljung–Box test is a test for up to twelfth-order serial correlation in the returns. The Goldfeld–Quandt test is a test for heteroscedasticity in the returns. The ARCH test is a Lagrange multiplier test for conditional heteroscedasticity in the returns. Tail parameter α gives the range of tail parameter estimates for a choice of m-values, i.e. a choice of empirical tail length. Limit move days indicates the number of days on which the futures price closes at the limit (limit up or down) for each of the contracts individually.

	Corn	Oats	Wheat	Soybeans	Soybean meal	Soybean oil
Mean	0.00687	0.00157	0.01007	0.01308	0.00489	0.00009
Standard deviation	0.895	1.012	1.113	2.588	0.862	0.086
Skewness	1.666	1.454	2.169	0.339	-0.660	1.081
Excess kurtosis	90.36	184.61	72.18	86.98	109.72	70.66
Jarque–Bera test	Reject	Reject	Reject	Reject	Reject	Reject
Autocorrelation ρ	-0.028*	0.027*	-0.047*	-0.010	-0.026*	-0.026*
Ljung–Box (12) test	33.59*	11.85	20.18	34.70*	35.49*	36.89*
Goldfeld–Quandt test	2375.22*	2288.27*	918.25*	1480.96*	985.58*	1328.57*
ARCH test	21.60*	0.132	105.82*	10.56*	10.09*	15.16*
Tail parameter α	1.75–2.01	1.55–1.85	1.95–2.30	1.78–2.12	1.78–2.32	1.95–2.35
Limit move days	34	34	5	28	24	22
Number of observations	10,211	10,208	10,303	10,436	10,437	10,435

Note
Asterisk indicates a significant rejection of the test at the 5% level.

twenty-two limit moves for all other contracts. The information in this table is rather homogeneous across assets and can be easily summarised. There is clear evidence of skewness and excess kurtosis. Thus, it is no surprise that the Jarque–Bera normality tests are overwhelmingly rejected. Ljung–Box tests on serial correlation in the returns and the reported first-order serial correlation coefficient (ρ) reflect the impact of the bid–ask bounce, the discreteness of the data or the infrequent trading effect. The last seems to dominate in case of the oats contract, given the positive ρ-value as bid–ask bounce domination is typically indicated by negative values for this coefficient.

The ARCH and Goldfeld–Quandt (GQ) test on heteroscedasticity illustrate the time-varying conditionality in the variance of the returns. The ARCH test is based on an autoregression of the squared returns on lagged squared returns, whereas the GQ test is a split sample likelihood ratio test for changing variance. Except for oats, all ARCH tests indicate significant time-varying conditional heteroscedasticity. The GQ test indicates that even for oats we cannot reject heteroscedasticity, although not of the 'common' ARCH type. In the light of this fat-tailed and time-varying conditional variance evidence, we next calculate the tail parameter index to give us an idea of an appropriate distribution. This parameter can easily be calculated by first sorting the returns in descending order. The resulting order statistics $R_{(i)}$, with $R_{(1)}$ being the empirically observed maximum return, are then used in the following estimator:

$$\hat{\alpha} = \left(\frac{1}{m-1} \sum_{i=1}^{m-1} \ln\left(R_{(i)}\right) - \ln\left(R_{(m)}\right) \right)^{-1} \tag{7.8}$$

as in Hill (1975). Because this estimator will only give unbiased results if it is estimated for the true tails of the empirical distribution, we will have to determine how many ($= m$) tail observations to use in the estimation. This is a complex problem, which is elaborated upon in Kofman (1994), but for this chapter we choose the pragmatic approach of computing the parameter for a 'large' range of m-values and reporting the $\hat{\alpha}$-range. If $\hat{\alpha} < 2$, this points towards a stable distribution with characteristic exponent $\hat{\alpha}$ for the futures returns R_t. If $\hat{\alpha} > 2$, a Student's t-distribution with $\hat{\alpha}$ degrees of freedom is a more likely candidate. In general, we cannot reject α to be equal to 2. Hence, the evidence is somewhat inconclusive in deciding which class of distributions is most appropriate. As there is some evidence that $\hat{\alpha} < 2$ for some contracts, we do not prematurely exclude the stable class of distributions.

Table 7.2 Sample split statistics

This table reports a set of descriptive statistics for returns and tests for three subsamples. The subsample selection is based on the frequency of limit hits/moves. Limit hits/moves predominantly occur in the months of June and July 1988. Hence, we distinguish a prelimit, a limit, and a post-limit sample. These subsamples correspond with, respectively, the first, second and third columns for each commodity. The descriptive statistics are the second, third and fourth empirical moments, and the first-order serial correlation coefficient. The tests are unit root tests on the levels of futures prices (note: not on the returns). Two tests are given, the augmented Dickey-Fuller (ADF) test, with a lag length based on the AIC for each commodity, and the Phillips–Perron (PP) test, corrected for serial correlation in the disturbances of an OLS regression of the futures price on a constant and the futures price one period lagged.

	Corn			Oats			Wheat			Soybean			Soybean meal			Soybean oil		
	Pre	Limit	Post	Pre	Limit	Post	Pre	Limit	Post	Pre	Limit	Post	Pre	Limit	Post	Pre	Limit	Post
Standard deviation	0.351	1.339	0.543	0.430	1.487	0.697	0.598	1.597	0.756	1.177	3.802	1.758	0.364	1.256	0.634	0.048	0.124	0.059
Skewness	7.096	1.171	−0.171	−6.004	1.305	0.181	1.387	1.876	−0.218	1.848	0.277	−0.829	0.846	−0.620	0.035	0.084	0.936	0.368
Excess kurtosis	161.5	45.3	4.4	206.5	102.4	9.2	26.8	43.2	8.1	42.6	48.3	11.4	16.7	63.6	11.1	28.7	42.5	16.5
ρ	−0.07*	−0.02	−0.09*	0.04*	0.02	0.02	−0.04*	−0.05*	−0.06*	−0.09*	0.01	−0.08*	−0.04*	−0.02	−0.07*	−0.04*	−0.02	−0.08*
ADF	−3.14	−0.67	−1.78	−2.60	−0.73	−1.81	−2.91	−2.15	−2.50	−2.15	−1.07	−2.29	−3.09	−1.16	−2.40	−1.64	−1.24	−2.92
PP	−18.6	−1.79	−6.67	−12.59	−1.81	−7.47	−13.95	−10.80	−9.83	−9.56	−2.77	−9.79	−13.57	−2.89	−12.11	−6.32	−4.00	−17.51

Note
An asterisk indicates a significant rejection of the null hypothesis at the 5% level.

Our next step involves an intertemporal analysis of the descriptive statistics. Because the frequency of limit hits and moves is rather clustered in the middle of 1988, we are interested in the stability over time of certain key descriptive statistics. These statistics allegedly illustrate the harmful aspects of price limits. Table 7.2 is based on a three-fold sample split with reasonably comparable sample sizes: 'prelimit' from January to April with 3,690 observations; 'limit' from May to August with 3,870 observations; and 'post-limit' from September to December with 2,880 observations.[4] The columns are sequentially ordered so that the first entry is prelimit, the second entry is limit, and the third entry is post-limit. The limit period coincides with the months for which we observe the highest frequency of limit hits/moves during 1988. Only for oats and soybean meal do we observe a few limit hits/moves in the post-limit period. A number of conclusions can be drawn from the reported measures.

First, for all contracts, the standard deviation unambiguously increases around the limit moves. However, this does not necessarily imply causality. Increases in the 'fundamental' (cash price) volatility could also lead to a higher frequency of limit hits (and/or moves). Secondly, skewness becomes more relevant during the limit period. Typically, prices are drifting strongly in a particular (upwards) direction with returns becoming positively skewed. Third, excess kurtosis (although being excessive for all periods) seems more so during the limit period. The occurrence of sudden large price changes obviously coincides with limit hits. However, this is not one-to-one related to interday realignments. If the futures price closes at the limit for a number of days in succession, we will observe large overnight price changes. Hence, we tentatively conclude that, even within the limits, price movements become relatively larger and more erratic. This conclusion aligns with the gravitation theory of price limits.

We observe that the first-order autocorrelation coefficient is significantly negative for the prelimit and post-limit periods. For the limit period, it is either insignificantly different from zero or significantly positive. Whereas bid–ask spreads are known to increase with increasing variance (see our first observation from Table 7.2), this finding is likely to illustrate the more than offsetting infrequency of trading during the limit period. These findings merely reinforce the need to model high-frequency data by carefully adjusting for microstructural 'noise' such as bid–ask bounce and thin trading either by specifying an AR(1) or an MA(1) model, see Miller *et al.* (1994). Finally, we report two unit root tests, the augmented Dickey–Fuller (ADF) test and the Phillips–Perron (PP) test, performed on the price series in levels. The latter test adjusts

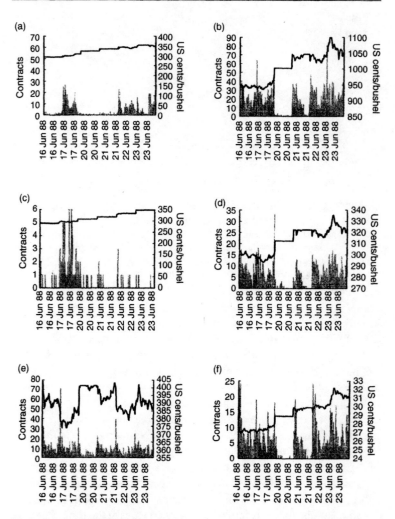

Figure 7.1 June 1988 agricultural futures prices and number of transactions. These figures display the futures prices (solid line, right y-axis) for each commodity's nearest-delivery contract during two weeks in the month of June 1988 at five-minute sampling intervals. The frequency of limit moves and hits during this period was particularly high. Also shown (bar chart left y-axis) is the number of transactions for each five-minute sampling period. (a) Corn; (b) soybeans; (c) oats; (d) soybean meal; (e) wheat; (f) soybean oil.

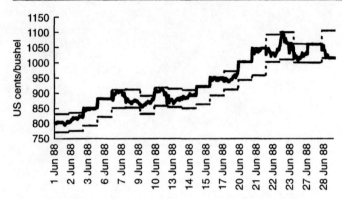

Figure 7.2 Soybean futures – price limits in action. This figure shows the futures price for soybean futures (nearest delivery is the July contract) for the trading month of June 1988 sampled at five-minute intervals. The horizontal line sections display the upper and lower price limits for each trading day based on the previous day's settlement price plus or minus, respectively, $0.30 (or $0.45 whenever the limits are stretched after two successive limit move days).

for serial correlation and heteroscedasticity in the residuals. Both tests indicate that we cannot reject that prices follow an $I(1)$ process. Interestingly, this is most evident in the limit period. Hence, in the long run, prices behave like random walks. On an intraday basis, however, it is still possible for prices to display mean-reverting behaviour.

We also provide some visual evidence of futures price behaviour around limit moves. Figures 7.1 and 7.2 illustrate price behaviour for the month of June 1988. Figure 7.1 is based on six trading days in the third and fourth weeks of June. The solid lines give the price movements for the six considered futures contracts, the bars give the volume in number of transactions per minute. All contracts, except for wheat, have a positive drift during this episode, with a number of successive limit-up moves. Usually, volume drops to zero when the price stays at the limit. The oats chart in particular shows the infrequency of trading during successive limit-up days, and the other contracts occasionally have zero volume, usually coinciding with a limit-up move. There does not seem to be a clear surge in volume immediately before or after a limit hit.

Figure 7.2 focuses on soybean futures for the twenty trading days in June 1988. The solid line gives five-minute transaction prices, the dotted lines give the prevailing intraday limits. Limits have been expanded for four days (21, 22, 23 and 28 June) after successive limit closes. The interesting phenomenon in this figure is the possibility of a 'rebounce' in

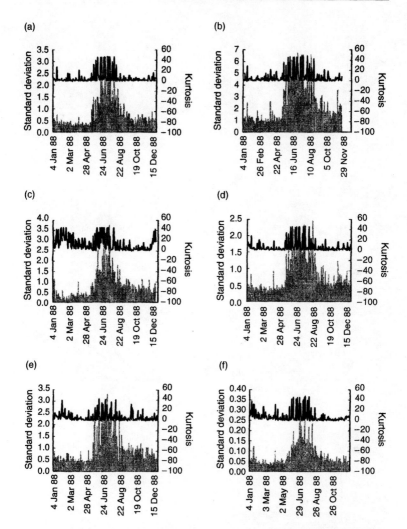

Figure 7.3 Volatility and jumps in futures prices. These figures display volatility (grey bar chart, left y-axis) and excess kurtosis measurements (black bar chart, right y-axis) for each commodity's full sample period (the 1988 trading year) at daily measurement intervals. Volatility (measured by standard deviation of prices) is computed over all prices at five-minute intervals. A similar procedure is used to compute the excess kurtosis measure. (a) Corn; (b) soybeans; (c) oats; (d) soybean meal; (e) wheat; (f) soybean oil.

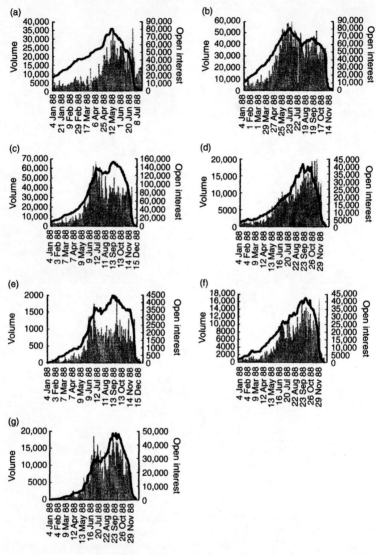

Figure 7.4 Liquidity measures. Shown are two measures of liquidity for each commodity's full sample period (1988 trading year) at daily measurement intervals. Volume (bar chart, left *y*-axis) measures the number of contracts traded per day. Open interest (solid line, right *y*-axis) is the measurement of outstanding open interest per day. (**a**) Corn (July); (**b**) soybeans; (**c**) corn (December); (**d**) soybean meal; (**e**) oats; (**f**) soybean oil; (**g**) wheat.

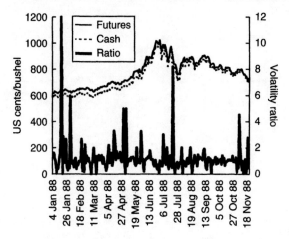

Figure 7.5 Soybean futures basis behaviour and volatility ratio. The futures settlement prices (solid line, left y-axis) and daily spot prices (dashed line, left y-axis) for soybeans' full sample of trading days are shown. The distance between these two lines measures the basis. Also displayed is the ratio of standard deviations of futures price changes divided by daily standard deviations of spot price changes (thick line, right y-axis). The price changes used in computing daily standard deviations are measured at five-minute intervals.

prices when limits are hit early on in the trading day (3, 7, 16, 21 and 23 June). Hence, prices are not always 'locked-in' after a limit has been hit, even if we consider that the underlying prices were drifting strongly upwards during this period. Furthermore, referring to Figure 7.1, trade still occurs (although to a limited extent) even if the price stays at the limit (as, for example, on 20 June).

Further evidence on price volatility, erratic price realignments and market liquidity surrounding limit hits/moves is provided in Figures 7.3, 7.4 and 7.5.

Figure 7.3 compares price volatility, as measured by the five-minute standard deviation (bars), and price jumps, as reflected by the five-minute excess kurtosis (solid line) measure, across contracts. Both measures drop to zero whenever there are no transactions in a five-minute interval. The 'boost' in volatility during the June/July limit month is apparent for all contracts. However, without further information regarding the 'underlying' cash price volatility, we cannot simply conclude that price limits increase volatility because the causality could just as well be the

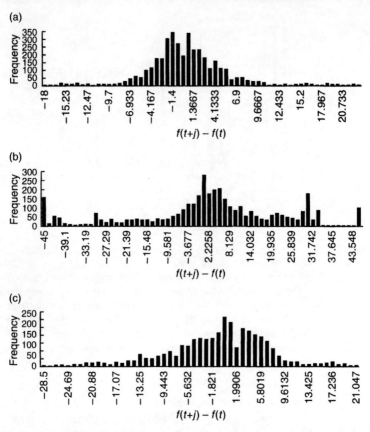

Figure 7.6 Folded distributions for soybean futures price deviations from the target price are shown by histograms of deviations of futures prices from their daily target price, i.e. the previous day's settlement price. Each panel is based on a subsample: (**a**) prelimit, January–April; (**b**) limit, May–August; (**c**) post-limit, September–December.

other way around. The excess kurtosis measure is to some extent more informative. It seems that there are many more peaks in this measure than can possibly be explained by underlying value realignments. We tentatively conclude that limits do lead to large erratic jumps in prices.

In Figure 7.4, the daily volume and open interest charts are shown. Interestingly, in terms of liquidity, the longer maturity dominates the nearest maturity for most of the contracts during the June limit month. This is perhaps best illustrated by comparing the July with the December corn charts. Evidently, this has nothing to do with evasive trading behaviour because limits on the longer maturity contracts were invoked at exactly the same time as on the nearby maturity. One reason may be that given the persistent upward drift in prices with frequently recurring limit moves, it may be wiser to set up arbitrage positions in longer maturities.

Figure 7.5, finally, gives a representative daily basis behaviour graph for the November delivery soybeans contract. The difference between the futures and cash prices actually narrows during the limit move days in June, perhaps reflecting overreaction of the futures price to changes in the cash price. The ratio of futures over cash price changes (in absolute terms) is given by the solid line. This is a measure of relative volatility that is more informative than the standard deviation plots given in Figure 7.3. Overall, the ratio is greater than one most of the time, reflecting a somewhat more volatile behaviour for futures prices than its underlying cash prices, which is a well-known phenomenon. There is some evidence of an increase in the ratio at the end of June and in early July, but this is not very conclusive, and we are led to conclude that the increased standard deviation of futures returns (implied by increased cash volatility) has driven limit moves rather than the other way around.

To investigate how truncation by price limits affects the distribution of deviations from the target (midpoint of the band), we also plot the intraday frequency histograms for prelimit, limit and post-limit for soybeans (Figure 7.6).

It is evident that the limits act as a 'mirror', i.e. the missing probability at the tails is redistributed proportionally inside the band.

Having discussed the empirical characteristics of the data, we proceed with estimating our target zone model. For that purpose, we slightly modify equation 7.5:

$$f_{t+j} - f_{t+j-1} = \delta_0 + \delta_1 \left(f_{t+j-1} - f_t \right) +$$

$$\sum_{i=1}^{2} \delta_{2i} I(.) \left(f_{t+j-1} - f_t \right)^2 + \delta_3 \left(f_{t+j-1} - f_t \right)^3 \qquad (7.5a)$$

$$+ \delta_4 \left(f_{t+j-1} - f_{t+j-2} \right) + e_{t+j}$$

by including a lagged dependent variable. This autoregressive term captures the bid–ask bounce and discreteness effects typically characterising high-frequency intraday prices, see Harris (1990) and Miller *et al.* (1994). For a dominating bid–ask effect, we expect δ_4 to be negative. Now, we can allow for a time-varying specification of variance and/or non-normal standardised residuals in equation 7.5a. The maximum likelihood estimates are given in Tables 7.3 and 7.4. Table 7.3 reports the log likelihoods obtained for the normal and Student's t-distribution models.[5] We perform a likelihood ratio test to determine which model is best.

We once again distinguish the three different time periods: prelimit, limit and post-limit. We conclude that the Student's t-distribution is most appropriate (far outperforming the normal distribution) in all cases.

Allowing for time-varying conditional variance results in improved performance for the normal distribution. However, Student's t-cum-GARCH is generally outperformed by the 'unconditional' Student's t-distribution with one exception (oats). Apparently, time-varying conditionality in variance does not capture the detected fat-tailedness in the futures returns very well in contrast with Yang and Brorsen's (1995) results. GARCH models are quite often found to be inappropriate for high-frequency data (see, for example, Guillaume *et al.*, 1995; Ghose and Kroner, 1997; Goodhart and O'Hara, 1997).

The parameter estimates reported in Table 7.4 correspond to the preferred model based on the reported likelihood ratio tests in Table 7.3. However, the parameter estimates of interest ($\delta_0 - \delta_4$) are rather similar for all four models. Except for soybeans (prelimit and limit) and soybean meal (limit), the constant δ_0 is insignificantly different from zero. The first-order term δ_1 is also frequently insignificantly different from zero. Whereas it is nearly significant for corn (limit), it does not have the negative sign required for mean reversion. The second- and third-order terms δ_{21}, δ_{22} and δ_3 are more often significant (or close to significance), particularly in the prelimit and post-limit periods. The cubic term typically has a mean-reverting sign (negative) in the prelimit and post-limit periods, and a gravitation sign in the limit period. The evidence supporting either hypothesis is mixed for the quadratic terms. Our non-linear model apparently performs best (in terms of significance) for corn and wheat. The somewhat disappointing performance of the other contracts is possibly attributed to a high degree of multicollinearity in the regressors.

In terms of fat-tailedness, we observe from Table 7.4 that, prelimit and post-limit, a Student's t-distribution with about three degrees of freedom fits the data best, whereas during limit the degrees of freedom fall towards the limit value of just a little over 2. Perhaps, paradoxically, in times when the limits are actively enforced, the stochastic process of futures price changes becomes much more fat tailed. What actually happens is that very small price changes become dominant with

Table 7.3 Target zone log likelihoods

This table reports the maximised log likelihoods for different distributional assumptions on the error term e_{t+j} in the following equation:

$$f_{t+j} - f_{t+j-1} = \delta_0 + \delta_1\left(f_{t+j-1} - f_t\right) + \sum_{i=1}^{2} \delta_{2i}I(.)\left(f_{t+j-1} - f_t\right)^2 + \delta_3\left(f_{t+j-1} - f_t\right)^3$$
$$+\delta_4\left(f_{t+j-1} - f_{t+j-2}\right) + e_{t+j}$$

It includes the unconditional normal distribution, the unconditional Student's *t*-distribution and conditional versions of both models. The conditionality we consider is heteroscedasticity of the GARCH type in the error term.

Models	Corn	Oats	Wheat	Soybeans	Soybean Meal	Oil
Normal						
Prelimit	−1,337	−2,111	−3,333	−5,819	−1,501	5,985
Limit	−6,614	−6,929	−7,298	−10,652	−6,368	2,589
Post-limit	−2,162	−2,850	−3,116	−5,694	−2,762	4,073
Normal-cum-GARCH						
Prelimit	−949	−2,047	−3,002	−5,203	−1,270	6,302
Limit	−6,519	−6,928	−6,445	−10,562	−6,274	3,170
Post-limit	−2,031	−2,728	−2,919	−5,429	−2,569	4,172
Student's *t*-distribution						
Prelimit	<u>1,621</u>	<u>1,534</u>	<u>−575</u>	<u>−2,842</u>	<u>1,053</u>	<u>8,890</u>
Limit	<u>−2,119</u>	−1,093	<u>−3,505</u>	<u>−6,310</u>	<u>−2,019</u>	<u>6,649</u>
Post-limit	<u>−408</u>	−802	<u>−1,247</u>	−3,655	<u>−754</u>	<u>6,157</u>
Student's *t*-distribution-cum-GARCH						
Prelimit	NC	NC	−578	−2,842	NC	NC
Limit	−2,126	<u>−951</u>	−3,505	−6,312	−2,020	NC
Post-limit	−406	<u>−796</u>	−1,246	−3,653	−755	NC

Note
We estimated the model per subsample. NC, the model did not converge. Underlined entries indicate the 'best' model based on a likelihood ratio test with the appropriate degrees of freedom (i.e. imposed number of restrictions).

occasional large (erratic) price moves. This confirms the empirical results in the exchange rate target zone literature.

Concluding our parameter estimates discussion, we find that there are signs of non-linearity in futures prices potentially driven by the existence of price limits. The size of the higher-order coefficients indicates that even far from the limits there is a discernible impact, in particular in

Table 7.4 Target zone estimates

This table reports the parameter estimates for the preferred model (based on the maximised log likelihoods for different distributional assumptions on the error term, in Table 7.3):

$$f_{t+j} - f_{t+j-1} = \delta_0 + \delta_1(f_{t+j-1} - f_t) + \sum_{i=1}^{2} \delta_{2i} I(\cdot)(f_{t+j-1} - f_t)^2 + \delta_3(f_{t+j-1} - f_t)^3 + \delta_4(f_{t+j-1} - f_{t+j-2}) + e_{t+j}$$

	Corn[a]	Oats[b]	Wheat[a]	Soybeans[a]	Soybean meal[a]	Soybean oil[a]
Prelimit						
δ_0	-0.003003	-0.002375	-0.010257	0.029811	0.004445	0.000484
	(-0.552)	(-0.665)	(-1.138)	(2.042)	(0.809)	(0.720)
δ_1	0.007121	-0.005947	0.018064	-0.014574	-0.006306	0.007675
	(0.418)	(-0.853)	(1.696)	(-1.447)	(-0.525)	(0.610)
δ_{21}	0.002819	-0.003506	0.010111	-0.003043	-0.004552	0.004441
	(0.176)	(-0.827)	(2.366)	(-1.492)	(-0.649)	(0.066)
δ_{22}	0.007859	0.006417	-0.006057	0.004075	0.005293	0.017246
	(0.458)	(1.485)	(-1.302)	(1.852)	(0.693)	(0.239)
δ_3	-0.004182	-0.001220	0.000406	-0.000175	-0.000716	-0.042534
	(-1.109)	(-2.140)	(1.139)	(-2.188)	(-0.770)	(-0.485)
δ_4	-0.127810	-0.010497	-0.071805	-0.113397	-0.084873	-0.062425
	(-7.951)	(-1.108)	(-4.748)	(-7.520)	(-5.272)	(-4.377)
v^*	3.91210	2.00146	2.86743	2.79616	3.36552	2.73104
	(7.155)	(2.246)	(5.501)	(5.470)	(6.703)	(5.118)
Limit						
δ_0	0.010739	0.006483	0.009501	0.139031	0.033276	0.001428
	(1.056)	(1.166)	(0.658)	(4.247)	(3.110)	(1.345)
δ_1	0.017771	0.000606	0.000304	-0.010499	-0.002773	0.005221
	(1.859)	(0.239)	(0.044)	(-1.080)	(-0.308)	(0.574)

	(1)	(2)	(3)	(4)	(5)	(6)
δ_{21}	0.003269 (1.827)	0.000065 (0.224)	0.000113 (0.135)	-0.000628 (-1.030)	-0.000233 (-0.129)	0.008424 (0.476)
δ_{22}	-0.003340 (-1.871)	-0.000140 (-0.452)	0.000058 (0.070)	0.000446 (0.743)	-0.000145 (-0.084)	-0.009411 (-0.539)
δ_{3}	0.000142 (1.779)	0.000004 (0.400)	0.000001 (0.200)	-0.000007 (-0.700)	0.000007 (0.088)	0.003575 (0.445)
δ_{4}	-0.008326 (-1.309)	0.000894 (0.397)	-0.028015 (-1.733)	-0.005905 (-0.897)	-0.002011 (-0.322)	-0.01743 (-1.995)
v^{*}	2.00171 (1.314)	2.00502 (2.728)	2.00153 (1.254)	2.00314 (2.553)	2.00252 (2.049)	2.00118 (1.943)
Post-limit						
δ_{0}	-0.003082 (-0.291)	-0.007682 (-0.795)	-0.001201 (-0.083)	0.022440 (0.760)	0.005359 (0.492)	-0.000928 (-1.021)
δ_{1}	-0.013946 (-0.818)	0.009600 (0.759)	-0.022652 (-1.256)	-0.014564 (0.873)	0.003224 (0.219)	-0.013765 (-0.852)
δ_{21}	-0.013872 (-1.736)	0.004733 (1.007)	-0.010572 (-1.668)	-0.003459 (-1.231)	-0.001554 (0.263)	-0.059533 (-0.679)
δ_{22}	0.014094 (1.590)	-0.004326 (-0.945)	0.013463 (1.968)	0.002840 (1.048)	-0.001319 (-0.226)	0.035877 (0.435)
δ_{3}	-0.002294 (-2.520)	0.000362 (0.978)	-0.001383 (-2.426)	-0.000154 (-1.540)	-0.000322 (-0.619)	-0.060206 (-0.582)
δ_{4}	-0.111858 (-6.374)	-0.011659 (-1.000)	-0.083156 (-4.953)	-0.108338 (-6.659)	-0.096579 (-5.363)	-0.058224 (-3.748)
v^{*}	3.69782 (6.081)	2.04374 (3.311)	3.16454 (5.384)	3.28203 (5.970)	3.15648 (5.418)	2.38543 (2.536)

Note
The t-statistics are given in parentheses.
a Student's t-density.
b Student's t-density in the prelimit subsample, and Student's t-density with GARCH distributed errors in the limit and post-limit subsamples.
* The t-statistics are based on $H_{:} v = 2$.

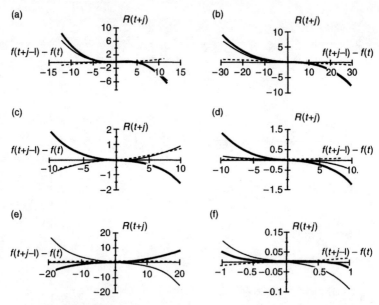

Figure 7.7 S-shapes in agricultural futures returns are shown in the fitted target zone models, based on the parameter estimates in Table 7.4. The dependent variable on the y-axis is the futures price change. The explanatory variable on the x-axis is the previous period's deviation from the target price. The thick continuous line indicates the fitted model for the prelimit sample; the dashed line indicates the fitted model for the limit sample; and the thin continuous line indicates the fitted line for the post-limit sample. **(a)** Corn; **(b)** soybeans; **(c)** oats; **(d)** soybean meal; **(e)** wheat; **(f)** soybean oil.

the prelimit and post-limit samples. However, the sometimes conflicting signs of the quadratic and cubic terms make it difficult to draw straightforward conclusions. Although the main hypothesis has been supported by our estimates, it is difficult to decide on the subhypothesis. For this purpose, we consider Figure 7.7 where the fitted model of equation 7.5 for the different futures contracts is plotted according to our target zone estimates.[6] To facilitate comparison, we plot the graphs based on the same model for each asset, i.e. the Student's t-distribution. If the target zone mean-reverting model is the true model, we expect a (increasing) negative deviation from the target futures price to generate a (increasing) positive futures return. If the gravitation model is the true model, we expect a (increasing) negative deviation from the target futures price to generate a (increasing) negative futures return. Analogous

(a)

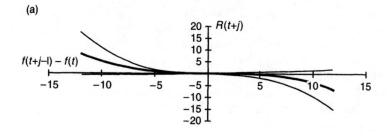

(b)

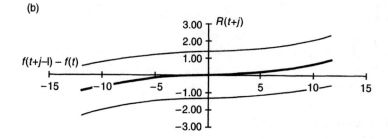

(c)

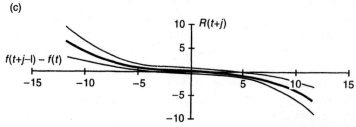

Figure 7.8 Confidence limits for corn. This is the same information as shown in Figure 7.7, but the information is split into the three subsamples to include the 95% confidence bands (thin lines surrounding the fitted model). (**a**) Prelimit sample; (**b**) limit sample; (**c**) post-limit sample.

conclusions can be drawn for positive deviations from the target futures price.

Looking at the graphs there is a clear difference among the three samples. The prelimit graphs display mean-reverting behaviour except for wheat. The post-limit graphs also reflect mean-reverting behaviour, mostly for corn, wheat and soybeans but not for oats. The limit graphs, on the other hand, are much less 'impressive' in non-linear terms. There is either no reaction (for wheat) or weak evidence of gravitation (for oats, corn and soybean oil). The cases in which we cannot reject 'no reaction' correspond to the random walk model. Formal model selection tests indicate that the random walk with drift model is regularly preferred. A clear exception, however, is given by corn, for which we do find evidence of non-linearity. To show this, Figure 7.8 repeats the fitted models for corn and includes the 95% confidence intervals.

Thus, when the fundamental cash price is strongly drifting upwards or downwards, so that it seems that limit hits (and moves) are imminent, the futures price process behaves like a random walk with drift. For 'normal' periods, price limits seem to have a mean-reverting impact on prices. As suggested in the introduction, we might be tempted to conclude that price limits are not the preferred regulatory tool in case of fundamental market realignments. In case of overreacting markets (when there is little evidence of fundamental realignments), limits do seem to have a moderating impact on price changes.

Concluding remarks

Price limit regulation is a hotly debated issue provoked by the occasional major realignment in prices. Despite their limited occurrence, antagonists argue that their very existence may deter prospective traders from entering futures trading. Protagonists, on the other hand, argue that the occasional mayhem and chaos sufficiently underline the need for even tighter price limits.

This chapter has made an attempt to identify the impact of price limits on traders' expectations, and hence the price discovery process. The current literature can be divided between those that argue in favour of the gravitation of prices towards the limits versus those that claim mean-reverting behaviour of prices bouncing back from the limits. We specify a target zone model for intraday futures prices that allows us to discriminate between these two competing hypotheses. By applying the model to a set of agricultural futures contracts, we illustrate that even without actual limit hits (or moves) for a prolonged period of time, there is a clear impact of the boundedness of prices. However, this impact is shown to be quite different from the impact of price limits during a period of frequent limit moves. Whereas we find evidence of gravitation during limit move periods, we discover mean-reversion during quiet periods.

We tentatively conclude that price limits are not the preferred tool in case of major market realignments. For regular market behaviour, they do, however, seem to have a modifying impact on volatility. Hence, a combination of price limits and (short-term) circuit breakers may well be an optimal solution.

Acknowledgements

The authors would like to thank the Chicago Board of Trade (and in particular Patrick Catania and Peter Alonzi) for insightful information on price limit behaviour at the Chicago Board of Trade and for the opportunity to present this chapter at the Eighth Annual Futures Research Symposium in Hong Kong. We are grateful to Joe Sweeney for continuous support and encouragement. Comments and suggestions by Bill Fung and Avanidhar Subrahmanyam have considerably improved this chapter. The authors acknowledge support from the ARC large grants scheme.

Endnotes

1 As an example, Jorion (1995) mentions that the US repo market is a creature of Federal Reserve Regulation Q. A market with daily turnover in excess of $500 billion has been created as investors switched out of bank deposits as a result of Q.
2 Note that the mean reversion hypothesis is not synonymous to its statistical counterpart. In this chapter, mean reversion implies price movements towards the target price, i.e. the centre between upper and lower price limits.
3 We distinguish between limit *moves* for futures prices closing at the limit, and limit *hits* for futures prices hitting the limits intraday but not necessarily closing at the limit.
4 Note that the exact number of observations differs slightly per commodity (for some contracts, we have more trading days than for others; see also Table 7.1, number of observations). The exact subsample sizes are given in Appendix 7.1 (contract specifications).
5 We also estimated the stable models, but these were invariantly dominated by the Student's t-distribution models.
6 We also compute confidence intervals for each of those fitted curves. The fitted curves-cum-confidence intervals are given here for corn only in Figure 7.8.

References

Bleaney, M. and Mizen, P. (1996) 'Non-linearities in exchange-rate dynamics: evidence from five currencies, 1973–94', *Economic Record* 72: 36–45.

Ghose, D. and Kroner, K.F. (1997) 'Components of volatility in foreign exchange rates: an empirical analysis of high frequency data', Mimeograph, Tucson, AZ: University of Arizona.

Goodhart, C.A.E. and O'Hara, M. (1997) 'High frequency data in financial markets: issues and applications', *Journal of Empirical Finance* 4: 73–114.

Greenwald, B.C. and Stein, J.C. (1991) 'Transactional risk, market crashes, and the role of circuit breakers', *Journal of Business* 64: 443–62.

Guillaume, D.M., Pictet, O.V. and Dacorogna, M.M. (1995) 'On the intra-daily performance of GARCH processes', Mimeograph, Zurich: Olsen and Associates.

Harris, L. (1990) 'Estimation of stock price variances and serial covariances from discrete observations', *Journal of Financial and Quantitative Analysis* 25: 291–306.

Hill, B.M. (1975) 'A simple general approach to inference about the tail of a distribution', *Annals of Statistics* 3: 1163–73.

Jorion, P. (1995) *Big Bets Gone Bad: Derivatives and Bankruptcy in Orange County*, San Diego: Academic Press.

Kodres, L.E. (1988) 'Tests of unbiasedness in foreign exchange futures markets: the effects of price limits', *Review of Futures Markets* 7: 138–66.

Kodres, L.E. (1993) 'Tests of unbiasedness in the foreign exchange futures markets: an examination of price limits and conditional heteroskedasticity', *Journal of Business* 66: 463–90.

Kodres, L.E. and O'Brien, D.P. (1994) 'The existence of Pareto-superior price limits', *American Economic Review* 84: 919–32.

Koedijk, K.G., Stork, P.A. and de Vries, C.G. (1998) 'An EMS target zone model in discrete time', *Journal of Applied Econometrics* 13: 31–48.

Kofman, P. (1994) 'Optimizing futures margins with distribution tails', *Advances in Futures and Options Research* 6: 263–78.

Krugman, P.R. (1991) 'Target zones and exchange rate dynamics', *Quarterly Journal of Economics* 106: 669–82.

Kuserk, G.J. and Locke, P.R. (1996) 'Market making with price limits', *Journal of Futures Markets* 16: 677–96.

Lee, C.M.C., Ready, M.J. and Seguin, P.J. (1994) 'Volume, volatility, and New York stock exchange trading halts', *Journal of Finance* 49: 183–214.

Ma, C.K., Rao, R.P. and Sears, R.S. (1989) 'Limit moves and price resolution: the case of the Treasury bond futures', *Journal of Futures Markets* 9: 321–35.

McCulloch, J.H. (1996) 'Real stock returns: non-normality, seasonality, and volatility persistence, but no predictability', Economics Department working paper no. 96-32, Columbus, OH: Ohio State University.

McCulloch, J.H. (1997) 'Measuring tail thickness in order to estimate the stable index α: a critique', *Journal of Business and Economic Statistics* 15: 74–81.

McMillan, H. (1991) 'Circuit breakers in the S&P 500 Futures Market: their effect on volatility and price discovery in October 1989', *Review of Futures Markets* 10: 248–74.

Margulis, Jr., A.S. (1991) 'Commentary: circuit breakers in the S&P 500 Futures Market: their effect on volatility and price discovery in October 1989 (by H. McMillan)', *Review of Futures Markets* 10: 279–81.

Miller, M. and Weller, P. (1991) 'Currency bands, target zones, and price flexibility', *International Monetary Fund Staff Papers* 38: 184–215.

Miller, M.H., Muthuswamy, J. and Whaley, R.E. (1994) 'Mean reversion in the S&P 500 Index basis: arbitrage-induced or statistical illusion', *Journal of Finance* 49: 479–513.

Pesaran, M.H. and Ruge-Murcia, F.J. (1996) 'Limited-dependent rational expectations models with stochastic thresholds', *Economics Letters* 51: 267–76.

Pesaran, M.H. and Samiei, H. (1992) 'An analysis of the determination of the DM/FF exchange rate in a discrete time target zone model', *Economic Journal* 102: 388–401.

Presidential Task Force on Market Mechanisms (1988) 'Report of the Presidential task force on market mechanisms', in Kamphuis, R.W., Kormendi, R.C. and Watson, J.W.H (eds) *Black Monday and the Future of Financial Markets*, Homewood, IL: Irwin.

Roll, R. (1984) 'Orange juice and weather', *American Economic Review* 74: 861–80.

Rose, A.K. and Svensson, L.E.O. (1995) 'Expected and predicted realignments: the FF/DM exchange rate during the EMS, 1979–93', *Scandinavian Journal of Economics* 97: 173–200.

Rose, C. (1995) 'A statistical identity linking folded and censored distributions', *Journal of Economic Dynamics and Control* 19: 1391–403.

Strongin, S. (1995) 'Commentary: on rules versus discretion in the design of impediments to trade (by A. Subrahmanyam)', in *Proceedings of the Research Symposium of the Chicago Board Of Trade*, Spring, pp. 201–5.

Subrahmanyam, A. (1994) 'Circuit breakers and market volatility: a theoretical perspective', *Journal of Finance* 49: 237–54.

Subrahmanyam, A. (1995) 'On rules versus discretion in procedures to halt trade', *Journal of Economics and Business* 47: 1–16.

Yang, S.-R. and Brorsen, B.W. (1995) 'Price limits as an explanation of thin-tailedness in pork bellies futures prices', *Journal of Futures Markets* 15: 45–59.

Appendix 7.1 Contract specifications

The data used in this study cover the time period January to December 1988. The intraday data (all frequencies) are derived from the Tick Data Inc. time and sales tapes. The details of the agricultural futures contracts traded at the Chicago Board Of Trade are given below.

According to Regulation 1008.01 Trading Limits, the following rules were active for our sample period:

> Price limits were symmetric above/below the previous business day's settlement price. Limits were lifted two business days before the cash month (= delivery month). For the first half of our sample period

(until 23 June 1988), limits were expanded by 150% of the current level if, for two successive business days, the market closed at the limit for three or more simultaneously traded maturities for a contract year. If there were less than three maturities remaining, this rule was changed to all traded maturities. For the second half of our sample period (as of 24 June 1988), the sequential limit days requirement was reduced to a single business day. Expanded limits remain in action for three successive business days. Limits remain at 150% for successive three-day periods unless at the end of such a period three or more maturities did not close at the limit. The limit expansion operated concurrently on the soybean complex futures. Limits reverted to 100% only if all futures in this complex met the conditions for reversal.

Futures contract	Contract size	Delivery (months)	Minimum tick size[a]	Initial limit[a]	Expandable limit[a]	Sample period	N[b]
Corn	5,000 bushels	Mar, May, Jul, Sep, Dec	0.25 cents/bushel	12 cents/bushel	18 cents/bushel	5 Jan–29 Apr 2 May–31 Aug 1 Sep–28 Nov	3644 3868 2879
Oats	5,000 bushels	Mar, May, Jul, Sep, Dec	0.25 cents/bushel	10 cents/bushel	15 cents/bushel	5 Jan–29 Apr 2 May–31 Aug 1 Sep–28 Nov	3688 3821 2699
Soybeans	5,000 bushels	Jan, Mar, May, Jul, Aug, Sep, Nov	0.25 cents/bushel	30 cents/bushel	45 cents/bushel	5 Jan–29 Apr 2 May–31 Aug 1 Sep–1 Dec	3689 3868 2879
Soybean meal	100 tons	Jan, Mar, May, Jul, Aug, Sep, Nov	10 cents/ton	$10/ton	$15/ton	5 Jan–29 Apr 2 May–31 Aug 1 Sep–1 Dec	3689 3869 2879
Soybean oil	60,000 lbs	Jan, Mar, May, Jul, Aug, Sep, Nov	0.01 cents/lb	1 cent/lb	1.5cts/lb	5 Jan–29Apr 2 May–31 Aug 1 Sep–1 Dec	3689 3867 2879
Wheat	5,000 bushels	Mar, May, Jul, Sep, Dec	0.25 cents/bushel	20 cents/bushel	30 cents/bushel	5 Jan–29 Apr 2 May–31 Aug 1 Sep–28 Nov	3689 3870 2744

Note
a Cents and dollars are all US.
b No. of observations in samples.

Index

agricultural futures 45, 47, 139, 144
ARCH 72, 72–73, 77, 79, 146
Asian Wall Street Journal 67
asymptotically rational expectations 79
attractor 8
augmented Dickey–Fuller (ADF) test *see* unit root tests

Bayesian error(s) 120–123, 130, 132
bid–ask prices 135, 137, 146, 148, 155
Brunner and Meltzer thesis 32
Budapest Commodity Exchange 42

chaos 9, 117, 120, 132, 162; *see also* Lorenz system
Chicago Board of Trade (CBOT) 43 96, 125, 139, 144; comparison with Tokyo Grain Exchange 45; history 43–44
Chicago Mercantile Exchange 56
China Zhengzhou Commodity Exchange 42; contract terms for mungbeans 52; growth in trading 53; history 50–51; management 54–56
circuit breakers 136, 137, 163
clearing house 21, 21–22
co-integration tests 70–71
cobweb phenomena 35
commodity futures exchanges 43
contract standardisation 22
credible reflecting barriers 140

cross-sectional regressions 91, 92, 104, 112
Cumby–Modest test 93, 105
currency futures contract 62

De Long *et al.*'s model 90

Edgeworth box 19
efficient markets hypothesis (EMH) 61–62, 77–79, 117, 118–119
Engle–Granger tests *see* cointegration tests
estimation: instrumental variable 72, 76; maximum likelihood 72, 80, 127, 156; non-linear least squares 72, 76; ordinary least squares 72
European Union Technical Assistance programmes 57
evolution of futures trading 20–21
exchange rate: US dollar/ Deutschmark 62–63, 73, 77, 80
exogenous disturbance 29
exogenous variables 68

Fama–MacBeth regressions 91, 92, 102
fat tails 143
Federal Reserve Bulletin 68
forecast bias 87, 91, 92
forward contracting 18, 18–20, 26

gains from futures trading 1
GARCH 118, 132, 144, 156
Goldfeld–Quandt (GQ) test 146

Granger causality test 94, 109
gravitation theory 148

hedgers: long 64–65; short 62–63
high-frequency data 144
Hill's tail test 143, 146

identification conditions 67
interest differential 66, 68, 73, 79, 80
International Kazakhstan Agro-
    Industrial Exchange 42; contract
    terms for wheat 48–49; demise of
    trading 50; history of development
    46–47
intrasample simulation: of futures rate
    75–76; of spot rate 75
irrational traders 87

Jarque–Bera test 77, 85, 146
Jicheng Information Network 56
Johansen procedure 71

Kazakhstan Securities Exchange
    (KASE) 50

lagged futures rate: as post-sample
    forecast 77–79
Lagrange multiplier test 109
Laguerre function 141
Ljung–Box Q statistic 85, 146

London Commodity Exchange 45
London International Financial
    Futures Exchange 45
London Metals Exchange 48
Lorenz system 117, 118, 120, 120–
    123

marginal rate of substitution (MRS)
    16
marginal rate of transformation
    (MRT) 16
Market Vane bullish sentiment index
    (MVBSI) 95, 98
Market Vane Corporation 95
maximum eigenvalue test see
    cointegration tests
mean reversion 138, 156
microstructure 112

Minneapolis Grain Exchange 43, 56
New York Coffee, Sugar and Cocoa
    Exchange 49
noise trader 87, 87–91, 95–102;
    model 91, 93, 105, 112; sentiment
    6–7, 87, 88, 90, 91, 92, 93, 94, 96,
    99, 107, 112; see also speculation
non-linear least squares 79
normal backwardation hypothesis 23,
    24

Pareto gains 1, 18–19
Phillips–Perron (PP) test see unit root
    tests
positive feedback trader 7, 94, 99,
    102
post-sample simulations: of futures
    rate 77–79; of spot rate 77–79
Poznan Commodity Exchange 42
prelimit graphs 161
price limits 135, 136, 138, 144, 162

random walk: as post-sample forecast
    77–79
randomness 117, 127, 130–1
rational expectations 5, 6, 16, 18, 28,
    33, 62, 107, 112, 120, 121, 122,
    130, 131, 140
rational expectations equilibrium
    (REE) 18, 27–28, 29, 32, 34, 35
rational expectations hypothesis
    (REH) 63–64, 71–72, 73, 130
rational traders 86, 88, 89, 90
regulatory intervention 1
residuals: conditional variance of; see
    also ARCH; diagnostic tests on 76,
    85
risk premium 5, 23, 62, 65, 68, 73,
    80, 87
root mean square error (RMSE) 75

S-shape 138, 141
safe asset 7, 88
sentiment index 95, 96, 102
sentiment: market 87, 88, 91, 92–111;
    see also noise trader
speculation 9, 22, 53, 65, 66, 68, 77,
    79, 86, 112, 117, 120, 121, 122,
    123, 125, 131

speculators 22
spot market 33, 35
spot price variability 34
stochastic paradigm of asset prices
    117
strange attractor 8, 9, 117, 120, 123
structural stability assumption 117,
    119, 124
Student's *t*-distribution 143, 156,
    156–161

target zone model 139, 139–144, 155,
    162
Theil's inequality coefficient 75
time-varying volatility 63, 64, 140

trading volume 26
traditional economic models 61
Treasury Bills 26
truncation 155

unit root tests: augmented Dickey–
    Fuller 68–69; Phillips–Perron 69
    70
unsafe asset 88, 90
utility maximisation 1

Warsaw Board of Trade 42
White's test 109

zero sum game 15